I0144878

BEFORE I FORGET

Stories from the Mountains & my Childhood

Bobby Adams

BobbyAdams @ Copyright, 2015
JesseHaleBooks@Copyright, 2015
Shades Creek Press, LLC
www.shadescreekpress.com

This is a work of storytelling as I have remembered life and experiences from my childhood, growing up in the north Georgia Mountains. Names, characters, places, and incidents are either the product of my own imagination and experiences or are used fictitiously, and any resemblance to actual persons, living or dead, business establishments, events, or locales, is entirely coincidental. If anyone is offended or embarrassed as a result of my storytelling, I extend my apologies. This collection of stories is intended to be humorous and entertaining. Perhaps the world needs a little more self-laughter.

All rights reserved. No part of this book may be used or reproduced in any manner, including internet usage, without permission from, Bobby Adams or Jesse R. Hale, DBA: Shades Creek Press, LLC.

ABOUT THE AUTHOR

Bobby Adams grew up in the foothills of the Appalachian Mountains, embraced and nurtured by its rich and complex culture; he was inspired to write this book by the people with whom he has shared moments and memories. His family was a medley of saw millers, bootleggers, coon hunters and preachers. Being the only redhead of five siblings gave Bobby a natural propensity to get into daily mischiefs, scuffles, routine appointments with the "hickory" and an ongoing conflict between his love of outdoors and the inevitable sunburn that only redheads can understand. According to his friends, he was the "class clown" as well as Class President of White County High School.

Bobby was born in the Charm House in Clarkesville, Ga. Bobby started working at his Daddy's saw mill at the age of 9. His fingers still show the signs of being bent and broken from rolling the logs up onto the carriage at the mill. He rode the bus to school from his first day until the day he graduated. With a lot of luck, and by the grace of God, Bobby obtained degrees from the University of Georgia and from North Georgia College. He then began a career in education, spanning 32 years that included teaching, coaching, and serving as Superintendent of Schools, all at Lumpkin County Public Schools in Dahlonega, Georgia. Bobby is married to Dr. Paula Early-Adams and has two children: a daughter, Brooke, a teacher in the White County School System, and a son, Brynnan, a student at the University of Georgia. His grandson, John Wilder, is the apple of his eye.

Grandparents on both sides of his family had small country stores. J. W. Sims grocery in Helen and the Adams store on Highway 75 north of Cleveland, Georgia, were stores where hard working men, still wearing their sawdust-sweat smelling overalls, would gather in the evenings around an old potbellied stove to swap tales and take a tug of whiskey if the occasion arose. Both of these congregating places served as a haven for tall tales and where stories would be told, lies perfected and humor would abound. Bobby developed a deep appreciation for the art of storytelling and for the stories themselves – true or untrue; so inspired, in fact that he has decided to preserve many of them in this book. Bobby loves to tell his stories. Bobby has tried to retell the stories as close as possible to the way they were told when he first heard them. I never get tired of hearing these great stories. The book was done with a lot of encouragement from his friends. I know that he certainly hopes you enjoy this book as much as he did putting it together. I know him well. He is my father.

Brooke Adams-Nix

First Edition
First Printing, 2015

Book design by Bobby Adams & Jesse R. Hale

Cover design by Bobby Adams, Jesse R. Hale &
Natasha Walsh
Final Cover Design and Production by Natasha Walsh

Proof-reading & editing by Melanie Blocker-Swope

Before I Forget

ISBN: 978-0-9838376-8-8
Copyright@2015 Jesse R. Hale
Shades Creek Press, LLC

Printed in the United States of America

In Recognition of the Author, Bobby Adams:

As a 21 year old graduating from the University of Georgia, I probably had learned all I could at that point in time about being an agriculture teacher. There was still plenty I needed to learn; and in most respects, much more I needed to learn about life. Fortunately, God blessed me with my first professional job as the agriculture teacher and FFA advisor at Lumpkin County High School in Dahlonega, Georgia. For the next 8 years I got what could be considered a "real" education. In that small student cafeteria every morning before the first period bell would ring, and again during lunch, Mr. Bobby Adams would provide those of us fortunate to be at his table, with a wide variety of stories, laughs, and thought provoking life lessons. Honestly, it was difficult to have a bad day at work when Bobby Adams was around. As a former history teacher, coach, and superintendent for that same school system, Mr. Adams was the coordinator for the student work-study program when I started working with him at Lumpkin County High School. The students loved Mr. Adams. It was not uncommon for them to come into my room and share something that Bobby had told them during his class. It almost always involved something about hunting or fishing. These two topics could always prove educational for those more important life lessons. With the exception of a few "stick in the mud" teachers, most all of the faculty and staff at the school loved Mr. Adams also. On many occasions I got to witness fellow co-workers (and more often the school administrators) looking down at their shoes, shaking their heads from right to left, murmuring affectionately under their breath, Bobby, Bobby, Bobby. In every case, it was due to something Mr. Adams said. The statements and stories told by Mr. Adams may be funny, but they also hold great meaning and life lessons. The fact is; Bobby Adams loves everybody. His mission in life must be to make others smile, or laugh out loud, as often as possible, because that is what he does. I have never witnessed a time when Bobby would not help someone in need. He genuinely cares for others. Another fact is; Mr. Adams tells the truth. He may not always be politically correct, but Bobby will not lie to you. These two characteristics make Bobby Adams such a unique person. Love and Honesty: two traits that make up the character of truly great men. These are the qualities that make Mr. Bobby Adams such a great influencer and role model. This may be the reason that Bobby Adams is the type of person you want to be around. I cherish times spent with Bobby Adams. Whether at the school building, out on a rabbit trail, in a mountain cabin, or horse barn, Bobby is the best story-teller around. His stories are real. His stories are interesting. There is no telling how many times people have told Bobby that he should write a book. To the delight of many, and to the benefit of all who get a copy of this book, it is exciting to serve witness as this project comes to fruition. We are all extremely blessed that Bobby Adams' book is finally available. We are fortunate to have these stories written down and in Mr. Adams words, "Before I Forget". Now the wisdom and humor in these stories can be preserved for all to enjoy. There is no doubt that this collection of stories will be worthy of reading over and over again. One thing is for sure; with or without this book, Mr. Bobby Adams will never be forgotten.

John (Chip) Bridges
Program Manager, Agricultural Education,Georgia FFA Advisor
Georgia Department of Education
1752 Twin Towers East
Atlanta, GA 30334

Young Bobby Adams as the Girls' Basketball Coach at Lumpkin County High School, 1972.

BEFORE I F0RGET

By

Bobby Adams

When I first began this project, I really didn't know if I had the ability to write and share the stories and tales that have been so much a part of my life. I wanted to put them on paper so that others could enjoy them as much as I did. My life has been a continuation of short stories. Some people might say that their lives have been a novel. I don't think that has been true for me. Short stories and tales of old times, and the lives of others have molded me in to what I am today. I kept telling my wife, my daughter, and son that I should write as many of the stories down as I could. My son, Brynnan, said, "Daddy you need to do that before you forget." I am sure there are lots of people that would have liked to share their lives and the lives of others if they had just done it before they forgot. Someone asked me how I made up all the stories that I tell. My answer to them was simple. I don't make them up. I have lived them. I have witnessed them. They are all a part of me. In my attempt to put these stories, jokes, saying, events or whatever you want to call them down, I have received a bunch of encouragement to keep telling my stories.

I hope that this book will provide entertainment for some, and insight for others.

I am sure that not everyone will like this book, but my life has not been like everyone's. We are all different and we have all been made to look, feel, and act as unique individuals with different likes and dislikes. Before I Forget is just me, Bobby Adams telling others, things that I thought should be shared. I didn't do this to make money, or achieve any type of success. I just wanted to tell my stories before I forget. I want to dedicate this book to all the folks that were responsible for its content. The names I have used are the names I remember. I haven't tried to change them. In doing so, I hope I have not offended anyone. Hopefully, this collection of memories will be passed on to others that will enjoy and see them as part of my life. There is no beginning and there is no end. I tell them when I remember them. When I get this published it will not be checked for spelling. It will not be proof read so that proper grammar is always used. I wrote it and the mistakes that are in this, are my mistakes. Public education did not cause the mistakes. So if you want to read this to be literary critics put it down right now and do not read any further.

I remember one time my mom was mad and she looked at me and said, "I am so proud of you." Mom had never said anything like that before to me, and it kind of caught me off guard. I said, "Why do you say that Momma?" She looked at me and said, "If it wasn't for you honey, I don't know what the people in this community would have to talk about." It was obvious to me that someone had been telling Mom something that she didn't want to hear about me. That is kind of the way my life was and has been. I have enjoyed my life.

I have had lots of fun. Sometimes you have to create fun. It doesn't come by chance. I have created this book so that fun can be shared. Some of the stories are not funny, but they all had a purpose in my life. I wanted to share as many of the stories and tales as I could remember. Much of the material is either a story that I remember or just my personal opinion. When you are the writer, you are allowed to do that. If the reader doesn't agree with some of the material in this book, that's ok. You can still enjoy the stories and tales. I just want to do this before I forget.

These stories come in no particular order. They are written as I remembered them, and when I remember them. Lots of times, days will go by before I think of a story or tale. I may be talking to a friend or listening to someone and it will remind me of an event or story that I want to share. Some of the stories may have been told before and if you are hearing them or reading them for a second time maybe you will enjoy them twice as much.

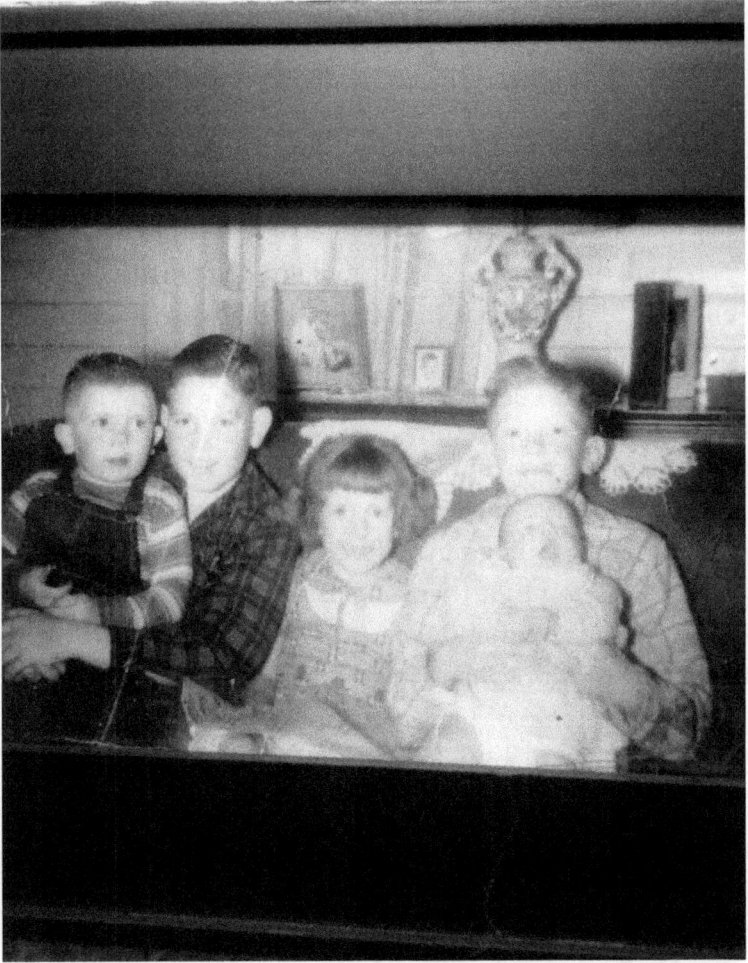

Bobby and his siblings; Bruce is holding Billy, Brenda is in the middle, and Bobby is holding Bradley.

UNINTENTIONAL EDUCATION

In the fall of 1969 I realized that come the next summer, I would have been in college for four years. I wasn't the smartest fellow in the senior class at White County Public school system in Cleveland, Georgia but I did know that most people graduated from College in four years. Not everyone but as I said most. I had started my college education at that glorious school in Athens known as the University of Georgia. I made it through one quarter before my Dad decided that I needed to come home and work and if I was serious about my education. Somehow he figured out that Allen's was not the library. If it was, then I was paying way too many fines. After graduation I was pleased to find out that the University had a library. It was a big one. I had walked by it several times. Dad decided that I could go to Truett McConnell College, a junior college located in my home town of Cleveland, Georgia, and haul lumber from his sawmill after and sometimes before classes started. I stayed at Truett for five quarters, and I had passed all of the courses that I had taken. I transferred back to Georgia in the fall of '69. I walked into the administrative office building and ask a lady if I could talk to someone about how to get out of college. She looked kind of funny at me then she asks, "Who is your counselor?" I said, "Don't have one; I didn't know I was going to need one." Well she directed me to a man that I had never met and only met him one time after that. I only know him as Dr. McElroy. Dr. McElroy asks me what my major was going to be. I told him I really didn't know but I would like to get out of school as soon as I could. I told Dr. McElroy that I had been taking classes in the mornings for the entire time I had been in college. That way I could go to work plus it allowed more time to study at that place they called Allen's. I was instructed to get him a copy of all my transcripts and then he would go over the courses that I had taken and we would see if I could graduate on time. I told Dr. McElroy that I was about as smart as I was going to get. My education was exceeding my intelligence. I told him that my head was not very big and I thought all of that knowledge that I was getting was making me top heavy and my head was starting to lean to the right. He laughed and said he doubted that. It was obvious I was dealing with someone who didn't know me. Two days later we reviewed my transcripts and he told me I could be an education major with a degree in History Education. That was the last time I saw my counselor. All I had to do was pass what courses I was taking and do my practice teaching and take one biology course and I could graduate on time, which meant in the four year time frame. I told him to sign me up for that. I don't know whatever happened to Dr. McElroy, but thanks for helping me get my unintentional education. That ladies and gentlemen is how I became a GEORGIA DOG.

GETTING IN HOT WATER

In 1953 my sister Brenda was born. I was 5 years old and had the run of the house. Mom had returned home with my new baby sister, and daddy had gotten one of Fletch Magness's girls, Josephine, to come and stay with mom until she got back on her feet. In those days there were no Huggies; so all of the dippers were cloth. People would boil water and then pour it over the diapers that had been bleached in Clorox to sanitize them. We had a washing machine. It was lots of fun to watch mom wash the clothes, and then she would get a pan and place it on the other side of the ringers that squeezed the water out of the clothes. They were then hung on a line outside to dry. I used to laugh when I would hear one of the older boys say, "We ain't had so much fun, since granny got her tit hung in the washing machine." I could visualize that; and to a little boy that was funny. Josephine had been boiling water to sanitize the diapers and I was in the kitchen watching her. She had poured some of the boiling water into a pan that was lying in the floor. I was busy watching, and Josephine asks me to hand her some washing powders that was on the table. Without thinking I took a step backwards, my heel hit the tub of hot water, and I just sat down in that pan of scolding water. I started screaming as any 5 year old would have done. Josephine quickly picked me up and ran for someone to help. My Uncle Roy was at the store, and he came running. He loaded me up in his truck and down to Dr. Neals we went. Dr. Neal examined my burns and said it would be a miracle if I didn't have some scars. He placed some kind of salve all over me; from the top of my knees to my belly button. I had to wear a thing that looked like a diaper. Uncle Roy carried me home and told mom I would be alright, but she had to put that salve on me once a day. Now momma had two kids in diapers. I wore that contraption for ten days. I had a few blisters pop up, but nothing really bad. I have thought about setting down in that hot water many times. I had no scars from that accident. Years later I would hear someone say, "Boy, I bet he got in hot water," and I would think, "Well, they might get OK, if they just had some of Dr. Neals old salve." It sure helped me when I got in hot water.

THE FIRST DAY OF SCHOOL

Mom told me I would have to go to Gainesville with her and my older brother Bruce to get me some school clothes. I was going to enter the first grade in the White County Public School System. I didn't really see the need for this, because I had some clothes that I liked to wear every day. Wearing overalls, or over halls (the country name) and going bare footed was my accepted attire. I thought that those clothes would be fine. However, mom didn't feel that way; so I knew that I would be making my way down to Gainesville before too long. We got in our new 1954 Mercury, and made what seemed like a long drive to Gainesville, Georgia. The square in down town Gainesville had several stores that had clothing in them so we knew we would have lots to choose from. Bruce and I would need at least two new pair of jeans and a couple of shirts, and a new pair of shoes a piece. We had been bare-footed most of the summer. I think the store was Gallant- Belks. It would later just be Belks. We also would go into the Sears-Roebuck store. It would become just Sears. I figured that Gallant and Roebuck must have died or something. After we had purchased my brothers, and my clothes, we would journey back to Cleveland. I remember looking at the grading that was taking place at Bells Mill and mom told us that a big lake would be coming before too long and we would have to cross a big bridge to get to Gainesville. That didn't worry me too much because I thought Gainesville was too far to drive to anyway. When we got home mom made us take our clothes and put them on the bed so she could look at them again. She wanted to make sure that her boys looked good in those new duds. On that first day of school, I wore some of my new clothes and went into Clara Hulsey's first grade class. I was scared to death. On the first day of school in 1954 the new White County School building did not have any desk. We sat on cardboard that was placed around the room. We sat with our little backs against the walls. As I sat there, I remember seeing Albert Jackson sitting to my right and Crandall Autry sitting to his right. Albert said to Crandall, "Will you be my friend?" I thought I wish someone would ask me to be their friend. That first day of school I still remember, and how scared I was.   Each year when school starts; I think somewhere there is a little boy or girl a little scared, and wanting to be someone's friend. I always hope they find that friend.

BACK FROM THE OUT HOUSE

My dad had lived his entire life drawing water from a well and going to an outhouse to take care of his body functions. My brother Bruce was 6, and I was 4. We couldn't wait to get our new bathroom in. We thought it would be great to go to the bathroom, and not freeze your back end off. There was nothing as terrifying as sitting down on that wood, and it have frost all over the top. In the mornings, Bruce and I would go to the bathroom together. He would sit on one hole, and me, sit on the other. There was no modesty in our house. Bruce and I would be in the bathroom doing our business, and at the same time planning what we could get into for that day. In fact, on several occasions Mom would come out to the john to get Bruce, because we would get to talking and forget that he had to go back in and dress for school. For dad, it was a hard adjustment.   Daddy said it didn't seem right to use the bathroom in your house. For months, I remember my dad saying that he would just go to the old bathroom. The meaning of bathroom took on a new meaning to me. The word bath had

17

meant getting a wash cloth, wetting it, and then rubbing all of the dirt off your face and hands. Now, with the addition of the tub, it meant getting in that thing and washing all over. I loved swimming in our new washing tub. The old number 10 galvanize tub would soon be a thing of the past. However, I do remember one time when dad had gone to the outhouse. It was a moonless night, very cloudy and very dark. There were some big oak trees in the yard and being little boys, we often would pee behind one of those trees. Dad had not taken a flashlight to the john, and I didn't know he was out there. By the light of the porch, I could see to the first big oak, and rushed to empty my bladder, and when you are 4 you can pee forever. I had just finished what I had gone outside to do, when daddy came walking back from the outhouse. I didn't know he was there and he didn't know I was there. When I stepped out from behind that tree; all I could do was scream, and dad yelled some words I had never heard before. When we realized who each other was, daddy looked at me and said, "Son go back in the house, now I can go finish what I came out here to do." He told mom that scare was better that any laxative. At that time I didn't know what a laxative was.

Bobby as coach & Defensive Coordinator at Lumpkin County High School, Dahlonega, Georgia

THE TIMES ARE CHANGING

Time, being the age that I am, has allowed me to see how things have changed in my home town and the surrounding area. Not just the increase in population, but the attitudes of people as well. In 1966 I was a freshman at the University of Georgia. The deer season was opening up on a Saturday, and I wanted to go deer hunting really bad. I got a ride home from Athens with Charles Hood. Charles, who is still one of my best friends, was from the Nacoochee Valley area. He was also going home so that he could go deer hunting. When we arrived in Cleveland, it was pretty late that evening. I went in the house and mom told me that all my brothers were camping. I asked if I could use her car to go hunting the next morning. Mom told me she had to take someone to Gainesville. Dads' truck was loaned out to one of his workers. So I said fine, I would just catch a ride. I got up at 5:30 AM that morning, got me some warm clothing on, and out the door with my British 303 across my shoulder. Mom and dads' house sat within 70 yards of highway 75. I walked to the shoulder of the road, and stuck out my thumb. I had on my red hunting hat, orange vest, a pair of blue jeans, big coat, and a gun strapped across my back. Three cars came by but the fourth car stopped. I opened the door to get in and the man said, "Where you going son?" I told him I was going to Tray Mountain to deer hunt. He informed me I was in luck because he too was going to Tray Mountain. I rode with this stranger up the mountain and got out of his car. I told him I appreciated the ride. He smiled and said, "I hope you get a big one." I did. I killed an 8 point buck. A gentleman hunting in the same area I was hunting heard me shoot and helped me drag the deer to the dirt road that winds up the mountain. He asked how I was going to get the deer home. I informed him that I had hitched hiked up there, and I was sure I could get a ride home. I sat down on the bank overlooking the road. The first car I saw coming up the mountain was my grandfather Sims. Papa saw me and the deer and a big smile came over his face. He said, "That's a nice one Bob, load him up and let's go home." I don't think that hunt could take place today, but in 1966 it did. That was a special time in my life. Things have changed since then.

TOO MANY POSSUMS

We had some colorful characters in the Asbestos community when I was growing up. One such person was Mr. Fred Freeman. Fred and his wife, Ms. Jesse lived just north of us on Highway 75. Mr. Freeman had been a veteran of the First World War. Fred had seen the horrors of war, but he came back to White County and raised a family at the foot of Yonah Mountain. He was our neighbor, and I always liked Mr. Freeman. He was always accommodating, and he had a great sense of humor. Fred could roll a Prince Albert cigarette with one hand. He was one of only two or three people that I knew that could accomplish such a feat. Prince Albert tobacco came in a red can with a picture of an English Nobleman on the front of the can. Today, I would say not many folks know about Prince Albert tobacco. Lots of the older folks in our community that smoked used Prince Albert tobacco. Occasionally, Mr. Freeman would come by our house, and ask if I could carry him to Helen to get him a pint of wine. He didn't own an automobile, and only drove his tricycle tractor. Sometimes, after having some of his wine, that could be a site to see; Mr. Freemans' side of the road would be whichever one he wanted it to be. On one of those trips we had made to Helen to get

Fred his wine, Mr. Freeman and I were on our way back to his home. We hadn't gone too far out of Helen, and Fred got his Prince Albert tobacco out and was rolling him a cigarette. He casually looked up while continuing to roll his cigarette, and said to me, "You know the automobile is a wonderful invention." I had carried Fred to Helen many times, and he had never said anything that profound before. I looked at him in a surprised way and remarked, "Well Fred, I guess it is. What makes you think so?" The look on his face and the words he spoke, have stayed with me for years. Fred turned to me and said, "If it hadn't have been for the automobile boy, the world would be knee deep in damn possums." I never thought about it, but I believe Fred may have been right.

FIRST BOAT

There is nothing as satisfying as when you buy your first boat. The second most satisfying is when you sell it. My buddy, Lanier Chambers and I had been fishing in an old boat that Lanier had purchased from someone. I really enjoyed those couple times we fished. Lanier called me one night and said, "Bobby, I want to sell the boat. Why don't you buy it for $1400? That's what I have in it. It is a good boat and really does great. I have added another live well. Man, you need this boat." He kept telling me what a good boat it was and I bought it. I was so proud of my new boat. I carried that boat from Georgia to North Carolina, to South Carolina, to Tennessee. I never got to hear it run. Something was always wrong with the boat. I saw Lanier a couple of months later and told him I thought that he was my friend, but he had sold me a piece of junk, and furthermore, I couldn't even sell it. Lanier said, "Bobby, let me tell you a story." This man had a horse, and his neighbor saw the horse.

22

His neighbor said that it was a pretty horse. The owner said the horse was a good horse and very smart. It would go get the paper out of the box. If you asked the horse how old it was; it would scratch it out on the ground. He would get a cloth out of your back pocket. Hearing all of that, the neighbor says gosh I would like to buy that horse. What would you take for the horse? The owner said $1400. So the neighbor paid him and took the horse to his new home. About two months later, the two men met on the street. The new owner of the horse said, "I can't believe you sold me that horse I thought we were friends, that damn horse has tried to kill me. He has kicked me, and that sorry thing has bit me on the butt twice. And he will not do one trick. And to make matters worse, I can't even sell him." The previous owner of the horse, looked at his neighbor and said, "Well, I couldn't either when I talked about it like that." That darn Lanier just smiled and walked away. The next day I placed an ad in the paper, telling what a good boat I had for sale. It sold for $1400 in four days. Lanier was right.

YELLOW JACKET PANTS

When spring time came to the Adams family it usually meant two things, turkey hunting and fishing. Both these tasks were taken very seriously. However, one came before the other; we were not allowed to have guns at age 6 or 7, so fishing was the first to get our attention. The preparation for turkey hunting would come later when we were more mature and knowledgeable. We would have to wait until we were 9 or 10 to do that sport. However, the preparation for fishing would be enough to keep our minds and bodies busy. First, you had to go find a good cane pole; one that was the exact length and size needed to haul in all those fish waiting to be caught. After that, getting your bait was next. It was during this part of the preparation, I remember finding little yellow bees going into a hole in the bank. Bruce, Clifford and I decided; there would be hundreds of little bee larvae in their nest. We could catch bream by the hundreds, if we could just dig that nest out of the bank. With a pick and shovel in hand, we started to dig. Bruce took the first turn digging. Somehow the dirt closed the hole and we didn't see those little yellow creatures. Clifford would take the second turn. He dug with all his muscle and power. And as soon as he struck that yellow jackets nest, there must have been a thousand of those little devils attack him. Now, I could have rushed in there and helped get those bees off of Clifford, but from the way he was screaming, I figured it would be best if I stayed back, at least until the screaming stopped. Thankfully, Clifford's mom, my aunt Louise, heard the screaming and came to the rescue. To this day, I think it may have been the only time in my life that I saw Clifford wearing yellow pants. His pants might not have been yellow, but with all those yellow jackets on them, they sure looked it.

BLUE BILL

It was either a house on 10 acres, or a Corvette. I had wanted a sports car for several years, but had never had a job that would allow me the opportunity to buy one. I had been teaching a couple of years, and I finally felt like maybe I could have me the sports car I had always dreamed of having. At about that same time, one of my best friends told me about a Chalet and 10 acres he had for sale in Northern Lumpkin County. After a lot of thought, I purchased the Chalet. My payment was $131.00 per month.   Not bad; the Corvette payment would have been $171.00 a month. The house was for 30 years. The car was for 4 years. I was making a whopping $378.00 a month teaching. After making the purchase, I decided it would be nice if I could rent a room or two to help make my payments on my house. Some college boys from North Georgia College would be ideal. One of the guys was Bill Christian. Bill worked in the dining hall with my future wife. Things were going pretty good.   I was usually at ball practice, and Bill was getting used to being alone at the house. Bill was at home one day, and as most of you know, the Chalets' have little balconies on them. It was extremely cold, and Bill was upstairs. Bill decided that rather than go to the bathroom downstairs, he would just relieve himself off the balcony. Bill did not expect that big puff of wind that blew the door shut. He also didn't expect the door to be locked. There Bill was in his underwear, on the balcony, and it was about 25 degrees. Bill decided that if he was going to survive, he would just skinny down to the lower level. He did, only to find the bottom doors locked as well. Lucky for Bill, the window over the sink was not locked, but the sink was full of dirty dishes. After turning three shades of blue, Bill crawled through the window, across the dirty dishes back into the house. When I returned home that evening, Bill told me of his plight. I looked at Bill and told him not to worry; no one in that part of Lumpkin County had complained about seeing a blue man in his underwear. Bill still doesn't think that was funny.

MOMS INTELLIGENCE TEST

One of the most delightful and happy times in my life was when I graduated from the University of Georgia. I could not believe I,

Bobby Lee Adams, could be graduating from college. It seemed like it had taken 20 years to get through that part of my life. I was not the most academically gifted student to enter that grand institution. In fact, I would say that if I had to get in the University of Georgia today, I would not be able to do it. You see, when I entered UGA you had to have an 800 on your SAT, and a B average or; be able to sign your name on a check that wouldn't bounce. The latter was the most preferred. Things have changed since I was in school. In elementary school, we didn't have IQ exams, no sir re. The Adams kids were administered poems to show our intelligence. My Mom would make us stand before one of our Aunts or Uncles and say, "OK, tell them what you learned." And we would say, "Had a little dog. Its name was Jack, tied its tail to a railroad track. Along came a train Choo Choo Choo, and that little doggie went Bow Wow Wow." Mom would smile and then say, "Ain't he smart?" If mom really wanted to showcase her sons smarts, she would say, "Tell them the other one." And we would dazzle our relatives with mind blowing brilliance, by saying, "Here I stand, black and dirty, if you don't come and kiss me, I'll run like a turkey." Naturally, we would have to run to mom, and then give her a kiss. It might not have been the most scientific test to determine our mental capabilities, but in our mothers' eyes, it made us as smart as any person that ever graced any prestigious University. I don't know which was more important, saying the poems or running and kissing our Mom. Looking back on it now, it didn't really matter, because it made mom smile.

OUT SIDE WITH A DOG

My friend, Billy Wayne Chambers was a one of a kind person. I am sure everyone that knew Billy Wayne could tell a Billy Wayne story. He was that kind of a guy. Once, Billy Wayne, Roy Ash Jr., myself and a few other friends of mine had gone to Steinhatchie, Florida to catch some sea trout. We decided that we would try to fine us a place that we might enjoy going to that second night we were there. The locals told us that there were several little bars around, but since we weren't local; we might get our butts beat. It seemed that the local men it that area didn't like men from outside the area coming to their bars. Well, we decided that we would risk it. That evening we headed out to a place called the "Crossroads Bar and Grill." It was a juke joint located outside of Steinhatchie. As we entered the bar, the smoke and noise kind of hit you all at once. As I looked around, I noticed that everyone was giving us the once over. Most of the patrons were male. There were, however, two girls in the bar that seemed to be getting all of the attention. We quickly found out that one of the girls was getting married the next day. Billy Wayne wasted no time in talking to the sister of the bride to be. After several beers, Billy Wayne says to this girl, "Hey, why don't you and I go outside?" All at once she started to scream, "GO OUTSIDE, GO OUTSIDE, I DON'T GO OUTSIDE WITH NOBODY BUT MY DOG." You could have heard a pin drop in that bar. All eyes were on Billy Wayne, and the screaming girl. Billy Wayne quickly scanned the room. All eyes were on him. Ole Billy just looked at that girl and started barking like a dog. Ruff, Ruff, Ruff. Suddenly, everyone in the bar started laughing, even the girl that was doing the screaming. We walked out of that bar without getting our butts beat, but if Billy Wayne hadn't of done a good imitation of a dog, it might have been a different story.

These are the Adams's kids: Back row: Bobby & Bruce, Front row: Brenda, Bradley, and Billy.

Maud Simms & Walt Sims

BROTHERLY LOVE

January 24th of 1946 was a special day. It was the day my brother Bruce was born. I was born two years later on March 22nd, 1948. Bruce was my mentor, my protector, my idol. He meant the world to me. As we were growing up, everyone would say Bruce and Bobby, or Bobby and Bruce. We were always referred to as one. My Brother was two years older than me, but it seemed to me that we were like twins. Bruce protected me when I was young, and after we reached adulthood, he and I usually talked at least once a day. He scolded me when he was angry with me. But he never tried to be anything other than a loving brother. It actually made me angry when Bruce got married. Bruce was married when he was a senior in high school. I thought; how could my brother love someone, and not want to be with me. Over the years I learned that love can go beyond one person. Bruce raised his family within shouting distance of where he and I were raised. He and his wife Tia had 3 boys. Bruce loved his sons with the dedication that only few fathers have. He was not without fault. I know that. Bruce was the one that always planned everything for his brothers. He would get us excited about a hunt or a fishing trip, or whatever it was he wanted us to do. Sometimes, he did it without thought for his wife. Bruce and Tia would divorce. Bruce tried marriage again, and that marriage would end in failure. Bruce never looked back. Bruce died at age 61. He had heart trouble. But he lived his life to the fullest. He loved the outdoors, and he loved his family. I have two other brothers, Billy and Bradley. I hope they can look upon me the way that I did Bruce. God intended for brothers to love each other. We do. Bruce was our example.

CAMPING GHOST

Camping out was a lot of fun when I was a boy. Now, I think a motel with black and white TV and no air conditioning is roughing it. In my youth there was something about lying on the ground with just a small blanket between you and the earth that made you feel like you were in tune with nature. A good king size bed, and a soft pillow with clean sheets, and a nice blanket is all the feel of nature that I need now. I learned as I got older, those rocks are made to go in gravel so it can be placed on roads. They were not made to go under my hip and back and make me sore from their presents under my blanket on the ground. Once, when we were camping just below Mr. Lat Sosebee's house on Joe Franklin road, two of the teenagers that lived on the road decided that they would place a sheet over themselves and pretend to be ghost and scare those kids that were camping. It just so happened that brother Bruce, cousin Clifford Cox, cousin Wayne Sims, friend Lamar Sosebee and I, all had our BB guns with us. When you have five 6 to 10 year old boys with BB guns, they are not afraid of NOTHING. This was unknown by those that wanted to frightened the grits out of us. When we first heard that WOO WOO coming from outside our tent, that was blankets placed over sticks, we immediately cocked our BB guns. Lamar peeped out. He told us it was two guys with sheets over them. Clifford told us to hold our fire until we could see the ghost really good. On his count of three, he gave the command to open fire. Now, our BB guns weren't powerful enough to penetrate the sheets, but they were powerful enough to make little red spots on the two guilty parties. We gave chase, but we couldn't catch them. No one ever confessed to trying to scare us, but there were two Franklin boys sitting in my Uncle Charles' living room with little red spots all over them. I still don't believe they were chigger bites.

THEM'S OUR FOOTBALLS

We had been practicing hard for a very important football game. The weather had been hot and our team had been working hard to prepare for a game that we desperately wanted to win. One of the Wilkins boys was our quarterback and like all of the Wilkins family, Ricky had a great sense of humor. The practice that day had gone exceptionally well and the coaches as well as players felt we had a good chance of winning the upcoming Friday night game. The football team usually went with shoulder pads and helmets on Monday after a game. On Tuesday and Wednesday it was full contact with lots of hard hitting and bunch of physical conditioning. Thursday, we would go helmets and shorts. Thursday was the day that the team would meet in the end zone and our head coach, who at this time was Coach Ken Davis, would give the weeks analogy on the practices and also give us our pregame pep talk. On this particular Thursday Coach Davis had the team in the end zone and he was giving one heck of a pep talk to the players. He was telling them the importance of this game and how they would have to play their hearts out. Our kids were getting really fired up, however about that time there was a beautiful lady from Dahlonega that walked out of the High School and came walking on the sidewalk that went right under the end zone where our team had gathered. This lady was the Dolly Parton of Dahlonega. All at once our Quarterback Ricky Wilkins started saying, "Coach, Coach, Coach," Coach Davis said, "What is it Wilkins?" Ricky Wilkins said, "Coach, I think that lady is stealing two of our footballs." Practice was over. The pep talk was through.

SMART FRIENDS

When I entered the University of Georgia, I didn't have the least bit of knowledge about college life. I felt very fortunate that my best buddy, and friend since second grade, was going to be my roommate. I kept thinking, he will be able to tell me how to act and what to do when we get to Athens, Georgia. Well Charlie Brown was just about as overcome with big town college life as I was. Charlie Brown, yes, my roommate was Charlie Brown. Not the cartoon character, but the guy that I had been going to school with since second grade. Charlie's dad, Mr. George Brown, had built a golf course in White County, and I found out later that my dad was the guy who did the grading to make Skitts Mt. Golf course. Charlie is one of the smartest guys I know. While we were in college together, I learned that not only was Charlie smart, but he always had a clever way of showing it. I never will forget the time that Charlie, who became a lawyer, and I were talking. I told Charlie that my marriage seemed to be falling apart, and I might have to ask him to be my attorney. Being the good friend that he was, and also showing how smart he was, Charlie just looked at me and said, "Gosh Bobby, I think I would have a lot better chance of winning if I represented your wife, Paula." Well, the marriage has lasted, and Charlie was probably right. Sometimes, I get the feeling that my friends know me too well. At least, I think Charlie Brown does.

PUT THAT IN YOUR PIPE

Coleman Canup hauled lumber from my daddy's sawmill for several years. Mr. Canup was a fellow who loved to tell stories of adventures that he had been privileged to witness or participate in and; there had been many. He and I once drove his old Jeep down the backside of Tray Mountain to the head of York Creek. York Creek and Curtis Creek come together at Anna Ruby Falls to form Smith Creek. We camped there overnight. There were lots of speckle trout in the creek, and we caught several of them and Coleman fried the fish. We had fish, fried potatoes and pork and beans. It was a fine meal and I remember it, like it was yesterday. Coleman said that one time he and his brother were watching his grandpa rock in his rocking chair. Occasionally, the elder Mr. Canup would pick up his pipe, puff a few times, and then lay it back on the floor. He then would nap a little. Coleman and his brother waited until he was napping and got the pipe. They picked up an old hen turd and stuff it in his pipe. The boys carefully laid the pipe back where they got it. They then hid around the corner of the house. In just a few minutes, it was time to puff on the pipe again. Mr. Canup placed the pipe in his mouth got one of the old long matches out of the box, swiped it on the floor and tried to light his pipe. After several puffs, the elder Mr. Canup yelled to his wife, "Honey, don't put my tobacco near the heater. It dries it out, and makes it smell like chicken sh—." Coleman laughed, and said his pap quit smoking shortly after that. You know it takes a heart attack, lung cancer or bypass surgery to make some folks quit smoking. I wonder if they just smoked a little chicken manure if it would have the same effect. I bet it would.

NAME THAT DUCK

My friend Lanier Chambers came by Mom and dad's house knocked on the door, stuck his head in and said, "You want to go duck hunting?" Notice, I didn't say someone went to the door to see who was out there. No, I grew up in a time when people gave you a courtesy knock. They usually gave you just enough time to get something over you if you were naked or hide behind a chair if there were no clothes or towels to grab. Since I had my clothes on, I grabbed my gun and out the door I went. Once in the truck, I asked Lanier where we were going. He said that he had seen some ducks on H.A. Allison's pond. We drove up, and sure enough, we could see two ducks on Mr. Allison's pond. Lanier told me to let him get hid behind the dam then make the ducks fly. I saw the barrel of his gun wave, which meant, I am ready. I jumped up and the ducks looked at me and went QUACK, QUACK. I yelled, "Lanier, they won't fly." "Throw a rock at 'em." He replied. I did. The ducks flew right over Lanier. Bam, Bam, the ducks fell out of the sky. We picked the ducks up and I said, "Lanier these don't look like wild ducks." Lanier said, "They don't, do they?" So we took off to Mom and Dad's to look them up in the encyclopedia. Spoon Bill domesticated ducks is what they were. Lanier and I were in route to another pond, and who do we see walking down the street behind the 5 & 10, Mr. H. A. Allison. Before I knew what Lanier was going to do, he pulled over right in front of Mr. Allison. "H.A. do you have any Ducks on your pond?" Lanier asked. "Well yea, I put two over there yesterday." Mr. Allison said. Lanier said, "H. A. you don't have them ducks anymore." "I don't?" He said. "No, we just shot your ducks, but we will buy you two to replace them." "Aw don't worry about it" said Mr. Allison. I don't think we ever bought him those ducks.

REGISTERED DOG

It is no secret that when I was younger, I coon hunted a great deal. I loved to hear the hounds barking in the distance, knowing that they would put that old coon up a tree. Another treat was to go see other peoples' dogs. One of my former football players, and coon hunting buddy was Randy Pruitt from Dahlonega. Randy would later serve as sheriff of Lumpkin County. Randy came up to me before practice one evening and said, "Coach, Lee Ralston has got a red bone gyp over at his house, and they say she is a good coon dog." Lee Ralston was a dog trader, and lived nearby. Randy wanted to go see the hound that Mr. Ralston had. After practice, we headed over to Lee's house. Lee had little dog houses everywhere. There was a dog tied to each of them. We were walking over to see the little redbone hound when a pickup truck with a dog box worth more than Lee's house drove up in the yard. A young fellow got out and asked if Mr. Ralston was around? Lee says, "Mr. Ralston died several years ago, but I am Lee." The young man proceeded to drag a pup out of the fancy dog box and said, "This dog is out of 3 bench champions, 2 nite champions, and has 8 champions in his pedigree." He pulled another pup out of the other side of the box. He says, "This pup is out of World Champion Bean Blossom Buck. He has 12 champions on his mother's side, and 6 champions on his fathers' side. I am going to trade you these two high bred pups for that little old redbone hound." Mr. Ralston placed his foot on the bumper of the gentleman's truck, looked at him and said, "Fellar, I come from a good mama and a good daddy, and you see what a sorry sumbitch I turned out to be. I am just going to keep my little redbone." Each time I hear someone talking about the breeding of a dog, a horse, and yes, sometimes people, I think of Lee Ralston. I think Mr. Ralston told it like it is.

THE CLUCKING HEN

There is nothing more protective of its young than an old hen. You let anything come around one of her little biddies, she will start to cluck, and before you know it, she will be flogging something or somebody. To me, that is the way most women are about their children. I got my introduction to religion at a little Holiness Church just below where we lived. It was a small church, with most of the congregation being related to one another. Not only did I get my first lessons in religion there, but I also got to see how protective my mom was of her little biddies. It was close to the 4th of July. Since we walked to church that evening, we were just a little late getting there. We had taken a seat near the rear of the Church. The preacher was preaching brimstone, hell fire and damnation. I could tell it was a good sermon because it was scaring me and he sounded like he was talking about me the whole time. Just in the midst of that good sermon, there was a loud KA-BOOM. The KA-BOOM had come from the area in back of the Church. There was only one thing back there. It was the outhouse, the privy, the john. Someone had just set off a big M80, or cherry bomb, and tossed it into the latrine. I smiled when the KA-BOOM went off. I would have loved to have seen that thing go off. One of the ladies sitting directly in front of us leaned over and whispered, "I bet it was one of those little Adams boys." My first thought was Dear Lord Jesus; I hope my Mom didn't hear her say that. She did. Mom tapped the lady on the shoulder and said, "My children are right here with me. Where's yours?" We followed mom out of the church all under her wing. I thought I heard a cluck. Thankfully nothing or nobody got flogged, but it was close.

GOOD NEIGHBORS

Our Neighbors were like family. They were people that came to help us when we needed help. They brought food when there was a death in our family. They looked after our livestock when we were out of town. We laughed with each other. We cried together. We played together. This is how it was with my family and the Magness family. The Magness family lived at the bottom of the hill in a house that everyone referred to as the "Old Jim Denton place." When I was growing up, the Magness family was a second family for me. Fletch and Dorothy Magness had a lot of children. The boys were Carlous, Harold, Donald, Jerry, Robert, Garvis, and Ricky. The girls were Ruthlene, Josephine, and Martha. Robert and Garvis were about my age, so each day we usually played together. But before we played, Dorothy always made the boys go get water from the spring that was near her house. They also had to cut wood for the cook stove that she had in her kitchen. I remember spending the night with them. It was a very cold winter night. When I got into bed, I soon found that you didn't move. The quilts were packed so high the sheer weight of the covers kept you from moving. There was only one wood heater in the house, and it was in the room that Dorothy and Fletch slept in. I also remember Jerry telling me to pour the water I was drinking out of the glass before I went to sleep. I asked him why? He told me it might freeze and break his mother's glass. Before Dorothy passed away, I visited her at the convalescent home. I loved Dorothy. She had a beautiful smile. She always referred to me as "Her Bobby." Yesterday, I read that preacher Robert Magness had passed away. That leaves Josephine, Garvis and Ricky. A lot of the people that I loved growing up have left this world. I hope my neighbors loved me as much as I loved them.

POOL HALL BLUES

Growing up just two miles out of Cleveland, Georgia was an adventure. We were far enough away from town to be considered country folks, yet close enough to hitch hike into town to go to the Princess Movie Theater or go to Stovall's 5 & 10. Both required only a modest amount of money for your enjoyment. Next to the theater was the Princess Grill, and in the same building, was a pool hall. For some reason, my mom thought that the pool hall was an evil place, a place where only hoodlums and trouble makers hung out. That might have explained why I liked to go in there so much. Each time we got to go see a movie, as soon as it was over, into the pool hall I went. If I had a dime left over, it would be spent in that den of sin. Mom had given me enough money for three people to go to see a movie. It was for my cousin Wayne, Brother Bruce and me. On the way there, Wayne and Bruce decided that they would go do something else. Unfortunately for them, they forgot to ask for their share of the loot. I proceeded on to the movie. After the movie, into the pool hall I went. Being true to form, I spent not only my money, but the rest of the money as well, which proved to be the wrong thing to do. It so happened, that Bruce and Wayne returned home before I did. Worrying about her red headed son, mom came to find me. Mom marched right into that pool hall, grabbed me by the shirt, and out the door I went. I had to confess that I had blown all the extra money in the pool hall. After my bottom healed, and I was able to sit down again, Stovall's 5 & 10 got a lot more of my business.

WHISKEY RIVER

While sitting in Church this morning I was looking out the window and saw a barn that sits in the middle of a big pasture that is located near the Church. I get lost in thought sometimes when I am sitting in Church. I guess the good Lord will have to forgive me for that. I don't know why but looking out that church window brought this story to my mind. I can't remember who the man was that started this story but I do remember sitting on one of the benches outside my grandfather's store, J W Sims Grocery in Helen when I heard the story. Many of those that sat on those benches were moonshine drinkers and were all filled with mischief. The gentleman said that the revenuers had been cutting down several of the whiskey makers copper stills lately and some of the men were finding it harder and harder to find a place that they could safely make their mountain dew. Many of the families that were located in the North Georgia Mountains depended on selling there fire water so they could buy clothes, food and other necessities for their family. One of the fellows that were a partaker of the spirits and sitting there was a fellow by the name of Pud Allison. Pud and his family were very well known in the northern portion of White County. Old Pud says, "Why I heared that them Revenuers have been getting so much of the whiskey that they wuz gest a taking hit rat to the Chattahoochee River and a pouring it rat in the river." Puds' brother was Rusty Allison. Pud and Rusty were men that I listened to a great deal when I was growing up. Rusty poked Mr. T. J. Tallant in the side with his elbow then winked at him, and looked at his brother Pud and said, "Why Pud, I have been hearing that those Revenuers have had a big impact on all of the Churches here in Helen." Pud looked a little befuddled and said to his brother, "Rusty how in the hell can Revenuers have a big impact on the Churches in Helen?" Old Rusty started laughing and said, "Why Pud every one of them has started their Sunday services off by singing "Shall We Gather at the River." Those Whiskey drinkers all laughed and so did I.

HE DID IT

When I was a young boy; there was nothing I liked to do better than to wrestle with my brother Bruce. Bruce was two years older than me, and I know many times he would hold back and not clobber me the way he would like to. You see, I was the kind of kid that my mama didn't want me to run around with when I was growing up. If they would have had drugs for hyperactive kids, when I was a kid, well let's just say; I would have been on a drip. I was off the wall on most days. I was out the door when I woke up, and back home when it got dark. I think sometimes my mom and dad thought there had been a big mistake at the hospital. Someone had gotten the wrong child. Surely that was what had happened. But through it all, they loved me. Once when Bruce and I were wrestling on the bed in the back bedroom of the house, I grabbed Bruce in a head lock and I did judo flip with him. It was beautiful. He sailed over my body, just like Roy Rogers would have done it. However, Bruce's left foot went through the window. It made a horrific crash sound. Fortunately, Bruce did not get a cut. But when mom come running back there to see what happened, I jumped off the bed. I pointed at Bruce, and said, "He did it." And with his leg still through the window it was hard for him to tell mom that he wasn't responsible for the broken glass. Bruce got a whipping. I got away. After that, if anything happened that might result in us getting a whipping, Bruce learned to tell mom real quick what happened. Man, sometimes I wish he hadn't learned so easy.

THE GIFT OF A ROCK

Growing up with an older brother and lots of cousins that all seemed to be about 2 to 4 years older than me was pretty darn hard. They would all seem at times, to think that I was too young to run with them. And maybe I was, but at least, I didn't know it. I found that there was one thing that made me, even if it was for a short period of time, equal to them. Whenever they made me mad, a good rock was one of the best equalizers of age difference that I knew. My brother and my cousins could probably all beat my butt. But with a good rock in my hand, I could hold myself in there with the best of them. I remember one time when my cousin Clifford made me mad. I don't really remember why, but I was mad at him. So, I did what I thought I should do. I picked up a rock and threw it at him. He asked me not to do it, so, I did it again. That time, I think I got him on the leg, so the chase was on. I started chasing Clifford; picking up a good rock, whenever he showed signs of slowing down. We had gone down into the pasture below my grandmother Adams house when I reached down to get a rock. Fortunately, before I hurled it at Clifford, I looked at it. It was one of the biggest arrowheads I had ever found. I didn't throw that arrowhead at Clifford. I did pick up another rock and whizzed it at him. I was kind of like Earnest T. on the Andy Griffin Show, but younger. Because of my rock throwing temper tantrum, Clifford went home. But later on, I gave Clifford that arrowhead. Today, Clifford has a beautiful collection of arrowheads. A lot of them would come from arrowheads that my brother and I gave him.

One of those would have never been in his collection, if I had thrown it. I could be explaining why Cousin Clifford got a knot on his head. Naw, I could never throw straight.

A SPEECH THERAPIST

There is none of my hunting buddies that I had rather go anywhere with than Howell Head. You never know what to expect. Now, first let me tell you, ole Hal, as we call him, is an excellent outdoorsman. I have made several trips to Colorado with Hal, and each time I have come back with some truly amazing memories. Hal is a true Southerner. He talks with that North Georgian, Appalachian Southern Redneck drawl. You know, just like I do, but more profound. We had been planning a trip out West, so Hal and I decided that we would go to a bar in Helen, eat and further plan our trip. At this particular time in Hal's life, it was between marriages. So ole Hal was always on the lookout for someone of the opposite sex to engage in conversation with, or maybe to dance the night away. We had been at the bar a short time when a very attractive young lady walked up beside us. The music was VERY loud and I was standing between Hal and this young lady. She leaned back and says to Hal, 'WHAT IS YOUR NAME?" Ole Hal leans back and says in his Southern drawl "HAAAL HEEAAD." She said, "WHAT?" I turned to her and said, "HOWELL HEAD." Then is when the real translation started. The lady then asked Hal, "WHAT DO YOU DO?" Hal says, "I WOORRK AAT MICCHHLLIN TAAR COMMPANNY." She said, "WHAT DID HE SAY?" I looked at her and said, "HE IS A SPEECH THERAPIST." "Cool" she said. The young lady went and sat down, and Hal said, "WWHATT TTHHEE HHEELL IS A SSSPPEECH TTHERAPIST?" I just looked at

Hal and said, "I think she likes you, Hal." I went home. Howell danced the night away.

TAKING ADVICE

When I first started teaching in Lumpkin County, I boarded with Ms. Ruby Abercrombie. Ms. Abercrombie was the Avon lady in Dahlonega. Nothing went on in Dahlonega without Ms. Ruby knowing it. She also knew just about everybody and who they were related to as well. She kept me up to date on all of the gossip and other important information that a new comer like me would need to know. She had her rules for her house. And she expected me to follow them. Ms. Ruby wanted me to be up at 6:30am and on my way to school by 7. There was to be no hanky-panky in her house. No women allowed in my room. No alcohol either. The $75.00 per month I paid her was for the room and one meal a day. It could be breakfast or dinner. I always had lunch at school. Things went well for several weeks. I could tell that Ms. Abercrombie was a lady that meant what she said. Actually I learned this the hard way. I had been working hard at school. The football practices were long and being a beginning teacher and coach, I didn't get in early. That getting up at 6:30 was killing me. I had been late getting up for a few days in a row. Finally one morning at the breakfast table, Ms. Ruby said, "Look here Adams, I am going to give you some advice. There's one thing I don't allow people to be around here; you cannot be a DRAG ASS. So you get up when you are supposed to get up, GOT IT." I was never late again. She and I remained friends throughout her life. It was great advice.

WHO WAS THAT MAN

I was doing some painting for a friend of mine, Ronnie Fain. Ronnie was remodeling a house for a gentleman, Mr. Paul Webb. I didn't get to know Mr. Webb nearly as well as I would have liked. He was one of those guys you could listen to for hours, and never grow tired. Mr. Webb was an attorney. Mr. Webb asked me one day if I said I had lived in Lumpkin County. I replied, "Yes sir, I lived in Lumpkin County for a number of years." Mr. Webb began to tell me this story. -----When he first started practicing law in Atlanta, it seems that a young lady from Lumpkin County had come to his office to ask if he would defend her in a case where she was charged with having a concealed weapon and attempted murder. After hearing her side of the story, he told her he would, and the first thing she needed to do was to go home and get her some good character witnesses. She asked him if the Sheriff of her county would be a good one; he told her that the Sheriff would be an excellent one, if she could get him. During the trial the Sheriff showed up to be one of the young lady's character witnesses. He was asked to describe the young lady. He gave her a wonderful character reference, saying he had known her for years, and he thought she was a mighty fine girl. Mr. Webb said that any lawyer worth his salt would not put a person on the stand, unless he knew what they were going to say. He said to the prosecution, "Your witness." The prosecution had no questions. They brought the trial to a close, and the Jury returned a "not guilty" verdict on the attempted murder charge, but a "guilty" verdict on the concealed weapon charge. The Judge fined the lady 4 or 5 hundred dollars, and the Sheriff came up and immediately paid the fine. The Sheriff then asked the young lady if she wanted to go get something to eat. They walked out of the courtroom together. Mr. Webb turned and said, "You know, that Sheriff must really think a lot of that girl." One of the other character witnesses for the girl said, "Well, he should. That's his daughter." That was unknown by either of the attorneys. Mr. Web passed away two years after he told me this story. I wish I could have gotten to know him better.

SIGNS THEY ARE A CHANGING

I was the baseball coach at LCHS for about 8 years and I loved every one of those years. My teams were successful but at the same time we had FUN. We laughed a lot. The young men worked hard at practice, and we won together and we lost together. In other words; we were always a team. I remember one game that we were playing against Dawson County and a young man named Danny Otter was my catcher. Danny and his wife Jan live over in Habersham County. Right before the game Danny came up and said, "Coach, I forgot my belt for my uniform." Being the considerate coach I was, I said, "Here take mine." And I drew my belt out of my pants. The game started and Otter's time to bat came up. Danny got a single and was on first base. Our sign to steal was very simple, a tug on the coach's belt. Everything looks pretty good at this point in the game, except, my pants were falling off. I didn't think anything about it when I pulled my britches up, but Danny did. I was looking in left field when I heard "YOUR OUT." I looked and there was Danny; thrown out at second base. I said, "Danny why did you steal?" He said, "Coach you gave me the steal sign; you tugged on your pants." He was right. We changed the steal sign. Just in case my pants were ever falling off.

MEANING WHAT SHE SAID

When I was growing up, we lived on a chicken farm near Helen, Ga. I wanted to go fast in everything. On a horse, in a wagon, bicycle, car anything that moved; I wanted to go fast. My Dad had traded Guy Palmer a milk cow for an old Jeep. That Jeep had no brakes what so ever. I mean it didn't even have a brake cylinder on it. So when I got in that jeep, I could go fast, whether I wanted to or not. We lived at the back end of a dirt road. I could drive that jeep and just fly all the way to twin tanks service station. There were a few folks that lived on that road. They were all Vandivers. Aunt Lou Vandiver was the oldest resident there. She was in her 90's and didn't like the dust that I created when I came flying by. She had asked me to slow down on more than one occasion. One day she stopped me and said, "If you don't slow that thing down; I will slow it down for you." How could this old lady slow me down? My goodness, she's in her 90's. The next day I came flying off the hill, there in the road was 4 boards with 16 penny nails all sticking straight up. I did mention that the old jeep had no brakes. I limped down to twin tanks with four flat tires. The bad part was I had to go back by her house and she was standing there looking at me with a smile on her face. My Dad made me go apologize to Aunt Lou. It made me realize you can learn a lot from an elderly lady, especially one that means what she says. Dad never did fix the brakes on that Jeep.

UNFRIED CHICKEN

My wife, Paula, is not a cook. It's not that she can't cook; it's she just doesn't like to cook. In fact, I would sell my oven but I wouldn't have a place to hide the Christmas presents. Many years ago before we were married, Paula and I were dating. She asked if she could cook a dinner for me. I was living in my Chalet in Northern Lumpkin County. I told Paula that I thought that would be a wonderful thing to do. I informed her that ball practice would be over about 5:30 or so, and I should be getting home around 6 that evening. I was filled with anticipation thinking about a good home cooked meal. I got home walked into my house, and there on the kitchen table was some beautiful golden brown fried chicken, green beans, and what looked like delicious baked potatoes. Paula was beaming with pride. We sat down and both started filling our plates. I bit into my chicken leg. I couldn't get the meat to turn loose from the bone. Maybe I am not trying hard enough. I twisted the leg a little harder. I watched and Paula was also struggling with her chicken. I looked at the chicken; it was golden brown on the outside, but raw as could be on the inside. Suddenly her smile turned to a frown and she said; "They told me to get it brown before I took it up and I did." Trying to comfort her and not laugh, I said, "Now Paula, don't worry about it. I bet they told Colonel Sanders the same thing, but I bet they told him to make sure it was done." Since that time Paula has never wanted to cook. I wonder if Colonel Sanders ever had that problem. I probably should have said something different.

KEEP THE WHORE

When I lived in Northern Lumpkin County, I had a neighbor named Tom McDonald. Tom and his sister Mamie lived right down the road from me. Both Tom and Mamie lived to way in their 90's. They were great neighbors. If you needed them all you had to do was call. They were super folks. I was in the woods one day and heard a tractor running so I go down to see who is on the dam of Whitner's Lake near my house. It was Tom bush hogging. He got off of his tractor, and was wiping the sweat off his brow. I said, "How's it going Tom?" Tom lifted his hat and said, "Pretty good. Have you been reading about Old Wilbur Mills?" Now Wilbur Mills was a congressman that had taken up with a call girl named Fanny Fox and had been in the news. I said, "Well, Tom a little bit." Tom looked at me and said, "If the taxpayers would buy me a whore, I wouldn't mind having one." I didn't really know what to say. So I said, "I guess so Tom." Tom then says, "Have you ever seen a picture of old Wilbur's wife?" No, I can't say that I have Tom. Tom says, "Well I have, and if I was him, I would just keep the whore." Sometimes honesty just comes out when you least expect it.

THE WAN WINE

When I bought my house in Lumpkin County, I soon learned that I had some really wonderful neighbors. Tom and his sister Mammie was an elderly couple that lived just down the road from me. Both were what you would call native Appalachian folks. Tom and Mammie lived in a small white house on McDonald Road. Tom had some great stories about the times that he and his friends made moonshine on just about every creek in that little valley. Tom told me this story about two of his neighbors. It seems that there was a family that lived down on the creek below the McDonalds farm. The man's name was Clayt Grizzle. Mr. Grizzle had an old female hound that had a litter of puppies. One of Tom's other neighbors that lived beyond the Grizzle place was Mr. Emory Anderson. Both men were friends of Tom and for the most part friends with each other when they were not feuding over something. Tom said that Emory had been visiting with him and they had been in to one of the jugs maybe a little too much. Emory decided it was time for him to go home. Let me point out that I was also a neighbor of Emory Andersons and I always liked Emory. I never got to meet Mr. Grizzle. I think he had passed away many years before I moved to Lumpkin County. After Emory left Tom's place he had to walk right in front of the Grizzles home. The old hound dog came out from under the porch and ran up behind Emory and bit him on the leg. This made Emory so mad that he went home got his gun and came back to the Grizzles place. The dog came running out again and Emory shot the dog grave yard dead. He proceeded on over to Toms place and told Tom what he had done. Emory then went home. Tom said that after Clayt got off of work he found his dog and came to him and ask who had killed the dog. Tom told him it was Emory. Well Clayt said, "I will just go shoot that Blankety Blank, Blank", and off he went. Tom said, "I knew Emory would be waiting at the wand wine." Emory had a slight speech impediment and Tom would try to sound just like Emory. Tom said he figured that Emory would be waiting at the land line so he took out a running as hard as he could through the woods to warn Emory of Clayt decision to kill him. Sure enough, Emory was sitting at the wand wine waiting on Clayt. Tom said, "I got between them and when Clayt walked up I jerked the gun out of Clayt's hand. I knew I could probably talk Emory out of shooting Clayt but I didn't know if I could get Clayt not to shoot Emory." Tom said, "I thought I had both men kind of calmed down.' Then Clayt said to Emory, "That old bitch dog has got four puppies and I am going to train them to be just as mean as their mother." Emory looked and Clayt and said," Yes a by dod I's got fo mo dam shot dun shells." Tom said he didn't think that Emory and Clayt ever liked one another, but at least they didn't kill each other.

EDUCATION THE HARD WAY

It was summer time and it was hot. I was helping Billy Wayne Chambers and his brother, Lanier, build a cabin on Cedar Mountain. I never learned a great deal about construction so; I was really hired for my physical attributes not my mental abilities. We had finished the outside walls up on the cabin and we were ready for the rafters. A friend of mine, Garland Seabolt, who by the way was a really good carpenter, was also helping us build this cabin. I had taken this summer job because I had some time before I would have to start football practice. It gave me the opportunity to earn some badly needed extra money. We were using 4x12x22 beams as rafters. And they were HEAVY. I got down off the building and laid one end of those HEAVY beams up on the side wall of the cabin then, I climbed the latter and was straining with every bit of muscle I had to get the beam up on the ceiling jost. Sweat was dripping in my eyes, and I was hot. Finally after I had stranded every muscle in my body, I got that beam up there. I looked and old Garland was just sitting there watching me. He looked over at me and said, "You know for a college boy, you are not very smart." Now that flew all over me. I looked at him and said," Yea, Why do you think that?" Garland smiled and said, "If that had of been me, I would have asked someone to help me with that heavy thing." Sometimes we get educated on the Job. Don't you think?

THE WALLET ON A STRING

White County was a very rural county in the 50's. We were beginning to get some paved roads. In the mid-50's we got a plant to locate here. We also were beginning to see the chicken industry bring us out of the poverty that had gripped the country since the great depression. I, like most people here, didn't know if we were poor or rich or what. We had most everything we needed and being young let us enjoy life to the fullest. We didn't have a recreation department, but man, we had FUN. If I was at my Aunts and Uncles place, we were exploring old mining caves or digging our own. We fished, hunted, camped out, and anything else that the seasons would allow. There was one thing that I had a ball doing. We would tie some cat gut fishing line to a wallet. We would put one dollar in it, if we had a dollar. We then would put it about half way out in the middle of highway 75. There was a big culvert about half way down the hill from our house near Asbestos road. We placed that wallet in the middle of the road and as cars came across the hill the drivers would see that wallet and you could hear tires squeal. Before those cars could stop, just as fast as we could, we would pull the wallet into the culvert. We got to hear lots of curse words and swearing when the drivers or there passengers couldn't find the wallet. I am sure there are laws that make that; plus other things we did for recreation illegal. But we were our own recreation department and we were probably way underfunded. Don't you think?

WHO'S THAT BLONDE

We are all blessed with good friends in our life. If I hadn't had the friends that I have had, where would my stories have come from? Believe me! I have had some great friends, and I still do. If it had not been for my friends I would have never finished High School. College would have never been in my vocabulary. Friends have always been there to help, to care, to laugh with, to cry with, to pick me up when I am down, and love me when I am unlovable. I don't get to tell my friends how much they mean to me. I guess, I (like most people) just take friendship for granted. One of my friends, Chris Black was playing basketball at the University of North Carolina in Charlotte, and he came home for a weekend break. Chris came by my house late on a Friday evening and said, "Let's go to Helen and have a beer." Which meant, let's go see how many beers we can drink before they close the bar. We proceeded to do that. It was late when we returned. So, Chris decided he would just spend the night with me. Chris had let his hair grow long, and he had bleached his hair to a golden blonde. Now—-my mom always came in and woke me up with a soft pat on my cheek. That Saturday morning I heard Mom open the door, she peeped in and quickly disappeared. In just a minute my dad came to my door. Dad said, "Bob who's in the bed with you?" I said, "It's Chris Black." Dad quickly said, "Good God, Frances thought you had a blonde headed woman in there." For many years my Mom and Dad laughed about that. Chris died way too young. I never got to tell him what a great friend he was. Our friends are great. We need to tell them. Don't you think?

THE WRONG GEAR

My dad always said a man could be educated and smart but not have one lick of common sense. Seems that dad has been right about a lot of things that I didn't see at the time. But common sense in its self is hard to define. I know people that think they have a lot of common sense but to me; they just don't know what common sense is. On the opening day of the Chattahoochee Wildlife Management Area deer hunt my brothers, my cousins and a few friends used to all go camping. It was a wonderful experience and there were always lots of laughs to be had. Me, my brother Billy and my friend David Wilkins were going to set up a camp on what was called the Martin Branch area of the refuge. My papa Sims let us use his old jeep to hook to a little trailer to haul our camping gear in. The road was steep and the hill was very slick. It also had some very deep ruts in it. Billy and I were going to push, and David was going to drive. As David was spinning those tires up the side of that hill, Billy and I started yelling "HANG HIGH DAVID, HANG HIGH." David shifted the jeep into high gear and that was it. It stalled half way up the hill. "Why did you shift into high gear David," Billy said in a bewildered tone. David replied, "Yawl were yelling hang high." Billy Replied, "We meant for you to stay on the high side of the ruts. Not shift into high gear." Oh well, I am not sure if common sense was needed here. But I think it was. Whenever I see my friend David, he always smiles and says, "Hang High, Bobby Hang High."

GRANNY GOSS

My grandmother Adams was a beautiful lady. She had long white hair that reached below the tops of her hips. She wore her hair in a bun. She raised 9 children. She had 4 boys and 5 girls. Granny Adams lived to be 93 years old and she died while reading the Atlanta Journal newspaper at her kitchen table. I don't know if reading the paper had anything to do with it or not. I somehow doubt that it did. Granny believed in two things for staying healthy, exercising and having a little totty of white moonshine before bedtime. My grandmother would walk up to Mom and Dad's house twice a day, once in the morning and then in the evening. She would go seven laps around Mom and Dad's pool. On one mornings walk my grandmother had completed her seven laps and sat down to rest a bit. There were 5 of her children and me sitting there. Before anyone said anything, I asked Granny, "Granny what was my Great Grandma's maiden name?" It was like the EF Hutton commercial. If EF Hutton speaks everybody listens. My Grandmother replied, "Well, I'll tell you. You grandma's maiden name was uh-----Goss." "Why mama, you never told us anything about who are grandmother was. Why didn't you?" Aunt Sarah said. Granny replied, "Well, they were some of them Goss women known to STEP ASIDE." I still laugh about that. I bet granny Goss would have been a real character. I bet she could tell me some real good stories. Don't you think?

GUNS AND ROSES

Recently I have been reading all of this crap about government taking our guns. Nuts saying get ready for blood shed. I mean some downright crazy crap. Let me please tell some of you a little bit of honesty. You are watching too much Fox propaganda. We have a constitution that contains a Bill of Rights. If these same people are so worried about constitutional rights, why not be as passionate about all of them not just the second amendment. Most of these gun idiots don't even know what former Presidents have done about guns. For instance they don't know that their big Republican hero Ronald

Reagan passed a series of gun control pieces of legislation. I think it was the called the Munford Act. The NRA was all for that legislation. We have an amendment that guarantees freedom of speech but you can't go into a crowd and yell Fire. There are laws affecting every amendment. Freedom is not absolute. Many people, Republican and Democrat, need to realize that we have laws passed when we feel it necessary to protect our citizens. Not many people have any more guns than I do. I love guns. I grew up with guns. I hunt. I target practice. I have no fear of someone coming to my house and taking my guns. If you do, get over it. Watch CNN or MSNBC for a change. If laws are passed, you like me should obey them. You can't pick and choose. If you don't like a law vote, Obama won, get over it.

DADDY THINKS HE IS SMART

When I learned to drive, I physically could not see over the steering wheel. So I would look under it. After all, I was 7 years old and anything that had a motor in it became a challenge. Needless to say, I loved to drive anything that would roll or ride. This feeling lasted for many years. In 1954 mom and dad bought a brand new Mercury. It was a two tone blue. And in that car I learned, that if you got to going backwards in R about 20 mph and jerked that thing in the D, you could spin the tires for a good while and leave a black mark on the pavement. Not bad for a seven year old. Well, that knowledge was carried with me into my teenage years. Mom and Dad had a 1965 4 door Impala Chevrolet. I was coming back from Helen on Alternate 75. There was a hill just before where Ridge Road came into the highway, and I had the bright idea that I needed to see how long of a black mark I could leave on that hill. Using the knowledge that I had acquired at the age of 7, I laid down one of longest black marks ever. It was a black mark that was unequaled by any of my red neck buddies. I still had a grin on my face when I passed the Ridge Road, but that is where I met the first vehicle since achieving my great feat. It was my Dad in his truck. I was in the house when Dad came in. He said, "Bob, don't you be spinning my tires off. They are too expensive for you to do that." I looked surprised and said, "Daddy, what are you talking about? I came through the Ridge Road. I didn't come up that hill." Dad said, "Come out here." Dad took me outside and instructed me to look under that rear fender. There was about an inch of rubber stuck to the top of the fender. From then on, I realized Dads are pretty hard to fool, especially one that had to stop because of tire smoke.

RIDE THAT BULL

Dad had bought a Jersey bull from one of our neighbors. It looked like a challenge to me. I believed I could ride that bull. I decided I would prove it. I tried for several days to catch that crafty old bull but to no avail. So being the ingenious little boy I was, I decided that if I could get that bull to eat some corn right under a big terrace in the pasture; I could then jump on his back and test my ability as a bull rider. It took several scoops of corn before I got that old bull lined up just right, but when I saw my chance, I made a mad dash. My hands were placed solidly on the bulls hips, I landed right in the middle of his back. I mean I nailed that landing. Even though it was very brief, and the dismount was not nearly as pretty, and the distance that I had jumped was nowhere near the distance that the bull through me. As soon as the breath came back into my lungs, I realized that bull and I were going to be enemies for a while. For several weeks I kept jumping on the bulls back till he would no longer buck. Well, that was no fun. I found that if I twisted the bull's tail he would buck. I did that for a while, and then he stopped bucking again. I am ashamed to say, but I broke the cartilage in that bull's tail. My Dad didn't know what I had done. He had the vet come and check the bull. The vet said the bull obviously had something called tail rot. The vet amputated the bull's tail. We kept that bob tail bull for several years. I never did tell my Dad why that bull's tail was broke. Over the years we had several of that old bull's calves. One of his bull calves was born with a natural bob tail. One day I told Dad, "I don't think that old bull likes me." Dad said, "If you had of broke my tail I wouldn't like you either." How did he know that???

HANDLE THAT CROWD GRANNY

One of my cousins was getting married and my grandmother Adams at that time was in her 80's. She had been asked to come down to Grace Presbyterian Church to sit in the reception line. Granny Adams had just got out of the hospital. She had recently had part of her colon removed. It was the first time and only time she had ever been hospitalized. This Church is a very large Church in the Decatur area and my cousin's family had been going there for years. So needless to say there were lots of folks at this wedding. After the wedding, my grandmother was sitting in a chair and as people would come through and greet my grandmother. They would say things like; hey Ms. Adams, it is so good to see you. Or Ms. Adams it is so nice of you to come down for the wedding, we hope that you are recovering from your surgery.   I kept noticing my grandmother would just shake her head up and down and grab the next person's hand. After about 30 or 40 minutes of this, I thought maybe granny is getting tired. So I go over to her and said, "Granny are you alright, do you want to rest?" She looked up at me and said, "I can't hear a word their saying; I got my hearing aid turned off."   My Granny knew how to handle a crowd.

DON'T JUDGE THE BOOK BY ITS COVER

You know it is hard to look at a kid in school and determine what they will become or how successful they will be. I am reminded of that each time I see kids that used to be students at school and or now successful whatevers. Imagine me seeing Jamie Satterfield on TV hunting deer or turkey. Jamie is now a Doctor, but loves to hunt and has a great hunting show. That reminds me of the time that Coach Price and I was walking across the area called the "bridge" at Lumpkin County High School. Several students were all just kind of milling around and one young man was playing his guitar. Several of the kids were listening to him play. He was playing pretty good. As we walked by Coach Price said, "I hope you can make a living playing that guitar-cause that is about the only thing you can do." Coach Price told me later that he hoped that boy has forgotten about him saying that. I would say maybe Zach Brown has forgotten it. But I wouldn't bet on it. He is making a pretty good living playing that guitar.

SLEEPING WITH GRANNY

Two of my best friends went to Helen and like lots of my good buddies they would stay until the bars shut down. Chris Black and Mike Wilkins had a wonderful time that night and after several of the brews they decided that it would be best if Mike would stay with Chris at Chris's granny Cook's house. Chris and Mike navigated the steps and Chris had Mike's arm as they entered the house. Chris of course was trying to keep Mike from waking his Grandmother up. The bathroom was located between the bedrooms in Ms. Cook's house. Just as they entered the hall, Mike whispered, "I got to go pee." Chris told Mike to go in the bathroom and be sure to be quiet, so that he wouldn't wake his Grandma up. Well, Chris turned right and went into the bedroom. He undressed and got under the covers. Mike exited the bathroom, but instead of turning left and going into the bedroom that Chris was in, Mike turned right. Now, Ms. Cook was an elderly lady and was sound asleep. Mike took his clothes off and jumped in bed. He thought he was sharing the bed with Chris, but when he heard the screams, he realized he had made a mistake. He was sharing the bed with Ms. Cook. Chris ran in to see what had happened, and Mike was trying to explain his mistake to Ms. Cook. Needless to say, sometimes we all get turned around, but if you do, I hope you don't have to explain why you were in bed with someone's Grandma. That might take years. Don't you think?

BURNING IN THE BED

When you are red headed, and have a light complexion, a 100 Watt light bulb is all you need to get a sun burn. I have always had trouble with sun burn. Many times I have gone to the beach and come back with, not just a sun burn, but with sun poison as well. I could be on the beach a few minutes, and I would look like a well-cooked lobster. So I know that the sun is not my friend. In fact, I don't like the sun. I want it to be cloudy all the time. With this in mind, I found it interesting that my niece, Brelan, asked me one day. "When, Uncle Bobby, are you going to come over and try our new tanning beds out?" Now, I love my nieces, and I would do anything for them, but getting in a tanning bed was something I had great reservations about. I know I burn real easy. But, being the loving Uncle I am, I told her, "Oh, I will come over in a few days." And I did. I went into their new tanning salon. They told me it would help prepare me for my summer vacation. I would be able to get a good tan. First of all, I wasn't planning on getting a good tan, but love is thicker than tanning lotion so I said, "Just tell me what to do." Brelan said, "Just go get in the tanning bed, take this little thing to put over your eyes, and turn the dial to 6 minutes." That sounded simple to me. I went into the room and took off my clothes. That was my first mistake. I wasn't supposed to take off ALL OF MY CLOTHES. I also thought where the nob said 16, was a 6. I didn't tell them about that mistake either. I didn't think it worth mentioning. However, the next day, I was burned in places people are not supposed to be burned. I could not touch myself where I needed to touch myself. Getting too much sun took on a new meaning. It hurt to put on my underwear. A pale man's bottom is not supposed to see a tanning bed. I am sure that is written somewhere, and if it isn't, it needs to be. Oh well, lying in a motel room with the air conditioner going is my kind of vacation. I don't want to get a tan. It's just not me.

RESCUE THAT BOY

We learned to swim at the big rock in the Chattahoochee River. The Big Rock is where lots of people learned to swim. The Big Rock is located behind what is now the Hofbra Haus. At that time it was the Chattahoochee Dining Room. We just called it the "HOOCH." Mr. Arthur Sutton and his wife Bertha had opened the restaurant in Helen. The restaurant was not nearly as important to me as the swimming hole located right behind it. When summer came, we were bound to end up at the Big Rock. My Mom made sure that each of her children could swim before she would let us jump off of that Rock. It was a great feeling to take three quick strides and jump into the River. That swimming hole must have been at least 6 or 7 feet deep back then. Just about every kid in Helen learned to swim in that hole. It seemed like it was far deeper than it was. But when you are young, swimming holes seem bigger and deeper. I remember one of the times that we were swimming at the big rock; there were several kids and some adults swimming in our favorite swimming hole. We were all having lots of fun jumping off the rock, and going down to see if we could reach things on the bottom of the river. I was sitting on one of the rocks watching everyone swim. Suddenly, a man on the bank, that I didn't know, started yelling, "MY SON, MY SON, SOMEONE HELP MY SON." I looked, and a kid I didn't know, was going under the water. My mom turned and jumped right into the water, grabbed the young man, and had him out of the water in just a flash. Mom looked at the man that was yelling and said, "He's alright. He didn't know it was over his head." I like to think my mom saved that young mans' life that day. I have thought about that day many times, especially what mom said.

Sometimes kids are in over their head, but sometimes there is not a mom or dad to rescue them. Maybe we should all be better lifeguards for the kids around us.

Bobby & his mother; I killed this big buck in 1963while skipping school. The principal excused me after I showed him the deer I had killed.

SHUT UP AND WHISTLE

One of the great whistlers of all time, that I had the privilege of knowing, was my Uncle Charles Sims. Uncle Charles would take us fishing or hunting, and he would be whistling. It was a beautiful whistle. It sound like someone had recorded it, and it would just come out of Uncle Charles' mouth so clear and pretty. Garland Vandiver was another fellow that I remember who whistled a lot. Those guys just knew how to whistle. I don't know why people don't whistle like they used to; but they don't. I guess with all the modern technology we have; they can just listen to the iPad, the DVD's, or whatever else is out there to make music. Both Uncle Charles and Garland loved music. If they didn't have an instrument to play, they just whistled the tunes that were in their head. It always sounded pretty to me. Most little boys want to learn to whistle. It is always a challenge for them to learn to whistle. They must get their mouths all puckered up, and make sound come out. I remember watching TV and Roy Rogers would whistle for Trigger. Trigger would come running when he heard that whistle. The Lone Ranger could whistle and Silver would get to him in a hurry. Rin Tin Tin would come running when he heard a whistle. I was bound and determined to learn to whistle. My Uncle Roy had bought some goats. I loved playing with those goats, but I could not get them to come to me when I wanted them to. I had to learn to whistle. I was outside one day playing with those stinking goats; and I do mean stinking, when suddenly, I was going to pretend that I was the Lone Ranger, the goat was silver; I puckered my lips and stuck my tongue in a funny position and a GREAT whistle came out. I HAD LEARNED TO WHISTLE. I would not let my lips change positions. It looked as though I had eaten a green persimmon. I whistled and whistled. I ran in the house where my brother and mom was, and whistled as loud as I could. After whistling for what seemed like an eternity to my mom, she said, "Bobby, if you don't stop that whistling I am going to stick a sock in your mouth." I stopped whistling. That was a relief to everyone. I learned a couple of valuable lessons that day. Everyone is not as excited about what you learn to do as you are; plus, those stinking goats still wouldn't come to me.

CAMPAIGN REFORM

In 1980 I decided that I would run for the position of Superintendent of Schools in Lumpkin County. Campaigning was a very hard thing to do. In that time period, you had to try to go door to door. You asked everyone and there neighbor to vote for you. For some reason dogs like to bite politicians. I had a couple of pair of pants torn by some canines that were bound and determined to see that I was not elected. After I was elected, I wanted to go to lots of those homes and say to those dogs; ha ha you mangy mutts I did it in spite of you. But realizing I only had so many pair of pants, I didn't. While campaigning, I learned that you would ask people to vote for you and move on. You didn't want to get bogged down with anyone to long. If you did, it would keep you from seeing the other potential voters. Once, I was in the Lumpkin County Co-op, and I was greeting some folks as they came inside, and I would ask them to vote for me. On this particular occasion there was a fellow by the name of Hoyt Grizzle in the store. I knew who he was but that was about it. I came up to Mr. Grizzle and said, "I am running for Superintendent of Schools and I would appreciate your vote." Hoyt looked at me and said, "Son, if you get elected, what are you going to do?" Now I had been campaigning hard, but no one had ever asked me that question. I didn't know exactly what to say. This was during the Iran hostage crisis, so I looked at Mr. Grizzle and said, "Well, the first thing I am going to do is try to get those prisoners out of Iran." Hoyt laughed and said, "My God boy, I am going to vote for you." Everyone in the store was laughing but I knew then; that I had better get myself better prepared to answer the tough questions. I took office January 1, 1981. The hostages were released on January 19, 1981. I saw Hoyt Grizzle on January 20th. I told him I took full credit for their release. He laughed and said, "I knew you could do it." Memories make for a good laugh, even if it is at yourself.

READ HIM HIS RIGHTS

Frank Baker served as sheriff of White County for thirty years. He died while serving as sheriff. Uncle Frank had married my dad's baby sister, Sarah. Aunt Sarah is also the only woman to serve as sheriff of White County. She would serve out the remainder of Uncle Franks' term. When Frank was first elected he had to drive his car. Most rural counties didn't have the money to furnish vehicles for law officers to drive. It was during this time that Uncle Frank came to our house one evening. He came in our house, and told my dad he needed our help. He wanted us to go with him to try to arrest a fellow that lived in Lumpkin County. He told dad to get his shot gun and come with him. He also asked if I would go. I think he wanted someone young and dumb. I was the perfect chose. Daddy and Frank rode in the front seat, and there was the unofficial deputy, Bobby Adams, sitting in the backseat wondering; what the heck have I got myself in to. We traveled inside Lumpkin County, which may have been a little out of Uncle Frank's territory, but this was in the early 60's and Miranda rights were nonexistent. We arrived at the suspect's house. Frank cut the lights off and slowly entered a driveway. When we stopped, he told me and dad to go to the back of the house, and if the guy came out running to stop him. Ok, by then my knees were shaking so badly the guy inside the house could probably hear them. We heard Uncle Frank knock on the door and say, "This is the Sheriff." Other than having bruises on my knees from them knocking so hard, the guy was arrested without incident. The arrested fellow was told to get in the back seat. That must have been where the young and the dumb rode in those days. I don't remember a lot of the conversation. But he was very pleasant, and I pretended to enjoy the conversation, while he smoked cigarettes. I sure am glad that he didn't come out that back door. I probably wouldn't have had clean pants to ride home in, and the smell of cigarettes wouldn't have been the only smell remembered.

GOD SENT DOG

Having a good coon dog was like having a sports car, or having a beautiful boat, maybe not as important as having a beautiful wife, but close. You get the picture. Most coon hunters like to prove that their dog is an equal to, or better than other coon dogs. To do this, you go to UKC night hunts. UKC is the United Kennel Club of America. They sanction the hunts and your dog can earn points and become a UKC Champion; if the dog is registered with UKC. I, along with my friend Ray Renzi, was attending one of the UKC hunts, and I drew out with a fellow who was a preacher, Ray, and another fellow whose name I don't remember. We were not hunting in the registered dog class. We were hunting in the Grade Dog class. This means our dogs were not registered but could compete anyway. The Preacher had a black and tan hound. I had a dog that was half black and tan, and the other parts I really don't know. She could have been a little bit of Adams, maybe some Thurmond, Goss, Pruitt, who knows, but she was a pretty good dog. The preachers' dog treed three possums. In the competition hunt if your dog gets so many minus points for treeing off game (anything other than a raccoon) they are automatically disqualified. After his dog had been disqualified for treeing three possums, we sat down and were talking. The preacher says, "I guess you fellars wonder how I got my dog." I said, "How did you get your dog Preacher?" The Preacher said, "I went to the Lord in prayer, and asked him to help me find a good dog. A few days later my boss at Fieldale told me there was a black and tan hound that had taken up at his house and he couldn't find the owner, so he wanted me to have the hound. God answered my prayers, and that is the dog I am hunting tonight." I remarked that I thought that was very nice of his boss to do that. Ray remarked about the same thing. The other gentleman who was with us was setting on a stump. The gentleman put a smoke in his mouth and looked at the Preacher and said, "Preacher next time you pray for a dog, pray for a COON DOG, not a darn POSSUM DOG." Prayers are answered, but maybe not exactly the way we want them to be.

SLING THAT ROD MATT

When my nephew, Matt Adams, was a young boy, he wanted to go striper fishing with his uncles on Lake Lanier and try to catch some stripers. Billy and I had gone to the lake a few times and we had been really successful. We caught several 20 plus pound fish and were itching to get down to the lake and catch some more big fish. Matt wanted to go with us, but he said he would like to carry a reel and rod of his own. The problem was Matt didn't have one. However, his dad, my brother Bruce had just purchased a brand new reel and rod that Matt didn't even know about at the time. His dad knew that Matt wanted to go so being the loving father; he told Matt that he could take his new fishing reel and rod with him. There was a stipulation. He informed his baby boy, that he had better take care of the new outfit or he was going to beat his butt. Matt promised and pleaded with his dad, saying that he would take care of his fishing gear and he really appreciated him letting him use it. The last thing Bruce said to Matt was, "Matt don't you throw my reel and rod in the lake." So with smiles on our face, we left pulling the boat and soon arrived at Little River landing. We quickly launched the boat and were on the way up the Chattahoochee. Everyone was getting the reels out wanting to catch a fish as soon as possible. Matt quickly got the new reel and rod rigged and was eager to make his first cast. It was a beautiful cast. I have never seen a rod and reel sail through the air going end over end as pretty as it did. Matts' first cast was his last. With a big splash and a loud ka chuc the reel and rod, that was once a price possession of my brother, would find a final resting place at the bottom of lake Sidney Lanier. In a pale shade of white, Matt looked at us and said, "I can't believe I did that. Daddy is going to beat my ass." Trying to console Matt with tears of laughter in our eyes, both Billy and I assured Matt the pain would not last long. Billy told him that he might want to say that a big fish jerked the rod out of his hand. We left it up to Matt.

DAD'S BLIND MULE

Sawmilling was a way of life for many families in White County, as well as lots of other counties in North Georgia. My dad placed a sawmill in most every county from Jackson County northward. They would purchase timber from individuals or the Federal Government and place a sawmill on site and cut the trees into lumber. In the 50's daddy and his brother, Uncle JC, cut over 5 million board feet of timber out of the mountains in Yahoola Valley in Lumpkin County. It was hard work. Daddy used mules and horses to bunch logs together, then a tractor would back up to them, and the driver of the tractor; would drive a grab into each log, and haul them into the sawmill where it would be turned in to lumber ready to go to the planner mills. My dad loved his old mules and horses. They, like the men that worked them, worked hard. In the summer time those animals would sweat so bad, they would look like someone had wet them down with a water hose. He told me that one time he had a mule driver that was bunching logs, and he would hear the driver shout, "Get up Bess, Get up Claude, Get up Bess, Get up Claude." After hearing the driver of the old mule say that for almost half a day, Dad decided to investigate. He walked out into the woods where the fellow was working the mule, and walked up to the man. Daddy said he looked at the man and asked, "Why do you keep saying Get up Bess, get up Claude, when there is only one mule?" Dad said the man put his finger to his lips and said, "SShhh, don't let him hear you. That old mule is blind, and he thinks he's got help." Daddy always got a good laugh out of that tale.

Mom & Dad

WHOSE MOTHER WAS THAT

My daughter, Ashley Brooke, was an only child for about 18 years. Needless to say, she became quite a "daddy's girl." Brooke would accompany me just about everywhere I went. It didn't matter whether it was hunting, fishing, working, playing, riding horses or whatever; Brooke was pretty much with me. I soon found out I had to be very careful of things that I said because Brooke love to repeat them. Now I was raised in a house where if a dirty word was heard coming out of a mouth, it would resulted in soap going into the mouth, and a mother would grow tired of swinging a tree limb. Dirty words were not tolerated. Daddy didn't say them. Mother didn't say them; and I never heard any of my Aunts or Uncles say any dirty words. How I learned to cuss must have been a miracle. That's the only way it could have happened. Since no one in my family cussed, those words that occasionally came out of my mouth must surely have come to me in my sleep. Ivory soap always tasted bad. Having a small daughter that listened to every word I said was a major concern. On one occasion Brooke accompanied me to get some supplies for a coon hunting event that I was helping put on. We had loaded several boxes of hamburger in the back of my truck. I told the fellow where we got the burger that I thought the meat would be ok if I kept the box tops on the burger to keep it from thawing. Just as we were leaving, one of my cousins' husbands asks me to stop by and help get his tractor unstuck. Brooke got into the truck. Brooke was standing in the seat. There were no seat belt laws at this time. We had only gone 2 or 3 hundred yards when I saw one of the box tops fly off and land in the road. I quickly pulled over and told Brooke to stay in the truck I would get the lid. Several cars came by and actually dodged the box top, but about that time a big bus that had LAKE CITY CHRISTAIN COLLEGE written of the side came barreling down the road. Bop, Bop, Bop, all three wheels flattened the box lid. That infuriated me. I said in what I thought was a very low tone, "Why you Mother." Out of the truck seat I heard, my little girl say, "Daddy, whose movferer wus dat?" It took a long time for me to explain to Paula, that no one's mother ran over the box top.

MIRACLE BEFORE YOUR EYES

Over the years, I discovered that my ears are not as good as they once were. The sounds that I used to take for granted, are not as crisp and clear as they used to be. I can no longer go into the woods and hear a turkey gobble on the distant ridges. I still enjoy the thrill of calling to the old turkey, and watching him strut as he makes his way toward me. My daughter Brooke has excellent hearing and since she liked to go with her dad on some of my outings, I thought Brooke might be kind of like a second set of ears. She was about 10 years old and I ask her if she would like to go on a morning turkey hunt with me. Naturally Brooke was more than willing to go. She and I got up way before day light. We put on our camo and out the door we went. Before long we were hiking in to a place that I had found. The area had lots of scratching and dusting; the signs that turkey hunters look for. Brooke and I walked out a long ridge and found us a good spot to listen for the sounds of the morning turkey. We hadn't been there very long when Brooke says, "Daddy can you hear that?" No, I hadn't heard anything. I asked her if it was a turkey gobble. "No" she whispered. I said, "What was it then?" "Can't you hear those turkeys walking?" At about the time she said that, I looked, and sure enough there was a bunch of turkeys walking in line coming right out the ridge. In the front was a big gobbler that had a beard that was dragging the ground. I thought this is great my daughter will get to see her father bag a big gobbler. I called a couple more times and the birds kept getting closer. I decided the big Tom was well within range, so I aimed my shotgun like I had many times before; the sound of the gun was loud. I watched as the big Tom took off running like a big ostrich. The sun was shining on his back as he went out of site. Brooke said, "Did you get him daddy, did you get him?" Embarrassment filled my body as I looked at my daughter. I said to her, and she still laughs about it, "Brooke you have just seen your first miracle, a dead turkey running through the woods." All she said was. "That was no miracle, you just missed." Kids need to believe their elders.

CHANGE IS HARD

I started working at my dad's sawmill when I was 9 years old. I carried the strips and slabs that were produced from cutting the trees into lumber. In all of my work experiences, I have found no work as hard as working at that sawmill. We worked in the summer when it was hot, and dad paid us just like any of his other hands. Wages was $1.00 per hour. I can't imagine a person trying to feed a family on $40.00 a week, but some did. You were always lucky if you got a full 40 hour work week in because of the weather. When it rained; you couldn't work. The roads would become too slick for the tractors and lumber trucks to navigate. My brother Bruce and I found out that Mr. John Denton would buy spring lizards for $1.00 to $2.00 per dozen, depending upon their size. In just about every place daddy had a sawmill there was a small branch or creek. So during our lunch break or as soon as the mill shut down for the evening; we would take some type of container, an old bait bucket, or empty gallon jug and catch spring lizards. Since we were too young to drive, we could usually talk one off the older men into waiting for us. They would ask us how many lizards we caught, and then take us home. Several times we made more money catching spring lizards than we did working for our dad at his sawmill. Daddy built a two story chicken house. It held 4000 chickens-2000 in the bottom, 2000 in the top. We fed the chickens and cleaned out the drinkers. In the winter we had to fill the heaters up with coal to keep the chickens from freezing to death. Winter meant cutting firewood and splitting it. We sold a lot of pickup loads for $5.00 a load. We also had to milk two cows in the mornings before loading the bus that took us to school. We didn't get to spend the money we made on just anything. That money was used to buy our school clothes for the next year. My son, Brynnan, has been trying to find him a job. I think it's harder for a teenager to find a job today than it was when I was a boy. It's not easy being a teenager in today's society. There's no more portable sawmills. It's against the law to hunt for spring lizards on Government land, and if you could; there's no more John Denton's to buy them. I don't have chicken houses. You push a thermostat to heat up the house. Small farms have all but vanished. I don't miss all that hard work. Times were a lot simpler when I was a young man. I am glad things have changed. But sometimes, it's just hard to except.

HE SERVED HIS COUNTRY

Perry Haynes was from South Carolina. Perry was known throughout the State of South Carolina for his involvement and support of archery. Perry loved to hunt with a bow. In 1998 we were going to Colorado on an Elk hunt, and Perry was going with us. He drove down from South Carolina and rode with us from Cleveland, Georgia to the Atlanta Airport. After we had unloaded our luggage and gotten most our bows and other luggage tagged and ready for transport, we went into the air terminal. Our gate was gate 40; one of the furthest away gates at the Airport. We were casually talking and placing our carryon bags on the conveyor for airport inspection. One of the attendants asked me if a small green bag was mine. I told her no but I thought it might be Perry's. Perry looked and said, "Yes, ma'am that is my bag." She immediately motioned for a police officer and pointed at Perry. The police officer told Perry to follow him. They got over to the side where a table was located. The officer asks Perry, "Sir, Do you have a gun in this bag?" Perry looked kind of shocked and said "No." The Policeman reached in to the bag and withdrew a small pistol. Perry said, "Oh, no I got the wrong bag." He tried to explain that he had two bags that were identical and he must have gotten the wrong one. I ask the man if we could post a bond or whatever we could do. He informed me real quick that Perry would have to be held for an arraignment in Court. They were calling for our plane to board. Perry said for us to go on and he would try to get to Denver, and we could come back and get him. We walked on to the gate. When we arrived at the gate; I looked out the window and saw a car speeding across the run way. I looked out the window and saw Perry and a man get out of the car. The gentleman was carrying Perry's' bag. They entered the terminal and I said, "What's going on Perry?" He told me he would explain things shortly. The man boarded the plane, placed Perry's bag over head and said, "Have a good flight Mr. Haynes." Perry said about the time we left him, the gentleman came up and said, "Perry, Perry Haynes what are you doing here?" Perry told him about his plight and the mistaken bag. The gentleman looked at the Police officer and said, "You put this man on his plane right now;" the officer said, "I don't have the authority." The gentleman replied, as he ripped Perry's ticket to shreds, "I am the damn authority. If it hadn't been for men like him; your ass would be working for the Japanese." The gentleman was a retired FBI agent and head of security at the Atlanta Airport. He also had been the 19 year old tail gunner on the plane that Perry flew during combat missions in World War II. Not only did they put Perry's bag on the plane, it still contained his gun. Two weeks later Dan Reeves, Coach of the Atlanta falcons was charged for having a gun in the safety zone in the Atlanta Airport and was fined $10,000. Perry Haynes was not only a renowned archer; he was a decorated pilot who flew many dangerous missions during the Second World War. He didn't get an elk, but we had a great time. Perry returned home and lived the rest of his life promoting archery in South Carolina.

HIDE THAT STILL

One of the things that I learned when I was a young boy was that a lot of the men that worked at my dad's sawmill liked to drink whiskey. They were usually hard working men, but on Monday morning a lot of those guys would be spending the weekend with my Uncle, the Sheriff of White County. Many times daddy would tell me to take his sawmill hands to the mill, and he would go by the jail and get the rest of his crew out of jail. It was kind of a regular thing for daddy to do. One time when we were sawing timber up in Rabun County, daddy had a sawmill near Tiger, Georgia. We were putting the mill up and three fellows came in and asked me who owned the mill. I told them the big tall fellow over there was the boss. They walked over to where dad was and talked to him; while we were busy digging holes and getting the sawmill put together. People were always coming in to talk to dad when we put a sawmill up. Some wanted jobs. Some wanted saw dust for chicken houses, and some might want lumber. Daddy was always very accommodating. We had been sawing for about two weeks when I ask dad who those men were that was coming in behind us every morning. As soon as we arrived, the three gentlemen that came in the first day we were there; would come in behind us. I thought dad may have given them a job. Well, daddy informed me that those fellows had a whiskey still out the road and they didn't want him to cut the big popular trees until the very last thing. Those trees hid their still. Dad told me not to tell any of the other hands about the still. I didn't, but three days later one of the guys decided they would investigate what was going on out where that morning pickup truck was going. They found the still. We figured we had about three more weeks of sawing. However, our crew found the still, and the fellows that owned it told them to help themselves to some of the brew. They did. We found our crew drunk at the mill for the next four weeks. If the mill shut down, they would go to the still and start drinking whiskey. Three weeks of sawing turned into six weeks of sawing. Dad said if he was ever going to get that timber cut, he would just have to hire a bunch of Preachers. Daddy said, "Naw, I couldn't do that, the Preachers that I know might let the temptation get to them and then I would be blamed for ruining a church." I always thought daddy might have been right.

DON'T SPEAK BAD ABOUT KIN

I had lots of cousins when I grew up. Uncle Roy and Aunt Marie had Roy Junior. Uncle JC and Aunt Betty had Larry and Lynette. Uncle LG and Aunt Pauline had Patricia, Cathy and Wayne. Uncle Bill and Aunt Ina had Billy, Jan, and Jimmy. Uncle Lovic and Aunt Frances had Dale, Sally, and Midge. Uncle Paul and Aunt Elene had Mike. Uncle Frank and Aunt Sara had Frankie.

Uncle Floyd and Aunt Thelma had Floweta, Dennis, and Charles. Uncle Kary and Aunt Louise had Clifford, Doris Ann, Karen, Connie, and Catherine. Uncle James and Aunt Inez had Dottie. The list goes on and on. But there has always been a lot of pleasure knowing that I have relatives all over the place. Sometimes when someone is talking about someone I know they will usually say something like; oh I better not say anything bad about them because they may be related to you. Usually if it is someone from White County, they are right. More than likely I am related to them. My father always kept up with members of his family. Dad loved his family unconditionally. As I have said before, my dad was a very humble man. He and I had gone to Mt. Yonah Lumber Company on a Saturday morning to get daddy's check for the lumber that he had sawed that week. This was a weekly event. Daddy did this every Saturday for years. The checks would be passed out to the men who had sawed lumber that week and then the men would stand around and talk. This Saturday there was a man that was really giving my Uncle, Frank Baker, Sheriff of White County, down the road. The fellow had been locked up for something he had done. Daddy just listened. Then the guy says something like this; and then that da—blanket blank wife of his did something and what a blanket-blank Bit—she is. Well the man didn't know that daddy was the brother of the women he was bad mouthing. Dad's face kept getting redder, and redder. I noticed that dad kept getting a little closer and closer to the man. All at once, BAM Dad was on top of the guy beating the stuffing's out of him. Finally someone grabbed dad and pulled him off of the man. We went home. I couldn't wait to tell mom that dad had got into a fight. I looked out of the window and I saw the man that dad had been fighting with drive up into our yard. Daddy told me to stay inside. Daddy walked down to the man's car and the guy said he was sorry he had said what he did about Aunt Sara. Daddy listened and said, "Talking bad about people's folks that they love will get you in trouble if you ain't careful." My daddy gave the man a black eye and good advice. I think both were well deserved.

THERE GOES MY TURKEY

My grandfather, John Walter Sims, most people just called him Walt, gave me my first lesson in turkey hunting. Papa had made some turkey calls out of some yellow popular boards, and he showed me how to take a piece of slate and rub over the edge of the box and make the sound of a hen turkey. Now there's lots of different turkey calls massed produced by call companies. I still think the calls that my papa made sound the best. I grew up loving turkey hunting. Each spring I can't wait till the season begins. Back in the early 70's, I had a brilliant idea. I had been hunting on a farm in northern Lumpkin County. I don't think I had permission to hunt on that farm, but I was taking my chances. I could get an old gobbler down to the edge of the field, but he would not come out in the field; so I could get a good shot on him. So, I decided if I could make me some kind of a decoy, maybe that old bird would think it was a gorgeous hen and rush out in the field with love on his mind. There was a young lady teaching art at Lumpkin County High School. She was our first art teacher. Cheryl Otter lived in Northern Lumpkin County and was a very talented art teacher. I asked Cheryl if she could make me a turkey decoy. There were no decoys on the market at that time. Cheryl made me a paper machete decoy. It was made of paper and some type of plaster. I had her paint it, and paid her $45 for her great work. I couldn't wait to slip back up to where I was hearing the old tom turkey. I placed the turkey decoy down in the field, and then I got in a wind row of trees and bushes and waited. I finally heard him gobble. I called a few times. I could tell by his gobble he was getting closer. With every gobble my heart would beat faster. The wait was exciting. Suddenly, I thought I heard an air plane. I looked into the sky. I didn't see an airplane. The sound was getting closer. It was coming up the field behind me. Oh, no there came the caretaker of the farm on his tractor. I couldn't dash out in to the field and get my decoy. He would see me. There was only time to lay low and wait. The gentleman saw my decoy. He stopped his tractor, dismounted scratched his head, and slowly walked toward my master sculpture. He walked around my beautiful decoy, looked at it, and then pulled it out of the ground. The last time I saw my master piece, he had it under his left arm going out of the field. All I could do was watch my master piece leave me riding under the arm of the driver on his tractor. I may not have been the first to use a turkey decoy in Georgia. But I would say I was the first person to see one ride away on a tractor.

GOD DARN FENCE

One of our neighbors was one of the first people in our community to get an electric fence. Just about everyone used barbed wire to build there fences, but our neighbor had decided he would put an electric fence up. Most people in those days had never heard of an electric fence, let alone seen one. Our neighbors' sister-in-law was a very religious lady. Her husband was a Holiness Preacher and a very good man. The preacher and his wife lived across the road and a little ways through some woods from our neighbor and his wife. Since it was only a short distance between the two houses, the preachers' wife and our neighbors' wife would walk an old trail that went through the woods and they would visit each other quiet often. It was only a few days after our neighbor had put his electric fence up that the preachers' wife decided to go visiting her sister. She did not know that the new fence that now crossed the trail was an electric fence. When she got to the fence, each time the preachers' wife would try to push the fence down so she could straddle it; she would fall down on her knees and start praying. When she arrived at her sister's house, she walked up onto the porch. There sat her sister sewing on an old shirt. The preachers' wife said to her, "You know sis; I have felt the spirit of the Lord many times in my life. But I don't think I have ever felt the Spirit as strong as I did when I crossed your new fence." Our neighbor had to change the route of his new fence. He claimed there was too much religion taking place on that trail, and it was getting harder to get his sister-in-law to visit.

SHINING LIKE A DIAMOND

Jimmy Vandiver was never a man lost for words. Jimmy could always say something regardless of the time or situation. I used to listen too many of Jimmy's tales when he would come by a little package store where I worked. We would set in some chairs and lean back against the outside wall. Both he and I enjoyed watching people and sometimes just the reactions that people would give would bring a smile to my face. Jimmy and I had been outside leaning in our chair for quite some time. There were some gas pumps and when people pulled up to the pumps I would ask them how I could help them and usually they would tell me how much gas they wanted or whatever. I think that sometimes Jimmy liked to say stuff just to watch the reaction of those around him. On this particular day we were sitting there and all at once a big green Lincoln Continental comes slowly pulling up to where Jimmy and I were leaning. This car had electric windows. The windows were so tinted that you could not see anyone in the car. The driver of the car was a middle aged lady with a fresh coat of paint on her face and hair. Her finger nails were colored green almost the same color as the car. Beside her sat a fellow that looked to be just a tat older than her. He was smoking a pipe. And he was dressed impeccable. It was not a cheap suit. The ladies window went down right in front of Jimmy. She looked at Jimmy over her glasses and said in a very heavy northern accent. "Oh Sir, can you tell me where the DEER LODGE is located?" Jimmy took his pipe out of his mouth and looked at me and grinned. He said, "Well ma'am you go through this little wide spot right up here across the bridge. That is Helen, Georgia. Then you will go across a mountain that's the Unicoi Mountain and go through a gap called Unicoi Gap. You then go down the backside of the mountain and at the bottom of the Mountain you will see a little hollow that is Moody Hollow. Then you go right on up just a little bit and look on your right. There you will see a big sign, shinning like a diamond in a dog's ass. It'll say DEER LODGE." That window went bzzzzzz right up to the top, and that lady took off. Jimmy had a big grin on his face and said, "I bet they can't find it, must of been a tourist." I couldn't have given better directions myself.

I WHIPPED YOU TOO HARD

My dad was a wonderful man. I never heard him raise his voice in anger. He never used profanity. He worked hard and tried to provide for his family. I know he wasn't perfect, but he always was loved by his wife and all of his children. His sisters, my aunts would always tell me that daddy was the best brother that they could have had. My grandmother told me that daddy never caused her any grief when he was growing up. He tried to be a good son to his mother. Dad never gave me but three whippings in my life. When you got a "whooping" from daddy, you remembered it. All three of those "whooping's" were for missing out of school. I had just been elected Superintendent of the Lumpkin County School System and daddy and I were going to Atlanta to get a part for dad's old bulldozer. I think we were going to the Allis Chalmers place. We were talking about my election and I was telling daddy how pleased, but surprised I was that I had won. Daddy said, "You know, I had saved some money for your brother to go to school on. He never missed a day of school in 12 years. But he got married and started a family. You would lay out of school to go hunting and fishing. I never thought you would do anything; but maybe sawmill. The only whippings I ever gave you were for not going to school. You finished high school. Then you decided to go to college. You went on to get your Masters. You taught school. Then you ran for Superintendent of Schools. Son, I believed I whipped you to darn hard." Maybe he did, but I have always been grateful for his encouragement, even if he did give me those three "Whooping's."

I LIVE RIGHT THERE

Helen was a sleepy little town for most of the early years in my life. There was the old hotel, Chief Westmoreland's garage, Zebbie Phillips little restaurant, Wilkco hosiery, Charlie Maloof's hardware store, and at the top was a bank. My great Uncle, Hane Sims had a Pure Oil Station, and right across from it was Warren Brown and Willard Tallents' tire and gas station. My grandfather, J.W. Sims had a little store just across the hill. It was located in what is now the parking lot for Betty's Country Store. Lots of local folks would hang out at one of those places and enjoy all of the stories and gossip that went with those meetings. One of the residents of Helen was a man by the name of Verge Adams. He would go to one of the down town stations and have a soda pop every day. Verge lived next door to my grandfather's store, which was just across the hill from the down town gas stations. Verge drove a green 1950 Chevrolet pickup. When Verge left the stations, we all knew he would start out in high gear, ride that clutch, and then let off of it; and it would jump and sputter across the hill. Needless to say Verge didn't care what side of the road he was on, because there was so little traffic; it didn't matter. On this particular day Verge had finished his drink and did what he had done every day for years. He started across the hill riding that clutch, and Ka buk, Ka buk, Ka buk right across the hill. Just as he crossed the hill and had gone out of our site; we heard a loud KA_BOOM. Every one of us took off running across the hill to see what had happened. There sat Verge's old truck pointing opposite from his drive way with the whole side of the truck bent up pretty bad. A black 49 Chevrolet with the front really mess up was in the middle of the road. Verge was getting out of his truck. The two drivers met each other in the middle of the road and Verge looked at the fellow and said, "What the hell's the matter with you, didn't you know I lived right there?" The gentleman said, "No sir, I am from Florida." I told you, there just wasn't much traffic in Helen in those days.

THE DOBERMAN GANG

I had stopped by Tom McDonalds' house to see when he wanted to rob the bee hives. We had 7 or 8 hives of bees and it was time for us to get some of that precious honey. I knocked on the door and heard Tom say, "Come on in, it ain't locked." Tom was sitting in his favorite chair and as usual was wearing his hat. We exchanged a few pleasantries and then I asked Tom if he thought we should get the honey. He didn't answer. Tom looked at me and asked, "You've heard about what happened to Henry didn't you?" Henry was Tom's nephew and my neighbor. I told Tom I had not heard anything about Henry. Tom began to explain. "Well, have you seen the folks that have moved in out the road where Henry's driveway is?" Before I could answer, he continued. "Them folks have got a big ole Doberman dog. Have you seen it?" I shuck my head, yes. "Well Henry stopped to get his mail and that big dog came out and chased him back into his truck. Henry got his pistol out of the glove compartment and shot into the ground to scare the dog off; he wasn't trying to kill it. The next thing I know, she is calling the Sheriff's office and here comes the law. She sicked the law on Henry." By this time I could tell that Tom was really upset about this thing with the Doberman. Tom said, "I'll tell you one thing, that ole Doberman better not come over here; I'll shoot it." I was kind of lost for words. Then Tom expressed his major concern. He said, "Have you ever seen that woman that lives in that house?" I shuck my head and said, "Yes." Tom continued, "Well, I will tell you this, if that man is feeding that dog to keep somebody from a raping his wife; he is wasting his damn dog food." We didn't get to rob the bees that day. The day was spent talking about the "Doberman Gang."

SAY I LOVE YOU

Growing up I never heard my Mom and Dad say "I love you" very much. They both showed it, but never said it very much, not to me or my brothers or sister. We always knew they loved us. They took care of us, fed us, carried us to the doctor when sick, and did everything that good parents should do. When Daddy got sick and I think realized that his life might be shortened he started telling us he loved us. We in turn started telling him that we loved him. I think he always knew as well. I tell mom I love her every day. I made a vow that I would tell my kids I love them if I get the chance at least once a day. It sure makes life great to hear your child say "I love you to." Don't you think?

NIGHT HORSES

Back in the 50's the Federal Government sold timber. I consider myself a conservationist but you got to know when to hug a tree, and when to cut one down. I have been called a tree hugger by some and a forest spoiler by others. My dad cut timber for almost 50 years. I used to tell those folks that didn't believe in cutting trees to try to build a house without wood; it would be pretty hard to do. Many of the early sawmills would set up inside the national forest and many of the men that worked at those mills would live in what they called little lions shacks. It usually consisted of four walls and some poles for rafters and usually number 15 felt paper. Sometimes they would have a wood heater in them. Folding cots and blankets was what the men slept on. The bathroom was the great outdoors. Baths were taken once a week. The bath was usually on a Saturday. Deodorant was non-existent. Smith Crumbly was a fellow who was helping cut a boundary of timber on the Chattahoochee Wildlife Management Area. Smith was staying in one of those shacks with his buddy. His buddy was a man by the name of Buck Robinson. Buck lived in Robertstown just north of Helen. Buck and Smith had been in the mountains for three or four weeks. Everything had been going pretty good when one of Buck's friends came by on a Friday evening after work. Bucks friend just happened to bring a half gallon of fresh moonshine. Buck liked moonshine better than water. It didn't take long before Buck was wasted. Mr. Benny Caudell also from Robertstown thought he would go check on Smith and Buck; since he hadn't seen them in three weeks, and he was a neighbor of both men. When Benny got there, he discovered that Buck was drunk as a cootie bear. Smith tried to get Benny to take Buck with him. Smith didn't like being there with a drunk on his hands. Benny tried to convince Smith that everything would be ok. He told Smith that Buck would go to sleep soon. Benny told Smith he would check on them later and said his good-bye. Benny walked to his truck and then decided he would go check on them one more time. As Benny got closer he could hear Buck talking in his intoxicated sleep. He heard Smith say, "I can't believe that damn Benny Caudell left me up here with a drunk man, and him a having night horses." Benny laughed, opened the door and said, "Buck I think you meant nightmares." Smith just snorted and said, "Go to hell Benny and you can take this man having night horses with you."

TINKS NASAL SPRAY

In the early 80's I was in a hunting club in Wilkes County. A friend of mine's father owned the Ford Place in Washington, Georgia. Ricky Linsey's family had the ford dealership for several years. Ricky and I had become friends when Ricky was a student at North Georgia College in Dahlonega, Georgia. Ricky's daughter, Hillary has been a successful song writer in Nashville. Her first hit was the song "Jesus take the Wheel." I had stopped in to see Ricky, and he told me that his cousin Gary Callaway might know of some land I could lease. Gary was also a friend that had attended North Georgia College. Gary found me some hunting land and after hunting there a few years; Gary's brother, Larry, offered an old house to be used as a hunting camp. It was the house that the man that started the University of Georgia's Red Coat Marching Band had lived in. His name was Mr. Hoye. The Hoye house is still being used as a hunting camp. One weekend I was at the Hoye house and decided that I would go hunting on a farm in the edge of Oglethorpe County. Another friend, Tim Miller had given me permission to go there. Tom Parker, who is a cabinet maker, heard that I was going to hunt on the Miller farm and ask if he could go with me. I told Tom I would be glad for him to go. Tom told me he would be waiting at his mail box at 6 am the next morning. It was a very cold morning when I picked Tom up. He was standing on the side of the road at his mail box just like he said he would be. Tom got in the truck and away we went. Now, being a cabinet maker Tom was around sawdust just about every day. Tom had lots of sinus problems. He was always squirting that Afrin Sinus spray up his nose. We were moving right along when all of a sudden I heard Tom start coughing, gagging, and heaving. He was yelling, "Pull over, Pull over, Uak Pull over." I very quickly pulled to the side of the road. I said, "Tom what's the matter are you choking, are you having a heart attack?" By this time he was throwing up. In between heaves, Tom said, "Hell no, but I just sprayed that damn Tinks' 69 doe in heat lure right up my nose. I thought it was my nasal spray." Some people might have said, "Can I do anything to help you?" Not me, I laughed until Tom said, "Don't you tell anybody about this." And then I laughed some more. I won't Tom. You know I won't.

ABOUT THAT BRA

Each Christmas I am always reminded of my shopping experiences with friends and family. First, let me say that I hate to shop. When I go to a store, it is to buy something; not to look at everything in the store or to try on 20 different items to see if I look good in them. I just want to go in, find what I want, pay up and out the door. I have found it much easier to buy for men than to buy for women. Give a man a good pocket knife or maybe a good hat, or tee-shirt that says FBI (female body inspector) and he's happy. It's pretty hard for me to buy for a female. I have found that the best thing for me to do is to ask the female what they would like for Christmas. Then I can go to a store that sells those items, get one, save the receipt because I know it is going to be the wrong color or wrong size, and give it to the female that wanted what she got but is not satisfied with it because it doesn't match the pocket book that you gave her when she wanted a pocket book. The receipt is the important thing because they can take it and exchange for whatever they really wanted. I have said all of this to show how difficult it is to shop for a female. My friend Billy Wayne Chambers and I usually shopped on Christmas Eve each year. We would go to Gainesville and get gifts that we knew people wanted us to get. Men know very little about purchasing female items. Billy Wayne and I decided that the JC Penny's store would have the female item that Billy Wayne needed to purchase. We go into the store, and you start to feel a little odd when you are hanging out in the ladies underwear section. Finally a nice young female sales clerk says, "May I help you two gentlemen?" I immediately pointed to Billy Wayne. Billy says, "I need to get a bra for someone." When I heard Billy Wayne say that, I knew this was going to be interesting. The nice young lady says, "Ok, what size?" Billy obviously had never been asked that question. Ole Billy Wayne looked at the sales lady and said, "Oh, I suspect they are about the size of a Big Orange." I think he should have just got her a pocket book and saved the receipt.

AN HONEST MAN

Ike McMurry was a fellow who lived in Turner County. Each summer Ike would help the Christian family plant, harvest and sell watermelons. Bill, Bob, John and Jim let Ike do most of the physical labor. Ike was not the sharpest knife in the drawer. As my grandpa used to say, "He's corn bread rose in the pan, but it didn't get done", or "his elevator didn't go nowhere, it just stayed hung up in the lobby." He was about a half bubble out of plum. Bill Christian had been told by his father to let Ike help him load watermelons and then to take the melons to the market and sell them. The elder Mr. Christian had told Bill what price they should get for the melons. If they were sold by the melon, Bill should get $2.50 per melon. If anyone would take five they could have them for $10.00. Bill and Ike had been having a slow morning, and it was almost dinner time. Bill told Ike that he would go to the nearby little diner and get him and Ike a burger. Bill reinforced the price of the melons to Ike before he left. Bill was gone a short time and when he returned he noticed there were several people standing around the melon stand, and there was old Ike arguing with a man. Bill walked up and asked Ike what was going on. Ike told Bill that the man driving that big fancy car got five melons but had not paid for them. Bill turned to the man and asked if he got 5 melons. The man said yes I got 5 melons and I gave ten dollars to that man. He pointed to Ike. Ike said, "You didn't give me any money." The man says, "Yes I did too, I bet he stuck it in his shoe." Bill was trying desperately to defuse the situation. He told the man he had known Ike a long time and he didn't think Ike was lying. The man said again yes I did pay him; I know he's put that ten dollars in his shoe. Bill looked around and Ike was sitting on box. Ike was undoing the laces in his shoe. Bill said, "Ike what are you doing?" Ike looked at the man driving the big fancy car with an angry look on his face and said, "You better hope that money is in one of these shoes." The man driving the car threw a ten dollar bill at Ike McMurry and drove away. After looking in both shoes Ike said; I told that man they weren't no ten dollar bill in my shoes. Ike McMurry didn't drive a fancy car, but he was honest.

THE FINE

I was working at Orbit Manufacturing Company in Helen, Georgia. They made ladies pants. My first job there was running a steam press. I was later hired to put little straps on the bottom of the pants. The straps snapped on to each side of the pants, and they could very easily be removed. I had just turned sixteen, and I now had my driver's license. I had been driving since I was 7 or 8 years old, but I had to take the test twice before I passed it. The young part time workers had to check each day to see if we needed to work. We usually asked David Wilkin whose father owned the company, if we were needed. I had driven my mom and dad's car over to the plant which was located on the South side of the Chattahoochee River. It was kind of behind what was at that time the Chattahoochee Dining Room. Mr. Wilkins had purchased the old Helen school house, and converted it into a sewing plant. When I arrived, I discovered that the parking area that had been dirt the last day I had worked was now covered with a fresh covering of tar and gravel. David stuck his head out and told me I didn't have to work. He also yelled, "Cut a circle." Well I couldn't disappoint my friend, so I spun out through the gravel. As I looked across the river, I could see the Helen Policeman running for his car. I thought if I can get to the highway across the bridge, I might be able to get away. Nope, didn't happen. He gave me my first ticket. It was for reckless driving in the Orbit parking lot. I went to see the Mayor, Dot Gadney. She told me she was only going to fine me twenty five dollars. Since I didn't have twenty five dollars, I knew mom and dad were not going to pay a fine for me; I went to my great uncle, Hane Sims. Uncle Hane loaned me the money and he also told me that Mr. John Edwards needed some help. I went to see Mr. Edwards, and he hired me to dig a ditch from the water tank in Helen to the top of the mountain. The ditch had to be 6 inches wide and 16 inches deep. He was going to pay me $1.00 per hour. I dug and cut roots, and then I cut roots and dug. After three weeks of blisters and sore muscles, I went to Mr. Edward's house and told him I was through. He said, "How much do I owe you, Bobby?" I hated to tell him. It seemed like it had taken months to dig that ditch. I said, "Mr. Edwards, I hate to tell you, but I have got 44 hours in digging that ditch." John Edwards pulled a roll of money out of his pocket and counted out forty four dollars. As he was counting he said, "Aw, don't worry about it. That man in Cleveland wanted $350.00 to dig that ditch with that machine." Suddenly, I didn't feel so bad.

THE FLASHING WOMAN

Graduating from the University of Georgia was quite an experience. I had successfully completed a program of study that would allow me to be a teacher in the school systems of Georgia. I was not what you call a model student. I had majored in morning classes. Lots of times I would sign up for a class and not know what I had signed up for until the day I showed up for class. I always wanted the classes to be in the morning, so I could have the entire evening to goof off. If there had been a degree in goofing off and having a good time, I am sure I would have gotten out as one of the top students in that program of study. My mom and dad had never insisted that I make good grades. While in public school the only question my parents ask was ---Did you make your pass? I guess they figured if I was passing then I was doing ok. After my first quarter at UGA, I tried to convince my dad that Allen's restaurant and bar was the library. He saw that I had written lots of checks there. I wanted him to believe it was for overdue library books. I don't think dad ever went for that, but it was worth a try. Later, I was actually glad to find out that there was a library on campus, but I believe I had been out of college two or three years when I found out about it. The day that I graduated from Georgia, my Mom and Dad made their second trip to Athens, Georgia. Their first was the day they dropped me out in the front of Reed Hall approximately four years earlier. On that wonderful day of graduation, there were about 250 people graduating with various degrees. I sat in a chair on the floor of the coliseum. Mom and dad sat in the stands overlooking the soon to be graduates. I could not see them. The Presidents of the various schools would say something like---Will all those students with degrees in Business please stand. Then they would confer upon them that they had graduated. I still could not find my mom and dad. I then heard the President of the School of Education say for those with degrees in education to please stand. It took me less than 30 seconds to see my mom leaning out over the rail with her Kodak 127 camera. It was flashing like it was hooked up to a police car. I don't know how many pictures mom took, but at one point I think dad was holding on to her foot so she wouldn't fall on to the stadium floor. I am sure there were at least 40 or 50 education majors blinded by a Kodak 127 flashing camera. One of the graduates sitting next to me said, "Who is that flashing that camera?" All I could say was, "That's my Mom, she's glad I made my pass."

TASTE LIKE CHICKEN

It seemed like the snows were more frequent and bigger when I was a boy. Maybe there not, but they seemed like they were. In the fall of 1956 my uncle Charles Sims had gotten me and my Brother Bruce along with his son Wayne and my cousin Clifford Cox to help clean his chicken house out. Back then you just backed your truck into the chicken house and started shoveling the chicken manure on to the truck. When it was full you would haul it out spread it on to your garden or field, or in this incidence, just pile in it in a field where you would later scatter it out. There were several piles of the chicken manure in a field off to the right of the road coming down the steep hill from Uncle Charles and Aunt Minnies house. It had not been scattered when a huge, deep, wet snow came that winter. Several inches of snow had fallen over a period of two days. We didn't have any store bought sleds. We used anything that would slide over the snow as a sled. It just so happened that we found an old 40 ford car hood. You talk about flying over the snow that thing would move. We had made several trips up and down the road when I got this brilliant idea. Why don't we move over to the right a little bit and slide down the hill and use the piles of chicken manure as jumps? Everyone thought that was a great idea. We also found that the more people in the car hood the faster it would go. Well with 4 boys huddled in the car hood, it was going to be an adventure. Not only were we going down the steepest part of the hill, we were going to back our starting place a little further back. When we came off that hill the wind in my face was taking my breath. The cold air was burning my eyes. I had a death grip on the side of that hood. My fingers were mashing into the metal. We hit the first pile of manure dead center, sending us flying through the air. It threw us not only over it, but over the second pile as well. The third pile of manure was a different story. We landed nose first. The sudden stop threw some over the pile of manure for others; it would be head first into the worst smelling pile of snow covered wet chicken manure in the world. Sledding came to a brief halt. We had to spit the manure out of our mouths and wash it off of our heads; we stunk for the rest of the day, but who cares when you're a little boy playing in the snow.

Some old fellas sitting and talking and telling some of these old stories you're reading in this book. They would gather around on the porch of Adams's store or around the pot-belly stove in the wintertime and chew the fat about everything. The one on the left is Andy Westmoreland.

DON'T PARK THERE

When my wife and I first got married we drove the worst vehicles you could possibly drive. Paula was driving back and forth to school in an old Volkswagen that barely was capable of getting to Dahlonega and back. I was driving a ford pickup truck that was wrecked when I bought it. But heck that's all we could afford. I was coaching year round. I was coaching football in the fall. I was coaching girls' basketball in the winter and baseball in the spring. There was a grant total of four coaches to coach everything that was offered at Lumpkin County High School. I was in my room teaching or watching a football film, can't remember which, but I would bet on the film. When the school secretary Ms. Corbin called me on the intercom and asks if I could take a call from my wife. Paula and I had not been married very long, but I knew it must be important. I told her I would be right down. When I got to the phone I said, "Hello." Paula sounded like she was crying when she said, "You better come home, the car won't crank." I said, "Don't worry I will bring some jumper cables and get it cranked." Then my new wife says, "THAT'S NOT ALL, I TRIED TO PUSH IT OFF-- AND IT RAN AWAY FROM ME." I then said, "What are you talking about?" She then said in a louder voice, "IT IS DOWN IN THE WOODS AGAINST A TREE.—BOO-HOO-HOO." I told Ms. Corbin I had better go home immediately to see what had happened. She got a teacher to cover my classes, and I left. When I arrived at my house, there stood Paula looking down the mountain. When I got out I could see the little orange VW neatly wrapped around a pine tree. Paula had tried pushing the little car off, but then it got to going so fast; she couldn't catch it. Trying to make her feel better, I thought I would add a little humor. I said, "Paula, that's a hell of a place to park." That was not the right choice of words. She cried harder. I called my neighbor,

Tom McDonald and asked if he would bring a long chain and his tractor. Tom showed up with his tractor and several chains. Tom turned the tractor off and looked down the mountain at the VW. He took his hat off his head and said; "That's a hell of a place to park." All I could hear was the BOO HOO's and a few choice words as Paula walked to the house. I never gave Paula any more advice about where she should park, neither did Tom.

JAIL BREAK PRAYER

Wallace Bell lived in Athens, Georgia. His brother was congressman, Tom Bell. Wallace and his wife, Maude, would come up to White County frequently to visit relatives that lived here. Wallace always seemed to have a lot more fun when Maude couldn't come with him. If Maude didn't come Wallace would look up his running buddy, Charlie Thurmond. One of the reasons Wallace liked to hang with Charlie was because he and Charlie could drink whiskey together and they always had a wonderful time. During one of their drinking escapades, it seems that Charlie and Wallace got locked up over in Habersham County. Wallace tried to get Maude to come to the jail and get them out. Maude told Wallace that he and Charlie had got in there without her help, surely they could get out. Two or three days had passed and no one had showed up to spring the two drinking buddies form the jail. Charlie began to get really worried and told Wallace it looked like they were in there for good. Wallace had an idea. He told Charlie that maybe they should pray and the lord might help get them out of the jail. Charlie listened to Wallace's suggestion and told him he believed that since he wasn't too good at praying, maybe Wallace should do the prayer. Wallace knelt down by one of the little cots and began to pray. He said, "Lord, I know that we haven't been the kind of men that You would like us to be but if You will help get us out of this jail we will try to be better men.

Lord we know we shouldn't have done what we did and drink all that old whiskey, if You will just help us out of this jail we'll do better. This is old Wallace Bell and Charlie Thurmond asking for Your help." As soon as Wallace said that, Charlie jumped up and said, "Oh hell Wallace you really messed up that time." Wallace said, "Why?" Charlie replied, "You told Him who we were". Wallace said, "Charlie I didn't mean to."

This is a picture of Comer Jackson, sitting in front of Adams's store. He was my neighbor, but better known for the good beer he made.

REFLECTION

Sometimes I try to reflect back on my youth just to remember things that might not mean anything to anyone, but they meant something to me. Like the time my dad took me to school after he had given me a butt beating for not wanting to go to school, then put me in his truck and drove me to school. Before I got out, he asked me if I needed anything, and said he would see me when I got home from school. It was his way of saying he loved me. There was one time when I went to Gainesville with my mom and a man in the drug store stopped us, as mom and I were leaving and he said, "Sir, I think your wife forgot to get her pocketbook." Momma and I laughed, and then I told the guy that she wasn't my wife, she was my mom. The smile on moms face told me; she enjoyed the compliment. I remember cutting grass for one of my neighbors and I worked so hard pushing that big old lawn mower. I was only 7 years old. When I got through they paid me a quarter. I didn't like those neighbors anymore. I remember seeing the men around the old store, and listening to their tales and hearing them talk about their hardships. I would watch my grandmother Adams walk with her hands behind her back. She always looked down at the ground as she walked. If any of her family lost a dime, she would find it. My grandmother, mom and other ladies would gather in what we used to call the "Old Café" building and they would put up a quilting frame and the ladies would all sew on a quilt until it was finished. It impressed me how neat the stitching was and it looked so cool for them to roll the quilt around the quilting frames. Occasionally the women would have a shower for someone in the café building. I never understood why it was called a shower. When I was a little boy, I thought someone was going to get a bath. I remember when my sister, Brenda, was standing by the TV, and when I ask her why she was standing there; she said well it said on the TV to please stand by. Some things you never forget. Reflecting back I had several close calls with death. When there was a wreck in our community daddy would ask if Bobby was hurt before he even knew who wrecked. Many of the people that touched my life in so many ways are not in this world anymore. Many have gotten killed or died of natural causes. As I reflect back in time, it makes me appreciate my friends and family. My memories are mine. They will be with me until I breathe no more. For the most part, they have been good memories. That is more of a reflection on my friends, and family than it is on me. All of us should take time and do a little more reflecting. When we look back on our lives, it makes everything and everyone in our lives a little more special.

WHAT A MAMA

Most people know that I love my Mom. She has been an inspiration to me my entire life. I rang her door bell and after several minutes of waiting, she opened the door and said, "Lord, I came to the door as fast as I could. That old arthritis has just about got me down." As I looked at my wonderful mother, I couldn't help but notice how frail she has gotten in her 84 years. She raised 5 children, lost one child at birth, and has lost a loving husband and two of her children have passed away. She is blind, has a pace maker, and has survived 13 major surgeries. She has no organs left that the human body can live without. We sat down on her old sofa and I placed my arm around her and ask if she needed anything. "No," she said, "I just hope all my children have a good Christmas." A tear came in my eye; just like they are coming now, but I know Mom can't see them. Men can love, but I don't think there is any love in the world that's greater than the love a mother has for her children. I hope my mom has a good Christmas. She deserves it. Merry Christmas Mom

Mom & Dad

DON'T SHOOT THAT BIRD

While serving as Superintendent of the Lumpkin County School system, I had many wonderful experiences. And I must say a few surprises along the way. My daughter was in the first grade and thankfully took after her mother in the intelligence department. Without my knowing, the elementary school had an art contest. The kids had to draw something to represent school bus safety, or things you shouldn't do on a school bus. Imagine my surprise when they called me and said "Mr. Adams your daughter won first place in the school bus poster contest. ---But we can't display it." Brooke was very talented in art. They wanted me to see what she had drawn. I go over to the school and there on a big white poster was a picture of a school bus perfectly drawn, even the lug nuts on the wheels, kids in the windows, the bus driver in his seat. And there in the middle of the bus was a little kid with hand out the window SHOOTING THE WORLD THE BIRD FINGER. I don't know how she knew not to do that. I guess it was just good parenting on my part. Don't you think?

I CAN FLY

My Grandpa Sims ran a little store in Helen. When I was growing up, my family made many trips up to papa Sims'. My Grandmother was a very sickly woman, and mom wanted to check on her almost every day. I always enjoyed the ride up to Helen, and as soon as we got there, I could find something to get into in no time. We would play hide and seek from the cars that came through Helen. There were so few back in those days, we found it fun to hide behind the big trees that lined the sidewalks of Helen. We could lie on the shoulder of the road and no one could see us. Maybe they could, but in our mind we were invisible. Another fun thing for us to do was to get on top of the ice house that was located next to the store. It was about six or seven feet tall but to us it was a sky scraper. We would jump off the top of the ice house and pretend we were soldiers attacking the enemy. I had watched a program on our TV that showed these army guys using parachutes to float behind enemy lines. If they could float behind enemy lines, so could I. I knew where my granny Sims kept her big umbrella and I was sure it would make a wonderful black parachute. I wasn't really sure if my Grandmother would think it was as neat of an idea as I did, so I didn't ask if I could use her big umbrella. Since she was sick a lot; I just slipped the umbrella out of her house without upsetting her. I figured that was the safest thing to do. I ran with that umbrella to the ice house. I was standing on top of the ice house looking down, when it occurred to me that all I had to do to get on top of the papa's store was to just lay a board down on the roof of the ice house and store and I could walk right to the top of the store. It would be a higher place to test my new parachute. In no time I was on top of the store. I opened my parachute and looked down at the ground. I was going behind the enemy lines. I stuck the umbrella parachute high in the air and jumped. My parachute quickly folded up, and looked like a funnel pointing toward me. That parachute was obviously defective. Fortunately, I hit the ground where it was soft and mushy. My decent was a little bit faster than I had thought it would be. When I carried my grandmothers' black umbrella parachute back to her house looking like a funnel, my mother saw it, and I believe to this day that at that moment was when child abuse began. I realized then that my behind was behind enemy lines.

Bobby riding the horse (Molly) backwards. Cousin Jan Marks is the girl.

ANNIE GET YOUR GUN

Taking an unpopular position is not easy. The easy thing to do is to agree with your friends and family and I guess then you can move on to whatever else is easy to agree on. Many of my FB friends and others have asked me to give my opinion on the current gun topic. Should we have any gun control legislation? My answer to that is YES. Whenever you have the population of White County killed in a year, I think it is time for our legislators to try to do something. Notice I said try. Gun legislation is not going to stop all gun deaths. But if it stopped one gun death, it would be worth something. When those planes killed over two thousand people in New York City, we had immediate action to try to make Americans safer. Those people died in one day. Yet, we have ten times that number killed spread out over a year and if the government hints at doing something, people jump out of their underwear. No one loves guns any more than I do. I hunt. I target practice. I have shotguns, handguns, black powder guns, deer rifles, and I will get more. I probably got more guns than most people do. But I think we should take a serious look at what might save lives in America. No one is going to come into your home and take your guns. That is bull crap. There is nothing wrong with having to have a background check if you are getting a weapon. I have had them; they don't hurt. Ninety percent of Americans believe that background checks would be OK. The remaining 10% is still trying to find their underwear. When someone says that responding to the deaths of 20 small children and 6 adults is a knee jerk reaction; that is hard for someone like me to accept. We have a Bill of Rights in our Constitution. But rights are not absolute. I can't go in a crowded facility and yell, "FIRE." I can't say anything I want to say just because I have freedom of speech. Every one that drives doesn't obey all of the traffic laws. We still have people getting killed in cars; that don't mean we don't need traffic laws. With rights comes responsibility, I think our founding fathers devised our Constitution so that when planes attack our people or when we recognize the need to protect our people from anything we should not step away from that responsibility just because some people jumped out of their underwear. I am not as paranoid as some people. I have faith in my country. I trust those in positions of power to do what is right for the majority of the people. Just because someone wants to try to do something that would save a few lives doesn't mean that my country has gone to hell in a hand basket.

To me it means my fellow man is dedicated to trying to make our world safer. This is just my opinion, now some of you can jump out of your underwear.

WHERE IS THAT LIGHT

Marvin and Laura Chambers lived at the foot of Yonah Mountain. Laura had three girls, Velma, Louise, and Dot. Ten years later the Chambers would have three boys Jere, Billy Wayne, and Lanier. Marvin drove the school bus for a number of years. I remember him stopping by the old Adams store on many occasions to get whatever groceries or items that he needed. The Chambers family owned lots of land at the foot of Yonah Mountain so all of the kids had room to roam as they were growing up. Marvin and Laura had taken an old 34 Ford that had no brakes and no head lights on a short trip. The plan was to get back before dark. But it had gotten dark before they could journey out Tom Bell road and reach their house. Tom Bell road was a typical North Georgia Road. It was red clay with ruts about a foot deep. If it rained, well let's just say that travel plans were put on hold. Marvin and Laura had turned in on Tom Bell road. It was a cloudy dark night, and you couldn't see your hand in front of your face. Rather than leave the old car there, Marvin had this bright idea. He had found a box of big strike diamond matches in the old ford. He told Laura that she could get out in front of the car and strike a match and he would drive toward the light. The trip from highway 75 out Tom Bell road would only be about a mile, so it wouldn't take very long at all for them to get home. Everything was going as planned. About a quarter of a mile out Tom Bell road there was a steep hill. We always referred to the hill as thrill hill. The road dropped of the backside to form a really steep hill. The last match Marvin had seen was at the top of the hill. When he got there he saw a match light on down the hill. Marvin was coming off of the hill and he was pumping the brakes heading to the match. Laura thought he is coming pretty darn fast. In fact he seemed to be going too fast. She had just lit a match. Marvin was coming fast; Laura jumped out of the ruts and ran up the side of the bank. The match didn't go out. Up the side of the bank Marvin came, until the old ford flipped over on its side. He wasn't injured, but quickly said, "Laura, why did you get out of the ruts and run up the side of the bank?" Laura said, "Because I thought it was safer than having you run over me in those ruts." Marvin Chambers didn't win that argument. He and Laura walked on to their house.

WHAT ON SANTA CLAUS?

When I was a small boy Marvin Chamber was one of the men that drove a school bus. He was our neighbor and he and his family was always very highly thought of in the Asbestos Community. We also had the Gerrells family that lived over near the Chambers family and they too were great neighbors. Mr. Roy Gerrells and his family farmed and raised Chickens. The Gerrells baby boy was my friend Ricky. Ricky is my age and has been a friend for as long as I can remember. Mr. Gerrells had told Ricky to go over to another of our neighbors, Mr. Carl Suttons' house and get a couple of roosters that Carl had caught the night before and had them in a coupe. Ricky didn't want to go get the chickens. Being a small boy, Ricky could easily find something more fun than getting old chickens for his dad. Finally Roy said, "Ricky if you don't go get them chickens, I am going to bust your behind." Not wanting to see nor feel the impact of bodily harm, Ricky finally tromped over to the Suttons house and got the chickens. He had both of the chickens by the neck and was walking back toward the Gerrells' house. Marvin Chambers had emptied his bus and was on his way back home. He spotted the young Gerrells's boy slinging the roosters by the neck walking down the side of the road. Knowing that the roosters were probably choking from the death grip Ricky had on them, Marvin slowed the bus and stopped. He opened the door, and since Ricky was just a small boy said, "Son, if you don't stop carrying them chickens that way you're going to kill them chickens, and Santa Claus won't come to see you." Ricky turned to Mr. Chambers and said, "SHIT ON SANTA CLAUS. HIS DADDY DIDN'T MAKE HIM COME AND GET THESE OLD CHICKENS." I don't know if the chickens lived or not, but I don't think Santa Claus came to see Ricky that year.

RED RUBBER

My cousin Kenneth Maness and I had spent a great deal of time making us some good sling shots. We had not only gotten us some sturdy handles; we had found some old red inner tubes. Back in the 40's and 50's inner tubes were either black or red. Actually the red was more a rust color than red, but everyone referred to the rust colored inner tubes as red. The red inner tubes were much better for making sling shots than the black inner tubes. That red rubber material would let you sling a cats' eye marble twice as fast as the black rubber. You could bust a coke bottle just as far as you could see one. We had not mastered the slaying of little birds with those weapons of mass destruction, but we tried. Nothing was safe from our new flips. Not a window pane or a coke bottle would be spared. After the first window pane, and Uncle Roy telling us he would beat our little butts blue if he caught us shooting out another window in any building in the same zip code; we gave up on the windows. Coke bottles would be our targets of choice. We broke so many bottles in was dangerous to walk barefooted anywhere around the Adams Store. We had taken a break from our shooting spree. I was watching Lassie and Kenneth had gone down to my Grandmother Adams to see if he could round him up some grub. I was being entertained by Lassie, when Kenneth stuck his head in the door and said, "Hey, can I borrow your flip?" I said "Sure, but where is yours?" He said he had left it on the sofa at our grandmothers. I handed Kenneth my weapon. He was gone just a short period of time when he came in and said, "Aunt Frances, would you mind frying me some chicken if I bring it to you?" My mother said she wouldn't mind at all. Soon Kenneth and I were eating fried chicken and it was delicious. Mom said, "You know, I can't wait until those little fryers that I have are big enough to eat." Suddenly Kenneth had this sly grin on his face. He said, "They are Aunt Frances. That's what we are eating now." There was no reason to ask why Kenneth had borrowed my weapon of mass destruction. The evidence was in our stomachs and on our plates. There was immediate legislation passed restricting the use of sling shots passed in the Adams house. Maybe our sling shots are the reason that they don't make red inner tubes anymore.

GET OUT AND PUSH

Growing up at route 4 Cleveland, Georgia allowed me the pleasure of being as happy as any red headed freckled face boy could be. I had no doubt that I would never get old and never want for a thing. My friends and family were always there when I needed them. Two of my cousins were like sisters to me. Sally and Midge Allen lived just at the bottom of the hill from my house and I could be at their house in just a few minutes. My Aunt Frances made the best chocolate milk that I have ever drunk. Sally was the oldest of the sisters. Midge was the youngest. Sally could drive the wheels off of a car. Midge and I would usually just set in the seat and begged Sally to slow down. The two Allen girls brother, Dale, always had a fast car. Once Sally, Midge and I got Dale's 40 Ford Coupe and decided, since Dale was working at the sawmill with his dad, we needed to take that Ford for a spin. And when Sally took a car for a spin, I mean she took it for a spin. We told my Aunt Frances that Sally was going to take be back up to my house. As soon as we were out of site, we were off and running. We would find a good dirt road and cut circles, or just see if we could spin the tires. Since Dale always had a big souped-up engine in his cars that wasn't too hard to do. On one occasion, Sally was going to back down a hill and get a good start at spinning the tires. She went a little too close to the ditch and there is where we stopped. Midge and I were sure that Dale would kill all of us. Sally told Midge and I to stop complaining and get out and push. We did. We just didn't know that if you got right behind the tires of a car that had a positive traction rear end in it that both wheels would spin, and mud would cover your entire body. Midge and I had to hide in our underwear behind a lumber stack while Sally washed our clothes, and Dales car. When Dale came in that evening he noticed his car was cleaner than it was when he left. We told him, we didn't have anything to do so we just washed his car. That helped explain why Midges' clothes and mine were still wet. He told us for washing his car; Sally could take me home in the Ford tomorrow if I came down there. The next day we were off and running again. I don't know how we or that car survived.

UNCOVER THAT WOMAN

My Grandmother Adams never knocked on our door in her life. If she came to the house and wanted to come in; she just opened the door and came on inside if there was no one inside, she would walk through the house and make sure everything was alright, and with her hands behind her back; she would walk out of the house and shut the door.   Granny Adams may have been the first neighborhood watch person in Georgia. I was on a break from school, and I had come home to spend a little time hunting and visiting friends back in Cleveland. I found out as soon as I got in from Athens that Mom and Dad were going out of town for the weekend. This was a rarity for them since most of their free time was always spent at home. My brothers were all going to be camping, so that meant I would have the house all by myself. Being the entertaining young man I was, I immediately started trying to find a young lady that might be interested in having a weekend of fun with yours truly. After I was successful at finding someone that wanted to party with me while mom and dad were out of town, look out Bars in Helen here we came. We had a great time drinking and dancing and listening to the music. After the junk joints closed down my date and I headed back to mom and dads. She had told her folks that if it was late when we got through partying she might just spent the night with a friend in Cleveland.   She did. That friend was me. Well, it just so happened that about 8 o'clock the next morning the neighborhood watch person came strolling in with her hands behind her back. I only had time to throw the covers over my friends head, and tell her to lay close and be still. Granny came in my bedroom and said,   "Where's your mother and daddy?" Me, "Uh, there gone somewhere granny." "Where did they go?" She replied. I said, "I am not sure where they went granny." "How long are they going to be gone?" Granny asked. With a quick reply I said, "Until Monday, I think." She then wanted to know what I had been doing, and where were my brothers. I answered her questions the best I could. My Grandmother turned with her hands behind her back and proceeded to walk out suddenly she stopped and said, "You better take those covers off of that girl, you are going to smother her to death." She walked out of the house hands behind her back looking down at the ground with a smile on her face. My Grandmother never told my Mom or Dad about that incident and neither did I.

REVENGE OF THE RABBIT

I always looked forward to snow in the winter. Not only did it mean that we could have fun playing in the snow, it meant we could track rabbits. We didn't have rabbit dogs, so the snow allowed us to track the rabbits and find them sitting in their beds. There was an old railroad track on a portion of the old Adams home place. The train ran from Gainesville, Georgia to Helen, Georgia. The train carried lumber from the big sawmill in Helen back to Gainesville. Paul Jr. Westmoreland told me that when he was a small boy that he and his brother Jere would go over with Daddy and the other Adams boys to watch the train as it carried its load to and from Helen. After the railroad quit operating, the site of the old rail tracks made a great place to track rabbits in the snow. The banks would over hang toward the old tracks, and rabbits would get up under the banks out of the snow. If the track went to the bank, but didn't show any sign of exiting old Mr. Rabbit was under the overhanging dirt. One of us boys would get a stick and try to punch the rabbit out while the one with the gun would wait for the rabbit to break and run. There was nothing better than fried rabbit, gravy and biscuits. The rabbits would usually run out a different hole than the one it crawled in to get under the bank. Usually that is what they did. On one occasion I was going to punch that old rabbit out of his hole. My brother had the shotgun. I had pushed the stick up into the hole several times but the rabbit had not tried to escape. I decided I would look in the hole to see if I could see the rabbit. I was down on all fours trying to peep in a dark hole when suddenly a furry critter came racing right at my nose. When rabbits run across your face and over your head and then travel down your back, across your butt and finish their dash down your legs; little boys cannot hold their water. Their pants will be wet and the snow will be orange. The brother holding the gun will be bent over laughing so hard that they too will have wet pants and changing snow color. It will not be caused by fear. No, it will be caused by uncontrollable laughter. We could hardly wait for the next snow, so we could get even with that rabbit.

All of these folks were friends and family. They are now all deceased. The little girl was my Aunt Sarah; she died at 83, only woman to ever hold the office of Sheriff in White County.

GOD'S LITTLE ANGEL

If you don't know who little Bence Allison is, you go right now on Facebook, find Darla Allison, and click on the picture of her baby girl. Bence is Darla and Jeff Allison's baby girl. Billi Kayl is Bences' older sister. They are my little nieces. My life has been wonderful. I have been blessed with a great family, mother, father, wonderful daughter, great son, outstanding wife, sister, brothers, cousins; I love them all. The friends and family that I have are my bridge. They have helped me get over the rough and rocky times. I am now the age I never thought I would be. So many memories I have that I want to share. When your life begins with a loving family and great friends, there is nothing better for you. Most in our family have been born healthy. However, my family does have a history of heart problems. My little niece, Bence, is probably one of the cutest little girls I know. Her big sister Billi Kayl, thinks Bence is the greatest thing since ice cream. All of us feel the same way about Bence. On Thursday, four month old Bence will be in a hospital. She will be having heart surgery on Friday to correct a heart problem that the surgeons say can be fixed. I have all the confidence in the world that this surgery will be successful. Science and medicine have come a long way since I was born. Most people are like me. They are nothing but an old softy when it comes to kids. I have held the hand of a friend as life left his body. Yet, I can't stop the tears from coming to my eyes when I think of little Bence having to go through this surgery. This writing is not about me. This writing is about little Bence. I am writing this to say to all of Bences' friends and friends of Bences' family. Please be a bridge for them. If you look up, mention Bences' name. When Bence smiles the world is a brighter place. God will guide the surgeons, and the Angels will hold her hand. Let's just be a bridge for a beautiful little girl.

THEY AIN'T THAT BAD

It is amazing to me, having spent many years around young people, the way some folks just write off our young folks. I hear people say, "Man we couldn't do that when we were young" or the classic statement, "Back when I was a kid bla bla bla bla bla. It is a shame how kids behave today." I guess some people forget that they were not exactly model citizens when they were young. I sure am glad that Frances and Herbert Adams didn't know all the things I did when I was growing up. I always laugh when I hear a parent say, "They don't make kids mind like they did when I was in school." That parent probably hasn't been in a school since they dropped out or graduated; whichever the case may be. I had lots of parents tell me to make their child mind at school. It was always my feeling that if a student was a problem at school; they were usually a problem at home. I remember one time a parent came to me and asked if their son could come back to school. He had been suspended from school for some infraction that I don't remember. I listened to the parent plea how bad that boy wanted to come back. I finally told them I would allow the boy to return. He returned but it was for a short period of time. He hit the Principal up side of the head and threw a phone at him just because the Principal told him not to be holding his girlfriend in an inappropriate way. I asked the Principal what happened and he smiled and said, "I don't think he liked the phone." He was one student out of 600. Someone later told me I made a mistake of letting the boy come back to school. I know the Principals head was sore, but I don't think I did. I think the boy made the mistake of not staying in school. The young man later led a tragic life. He died at a very young age. I don't like to hear people talk bad about our schools or kids. I always try to remember that old saying that still rings true today: There but for the grace of God go I. Try to remember that. It makes our kids look a whole lot better. Don't let the actions of one kid make you think all kids behave in a bad way. Go visit a school; you might be surprised at how good they are.

SLOW TALKING

Spring time had been slow coming that year. There had been several below freezing days in March. I had to delay baseball practice because of the cold weather. We were throwing and doing drills in the gym but we really wanted to get outside. Some of the other schools had started their spring break and their students were out of school. Spring break for Lumpkin County would not come until the second week in April. Since one of the schools in our area, Dawson County was out, there was an old Dawson County boy that came up to our school. One of my students came in and asked if the boy could come in and visit with us. I told my student if the young man would sign in at the central office, and not interfere with my class it would be ok with me. I remember young man came in and sat down in a desk that was right in front of the boy who had asked if he could come into the room. The bell rang and I thought since we had a visitor, I would allow him to introduce himself. I told the class we have a visitor from a neighboring school and I would like for him to introduce himself. The young man stood up and said in the slowest southern drawl I have ever heard, "Mmmyyy nnnammes Haaaroold Chhesssteer." Needless to say, everyone started to laugh. The young man just looked around the room and said, "Ifff yyoou thank III ttallk ssloow youss ssshoulld heaaar mmy ssister. Tthherre wwas ann old bbooy aaskk her iff ssheee wanted tooo haavve sexx, beefoore ssshe ccoouuld aaannswwer, theey all rreaadie hhaad." Class was over.

SHOCKING DOC

We had planned a trip to Nebraska to go pheasant hunting. I, unfortunately, didn't get to go. My Brothers, Bruce and Billy along with several of our friends went to Beatrice, Nebraska. Being the first trip out there; it was decided that they really needed to see if they could find someone that had a bird dog that could go on the hunting trip. Unfortunately not many folks with a good bird dog will loan you their dog to take to some place, unless they are going with you. Billy and Bruce found that there was a retired Veterinarian that sold bird dogs. They went to the Doctor and purchased an old brittany spaniel. The dog's name was Doc. Doc made the trip with my brothers and friends, and from what they told me; he did a good job on the bird hunt. One of the things that they discovered about Doc was that he didn't like to come to you. So to correct this problem my brother Billy had purchased a shocking collar that is used to train dogs. You could yell Doc's name and if he didn't come; you simply applied a little jolt of electricity my means of the collar, and Doc would immediately know he should obey. Doc was kept in a kennel right outside of brother Billy and Sadie, my sister-in-law's house. Occasionally, Doc was turned loose from the kennel and allowed to run free. Since he was near a heavy traffic highway, he was always made to wear his training collar, just to make sure he didn't get near the road. One day Billy and Sadie were sitting in the house and old Doc kept barking. He would start barking and Billy or Sadie would yell at him to stop and he would. But soon he would resume his uncontrollable barking. After this had gone on for quite a while, Billy said, "If he doesn't stop that barking, I am going to get the controller for the training collar and give him a jolt." The barking would stop, then it would start, it would stop, then it would start. Billy goes to find the controller. He found his three year old twins Megan and Zack in their bedroom playing with the controller for the training collar. They had discovered that when you mashed the button a light would come on, and when you let off of it the light would go off. From that point on, I always thought that old Doc was a lot quicker to come to you than he was before the twins found that controller. At least I think he was.

AGING OF A DOG

When I got our Golden Retriever Amos for my son, he was just a puppy. Brynnan was four years old and Amos was 2 months old. My Son just turned 17. Amos is 13. Amos has been a member of our family for 13 years. Amos has been one of the most loving animals that I have ever had. He has never been aggressive toward man or animal. He never got out of his hyper stage until he got so old that he could no longer be hyper. He was a very easy dog to train. He loved to please me. The people who deliver our paper always throw it out at the bottom of our driveway. After watching Amos tear up several papers, I decided I would get Amos to fetch my paper to me. It didn't take long to do that. I could say PAPER AMOS and he would go find the paper, regardless of where the folks had thrown it, and bring it to me. He would not even break the plastic wrapper that was wrapped around the paper. He has always loved to ride. He would jump in the back of the truck and stick his head into the wind. He loved to ride on the four-wheeler with me. He rode on the back seat. I didn't have a carrier for him to ride in; he just sat right on that seat and slobbered all over me. He loves to swim. I would take Amos to a lake or stream and he would be in the water before I knew it. He would fetch a stick, or if I shot a duck; he would retrieve it. Amos can't hear me say PAPER AMOS any more. He no longer can jump into the truck. He would love to get on the back of the four-wheeler, but he can't. When I turn him loose he will still go wade in the water, but his joints just will not let the aged dog swim. We have him in the lot with Brynnan's new German Shorthair, Willie Bell. He lets her sit on him. She pulls his hair and occasionally lays her head on Amos like he is her pillow. Amos can't see me as well as he once could. When I speak to him, I have to speak very loud, and he looks around to see where the sound is coming from. Old dogs are not too much different from old people. We love them, take care of them, and they love us back. I just wish dogs didn't get old so quick.

ALZHEIMERS AIN'T FUNNY

Not all of my stories are told to be humorous. Some are told just to be shared. They may give insight to some or it could be that I just wanted to tell it. I guess this is just a story that I wanted to share because I have thought of it many times. Each time I talk with someone about a parent or loved one that has memory loss it brings me to a time when my oldest brother Bruce and I were turkey hunting over in Lumpkin County. Bruce and I had got one of our friends to let us out where you turn down to Dockery Lake on Highway 60. Our goal was to hunt down the mountain and come out somewhere in Yahoola Valley. Our father had sawed over three million board feet of lumber out of the valley back in the 50's. Bruce and I had been small boys but we still remembered the fishing in the mountain stream that bears the valleys name. The headwaters of Yahoola Creek contained some excellent trout fishing. We also knew lots of the families that lived in Yahoola Valley. We hunted down the mountain without any luck of hearing a gobbler. We came out at Walter Caldwell house. Walt had served on the Board of Education when I started teaching at Lumpkin County High School, and my dad had always been very fond of Walt Caldwell. Mr. Caldwell was sitting in a chair on his front porch. I saw Walt and told Bruce we had better speak to Walt or he would be mad at us. We walked up into Walt's yard and I said, "Hey Walt, how are you doing?" He threw up his hand and said, "Hey Bobby, Bruce how are ya'll doing? Come on up and set a spell. How are Herbert (my dad) and JC (my uncle) doing?" I told Walt that Daddy was doing ok, but Uncle JC had passed away. We talked for a few more minutes about the days when dad had been sawing the timber in Yahoola Valley. After we chatted for a while, Bruce said, "Bob, we need to get on to where the boys said they would pick us up. If we are not there they will worry about us." We told Walt bye and left. The next Monday after school, I went to Valley Sports. It was a sporting goods store that Walt's nephew, Ernest Caldwell and his wife Glenda was operating. I told Ernest I had seen his Uncle Walt over the weekend, and Ernest said, "Yea, it's bad about Walt." That kind of shocked me, and I said, "What happened to Walt?" Earnest told me that Walt had Alzheimer's disease and didn't even know his children. It was hard for me to believe that my friend could not remember his family when we had talked about things that had happened 35 or 40 years ago. Neither I nor my Brother thought there was anything wrong with Mr. Caldwell. Alzheimer is a strange disease, that's for sure.

WHAT TIME IS IT

We had a big camp on the Chattahoochee Management Area. Deer season was in full swing and our annual camping trip was here. I have to confess this camping trip would also be kind of like a beer fest. Everyone that camped would chip in a few dollars and a truck load of beer would magically appear. On this particular camping experience my good friend Ed Bentley had been select to be our chef. He was selected mainly because he was the one standing next to the stove when it was time to eat. We never knew who would be camping with us. There would be days when we would wake up and a new face would be in the camp. Where some of the folks came from would be a mystery, but no one really cared. I don't know whose idea it was to pull a joke on a fellow new to our camp. I think his name was Pearce Marks. I believed he owned Mark's Oxygen Company. Ed Bentley had given a great lecture on the need to get in the woods early if you were going to be a successful deer hunter. Ed had told everyone they had better get to bed if they were going to get up early and kill a big buck. Taking Ed's advice, Mr. Marks hit the sack about 10:30 that evening. We let him sleep till about 1:30. Ed Bentley woke the gentleman up and told him it was time to rise and shine. He had slept about 2 hours. While he slept we plotted a little scheme. Ed had also noticed that Mr. Marks did not wear a watch. Ed told the Marks fellow that he would have his breakfast fixed in just a bit. He also told him that I would take him to where he wanted to hunt. After he had hurriedly eaten his breakfast, I carried him to where he wanted to go. I told him it would be daylight soon and I hoped he got him one. He sleepily got out of the truck. I then turned around and right back to camp I went. All of the conspirators laughed and decided that we would go to bed. That next morning about 10am Mr. Marks made his way back to camp. He thought we were just getting in from our hunt. Some of us were actually just getting up. Mr. Marks said, "You know when you let me out; I got to my stand and it seemed like it didn't get light for hours." He said he thought he might have actually gone to sleep for a while. As Ed Bentley was pouring himself a cup of coffee, Ed said, "You know it did seem like it took a long time for it to get daylight this morning". Thinking back on it, I would say Ed Bentley was right. We were sleeping in a dark tent.

WHO TIED THAT GOAT?

My Uncle Roy was daddy's oldest brother. I remember him as being a man that had a big smile, walked somewhat stupped over, and liked to drink whiskey. I wish he had lived longer so I could have gotten to know him better. He passed away at age 47. I think it had something to do with his love of whiskey that made his liver go bad. I remember him as a man that loved animals. He had dogs, horses, and cows. He owned the first Weimeraner dog that I ever saw. It was a big blue grey dog. It was a very beautiful dog. Uncle Roy was always buying animals. Once he bought two billy goats. I loved to play with those old goats. People that have been around billy goats know that they have a very bad odor. The male goats like to urinate on their beard. They will drag their beard across a nanny goat to mark them as one of their herd. That goat pee really stinks. I had a little red wagon and I would tie a rope around one of those goats neck set down in that little wagon and hold on. I didn't care where that goat went just as long as it was pulling me with it. When one goat would pull me to the point it was exhausted; I would then go get the other goat. I decided that those goats would be fun to ride. One day I tried riding those goats. It was fun they would throw me off by running and then stopping real quickly and right over their head I would go. Of course I had not thought of the smell, I was having too much fun. That evening I had tied the goats back up and headed for the house. Mom met me at the door. YOUR NOT COMING IN THIS HOUSE SMELLING LIKE A BLAME BILLY GOAT came echoing out of her mouth. She came out on the porch holding her nose and made me strip down to my jockey shorts. She single handedly grabbed my smelly clothes and carried them to a barrel and quickly found a match and burned my clothes. While I stood on the front porch in my underwear for the entire world to see,

Mom made a quick trip to the store and I heard her say, "Roy Adams, if you let my son play with those stinking goats again, I am going to give you a whipping." She turned and then came marching back toward the porch. I was ordered into the house and into the tub. The next morning we woke to the smell of billy goat. Somehow during the night those two goats got tied to our screen door on the front porch. We never found out who did it. I wished Uncle Roy had lived longer. He and I could have had lots of fun.

SMOKE THAT CIGARETTE

My Uncle LG Adams was a one of a kind fellow. He was my daddy's youngest brother. You never knew what was going to happen when Uncle L was around. I think that is one of the reasons I loved him. Uncle LG and Aunt Pauline had three children, Patricia, Cathy and Wayne. We all grew up together, and were kind of like brother and sisters instead of cousins. In Uncle L's later life he experienced a great deal of sickness. He lost a lot of the circulation in his legs and had to have one of his legs amputated due to bad circulation. Through all of sickness he continued to smoke. I would try to get him to quite but I was never successful. However, even during his sickness and stays in the hospital, he never lost his great sense of humor. His smile and laughter I have never forgot. He came home after a stay in the hospital and I stopped by to see him. The road to my house goes right by where Uncle L lived. I asked him how he got to come home so soon. The day before I had stopped in at the hospital to see him and I was told by one of the nurses that he would have to stay a few more days. Uncle L said, "Well, they said I couldn't smoke in the room, so I was going to slip outside and smoke. I pushed this IV bottle down the hall and I saw a door that looked like it went outside. It was dark so I didn't think they would see me. I had on one of them hospital nightgowns, you know them kind that is open in the back." I said, "Yes, I saw you in your hospital gown yesterday." He continued, "When I opened that door it was blowing snow, and it was cold as crap out there. I had just got that darned old IV bottle out the door, put the cigarette in my mouth and the wind blew my first match out. I had one more so I struck it. I got two or three quick puffs off of that cigarette and though it was so cold; I would just go back in the hospital. You know them dang doors lock when you shut them? I pushed that darn IV thing all the way around the hospital in my gown freezing to death, trying to find a door I could go back into the hospital. With that gown split in the back, I thought I was going to freeze my butt off. I ended going all the way around to the front door. I think I may have been the first person ever send home from the hospital for smoking." Uncle L laughed, and so did I. The picture of him pushing that IV around in his split hospital gown still comes to my mind. He was a good Uncle.

SUDDEN SUMMER

Several of my friends had just graduated from High School. As soon as their graduation was completed, several of us White County boys headed out to Panama City, Florida. We had rented us a big house and were having a great big time. It was hot and of course since it was sunny, I didn't venture to far away from our estate. There was a good refrigerator in our rented castle and it served the purpose of keeping the beer cold. We had been very fortunate, only a couple of the crew had been locked up and sentenced to pay a fine for public intoxication. One of my friends was Chris Black. Christopher

Clair Black may have been one of the best athletes to come out of White County High School. He would go on to play college basketball at the University of North Carolina at Charlotte. While we were on this graduation celebration Chris had gone to a local drug store and purchased some kind of hair bleach that was called---SUDDEN SUMMER. It was supposed to lighten the color of your hair. Chris had a natural sandy brown hair and thought he wanted his hair a little lighter. Since we were on the beach this would be a perfect place to bleach his hair. Before this cosmetology session would begin, we would have to consume a large portion of the beer that was in the frig. After having done so, Chris decided; it was time to practice his cosmetology skills. He and I were out in the back yard of our rented complex and Chris would put a little of the bleach on his head. After putting what he thought was the correct amount on his head, while we waited; he made frequent trips to the frig. Maybe 45 minutes later Chris proclaimed that he had gotten the exact color of hair he wanted. He then made several more trips to the cooler. After having made several trips to the cooler and frig, Chris kind of went to sleep in a lounge chair. I let Chris sleep for about 20 minutes and then I took it upon myself to make Chris's hair look better. I poured the entire bottle of SUDDEN SUMMER on Chris's hair and rubbed it in without wakening him. I then went inside the house and slept for a couple of hours. When I got up I went out, and there laid my friend with bright WHITE hair. Chris woke up and said, "Damn, look my hair it's white. I must have slept in the sun too long." I just agreed and said, "I believe you are right, definitely too much sun".

BISCUIT POISONING

I have suffered from biscuit poisoning for a number of years. That is what made my waist expand as I have aged. At least that is what I tell my son. My waist size is easily expanded. I can look at a biscuit, and then I have to let my belt out two notches. I used to be able eat as much as I wanted with no weight gain. If increasing my IQ was as easy as increasing my waist size, I would be the smartest man in the world. My son is 17 and I am 65. I know sometimes he probably wishes he had a young dad that could do all of the things a 17 year old likes to do. Unfortunately he is stuck with me. I keep telling him I will try my best to lose weight. I would ride the bicycle but my knees keep hitting me in the belly. I always tried to stay in good physical condition and then I had a few heart blockages. Then after the heart blockages came back surgery. After the back surgery, came open heart surgery. This thing they call aging is about to kill me. I hope I can overcome it. Now that I have reached the age that everything that was going north is heading south, my appreciation for life is a whole lot greater. Gravity is taking on a new meaning. I used to stand in the bathroom look in the mirror and smile. Now, I look in the mirror and I have to put on my glasses to see if I am smiling. I am not complaining about getting old. It is just a hard thing to do. My mind will still write a twenty year old check but my 60 year old body can't cash it. I have tried to except aging gracefully. It is just not going to happen. I have always known that people are born, then they age and at some point they die. I am going to try to put off that last part for a long time. As I have gotten older, I have discovered a number of things that I didn't know. I didn't know that you could turn over in bed and pull a muscle. If you and your wife are lying in bed and have romantic feelings, you will get a leg cramp and it will make you jump out of bed yelling things that are not romantic to your wife. You can get a cold and keep it as long as the money holds out to buy medicine. I know that exercising is important. Every time I have the urge to exercise, I just lay down until that urge is gone. All of us need to try harder to get in better shape. I did give up smoking, drinking and looking at beautiful women. I just haven't been able to give up lying.

DOG IN A HOLE

Jimmy Vandiver pulled up in our yard one evening and asked if I would go with him over to the Hamby fjord which is located on Dukes Creek. The property is now part of Smithgall Woods. This is the property that the late Charles Smithgall sold to the state. In the 50's and 60's it was privately owned. Jimmy got two cans of dog food out of his car and we started our walk. As we were walking in he explained that the reason we were carrying the dog food was because one of his dogs and been chasing a squirrel and had fallen in an old Gold mining shaft. When we arrived at the old gold mine shaft Jimmy opened the dog food and chunked it down into the deep pit. He threw a small stone into the shaft and I heard water splash as it hit bottom. Jimmy told me he knew the dog had water, but did not know if he was injured from the fall. Jimmy ask if I would mind bringing the dog food over next week and he would try to figure out a way to get the dog out of the pit. I agree to carry the dog food over and feed the dog. The next Saturday Jimmy pulled up and ask dad and me to go with him to feed the dog. He had a plan to rescue the dog. He told dad to bring his power saw and instructed me to get an axe. The three of us carrying dog food, a power saw and an axe walked over to the pit that had been the home for Jimmy's dog for several days. When we arrived at the pit Jimmy called the dog, and we could hear him whining. Jimmy told dad to cut a popular tree that was about 30 to 35 feet tall. Jimmy told us to make sure that the limbs were left long enough that they could be used as steps. The three of us pulled the popular tree that was going to serve as a latter to the edge of the shaft. I asked Jimmy what we were going to do. He told me we were going to put the log butt first into the hole and then I was going to climb down the popular and get the dog out of the hole. Sound like a plan to me. I wasn't too sure about the part that I was going down the tree to get the dog, but since I was the youngest and dumbest; it kind of made sense to me. We pulled the butt of that tree to the mouth of the pit. We started to raise the tree. When we got the tree to a pivot point Jimmy said, "OK, now push." And push we did. That tree went yeeeoon, completely out of site. We could not even see the top of the tree. Jimmy looked over into the mining shaft and said, "Deep ain't it." Daddy said, "Jimmy, we can't cut a tree that will reach the bottom of that pit." I said, "And if you could, I wouldn't be the one going down it." We fed the dog a few more days in the hole, and Jimmy Vandiver got some of the Army Rangers from the ranger camp in Dahlonega to bring their rope latters over to rescue the dog. The dog was unharmed and I didn't have to go into that deep hole. Both of us were pleased.

GETTING REFINED

Most of the people that I know are regular people. They are not snobbish. They speak to you when they see you. They don't care if you drive a fancy car or a broke down pickup truck. They love their families and do the best they can to look after them. Some live in mobile homes, others may live in a big house. I didn't know why they put more than one fork on a table until I was nearly 30. I ate with some friends once and I had never seen so many forks and plates and eating utensils. I would wait to see which one they picked up; then I would pick up the same one. I made it through that dinner without a major blunder. You could probably say that I was not a refined gentleman. When mama put food on our table you got a fork and a plate. That was all we needed. You never left your hand around the food for too long. You could have very easily gotten a fork stuck in it. We never had a dessert. Mom just fixed the basics and that was it. Sometimes she would make a cake, and when she did, that thing was set on the table and it disappeared in a flash. During my tenure as Superintendent of Schools of Lumpkin County, I was asked by a representative of a book company if I would attend a dinner, and then go to the Opera at the Fox Theater in Atlanta, Georgia. I had never been to an opera, and I thought this is a time that I can kind of make myself more in tune with a higher class of culture than I was used to. I should have known it might be a little bit over my head when he said it was formal attire. That meant wearing a tie to me. But to me on the safe side I rented a tux. I showed up. We ate at a fine restaurant where they had too many forks on the table, and then we traveled on to the Opera. It was some kind of fine. I mean they had two women that could really sing, I guess, if you like Opera. I couldn't wait to get myself out of that misery. We came out of the theater and the book salesman said, "Well Mr. Adams how did you like the Opera?" I looked at him and said, "It wasn't that bad, and if you like that kind of singing; you bring yourself up to Dahlonega, Georgia on the third weekend of October. We have what we call Gold Rush. And if you liked that Opera, you will love hearing Mama Lucy Cain and her daughter Bedele Nix do the hog calling contest. They have won it three years in a row." That salesman never came to Gold Rush. I don't guess he wanted to be in tune with my class of culture.

CHECKERED FLAG

I have been a fan of racing since I watched Roy Farris and Dale Allen drag race through the Freeman straight on Hwy 75. The straight started just below where I was raised, and it gave me plenty of opportunities to witness young men in their souped up cars drag race. From drag racing to oval dirt track racing was a natural evolution for me. On Friday night we would go to Banks County to the dirt track that Tommy Irvin ran. Then on a Saturday night we would be at the Toccoa Speedway and watch Bud Lunsford, the Irvin boys and Barrons try to prove who was king of the dirt track. A few of my friends decided that we would build us a race car. We, mostly they, purchased a 1940 ford coupe for $400.00. We tore the interior out of that car and then welded a roll cage in it, and we were ready to race. One of the guys that had been working on our race car was Dude Robinson. I always liked Dude. He had a contagious grin and a good nature. He also loved to race. Dude decided that he and I would pull our jalopy to Toccoa Speedway. Once there, Jere Westmoreland was going to drive it. We hooked the car to the back of Dude's 1956 Crown Victoria Ford and started towing the car to the race track. Our journey to the track would take us through what was called the Sisk Straight in Habersham County on highway 17. Dude and I were trying to get the car to the track so Jere could get her warmed up for the race. At the lower end of the Sisk straight are some pretty good little hills. As we went over the last hill I looked to my left and I saw the race car that we were towing break away from us. I said, "Dude, the car is loose." Dude hit the brakes on his Ford and the race car when sailing passed us. If I had of had a checkered flag, it would have been waving. The race car went into the ditch, up the bank and then it tipped over on to its top. We got out of the Dude's car and surveyed the damage. With the help of some folks that had witnessed the escaped race car; we pushed the race car back on to its wheels. Dude got in the car and kicked the roof back out and we re-hooked the car; this time making sure the car would not break loose and pass us. We finally got the car to the track that evening. We didn't win the race at the Toccoa Speedway that night, but I still have the memory of that old race car winning the race through the Sisk straight.

DON'T COME THAT WAY BENNY

Smith Crumbly was Aunt Lou Vandivers brother. To say that Smith was a stubborn fellow would be an understatement. Smith Crumbly worked at my dad's sawmill for a long time and was always liked by everyone that knew him. Smith had an accident in his youth. He actually had gotten his head hung in a syrup mill and lots of folks though that it was a miracle that he survived. Smith kind of snorted when he talked. He would come up to me and say, "ZZZZZZZZ, Hey red you got a smoke? I left mine on the mantle?" Smith always left his cigarettes on the mantle. He would begin his speaking with a sound like someone snoring. Smith loved to coon hunt. He and a couple of his friends, Benny Caudell, and Buck Robinson were going to go coon hunting up on Smith Creek below Anna Ruby falls. Buck and Benny lived in Robertstown, and at that time; there was only a trail up to the falls. Unicoi State Park had not been built. Buck couldn't talk plain and Smith snorted when he talked. Benny, Buck and Smith let the dogs loose and it wasn't long before the dogs were hot on the trail of an old raccoon. Benny said the dogs were getting closer and closer to the falls. When they actually got to the falls, they didn't slow down. It was a cold January night and it was freezing weather. The dogs were running yeow, yeow, yeow. Benny says to Buck and Smith, "Boys, we can't go around that way; we will be on top of the falls." Smith says, "Benny don't tell me which way to go. I was born and reared in these here mountains. I know every pig trail around here." Benny pleads with Smith to not go around that way. Buck says, "Don't argu wif dat dam ful Benny. Him fanks his noses everfang." After a good bit of arguing with Smith, Benny finally says, "OK Smith, be a damn fool and go on." Buck says, "Ah Benny uh taint tel him a dawn fang wet him go." Smith is carrying an old kerosene lantern. He goes up and starts to cross the head of the falls. He doesn't see the half inch of ice on the rocks. He starts to slide. Benny said it looked like a ballet dancer. Smith is rocking from side to side. The light is shining, and then it suddenly—goes over the falls. They hear him fall, the crash, and then light goes out. Buck starts to cry. "Oh no, Benny, mith is dead what tan we do?" Benny looks and says, "Buck we will have to go to Robertstown and get some men to help us get his body out of there." Both men are completely distraught. They start walking away to get help. As they are walking, they look back. Suddenly a match lights, and the lantern starts to glow, then it starts to wave. They hear this snort zzzzzz and a voice yells, "HEY BENNY, DON'T COME DOWN THAT WAY. IT'S ROUGHER'N HELL." Smith lived to coon hunt again.

CHEAP RACE TEAM

Going around a quarter mile dirt track doesn't look too difficult. It probably wouldn't be if you were just out for a test run. But you put about 15 to 20 cars lined up nose to tail and have that 400 plus horse power engine tuned to perfection, you had better be pretty darn good at steering a race car. North Georgia has been very blessed with some drivers that could smoke those tracks. Not only did we have men but one of the early female drivers of a race car was from Lumpkin County. Sarah Christian was Tommy Christian's mother. She was one of the first female stock car drivers in America. I guess Tommy got his desire to race from his mother. Tommy is no longer with us, but he was my friend and I want share this story with you. Tommy owned an old late model race car, and it wasn't all that bad. He was going to race his car over at the Toccoa Speedway. Tommy wasn't that bad of a driver, but Tommy thought he would get Doug Kenimer to drive his car. Doug Kenimer had been driving race cars for a long time, and was at one time the National Dirt Track champion. Doug and I were talking and he asked me what I was doing Saturday Night. I told Doug that I didn't have any plans. He said well since you don't have any plans, would you like to go with me and fat boy Christian to the Toccoa Speedway on Saturday night. Doug called Tommy "fat boy." I told Doug that I would go with him and Tommy. We arrived at the track and unloaded the car. When it came time for the late model hot laps, Doug got in the car and fired it up. He went out on to the track and was going to see how the car was handling. He was going pretty well, and then the car started cutting out. Doug pulled into the pits. He told me to take the gas filter off to see if it had water in it. I did. No there was no water in the gas. Doug got back into the car and started the race. The car was sputtering all around the track. He pulled in and told Tommy there was no reason to ruin his car and it would be better just to shut it down. We were watching the race and Doug looked at Tommy and said, "Fat boy did you put any gas in that car?" Tommy Christian smiled and said, "Why hell no, I forgot to." Doug looked at Tommy and said, "Damn Tommy, I knew we were a cheap race team, but I didn't know we couldn't afford gas for our race car." We all laughed and watched the race with Tommy's car sitting there in the pits out of gas.

REAR ENDED

I wanted to write this down while it was fresh on my mind. My buddy Bill Christian got into town yesterday. Bill goes to Little Rock, Arkansas every three weeks to get his meds. Bill has been doing this for three and a half years. If you don't know Bill Christian, you are missing something. He knows more people, and can remember people's names, better than anyone I know. There is something else about Bill that I have noticed. If anyone is going to get hit in the rear by another driver, it will be Bill. Bill had driven through heavy traffic and gotten all the way into Cleveland, Georgia yesterday, only to be rear ended right in front of the White County Courthouse. Bill called me and left a message that he had been in a wreck in front of the Courthouse, but I didn't get the call until about 30 minutes after it had happened. By then Bill had been able to get our friend Joe Campbell to come and pick him up. It hadn't been too long ago I was going down highway 129 south out of Cleveland, and there at the red light, where WalMart is located, was Bill Christian with another car in the rear end of his truck. Luckily Bill wasn't injured in that accident. I was going down the highway not long before that accident and one of my friends called and said, "Bobby, Bill Christian has been in a wreck on Highway 75. Someone has run into the rear of his truck." I immediately called Bill. I asked him if he was hurt. Bill said, and I quote, "Hell, yes I am hurt. A guy just ran into me running about 60 mph. I was pulling to the side of the road when I met a funeral procession. This guy ran into me, and I finally got out of my truck and he asked if I was hurt. I told him the same thing I told you. Hell yes, I am hurt. Then he asked why was I pulling to the side of the road? I told him there was a funeral procession coming. He told me in Florida, he didn't stop for funerals, I told that SOB; it was obvious that he didn't stop in Georgia either." And that ladies and gentleman is Bill Christian. Please do not run into the rear of his truck.

FOOLISH BOYS

Sometimes when you look back on some of the things you did, it makes you realize that we all have our "dumb moments." We were just young boys and had started fishing with our Grandfather Sims. He would take us over to Hiawassee, Georgia to Lake Chatuge and we would catch bream, blue gill, catfish, bass, just any fish that would bite; we would catch. Fishing began to be an obsession of ours. My brothers and I loved to fish. We would catch spring lizards for bait. We would dig worms for bait. We would knock down wasp nest and use the lava for bait. If it crawled or wiggled, we would use it for bait. Anytime we heard someone make a suggestion about bait that would catch fish, we were bound and determined to try it. There were a couple of ponds across the road from what used to be Twin Tanks service station on the out skirts of Helen,

Georgia.   At one time either Jimmy Vandiver had a gravel business there, or the county had bought gravel and dug the holes that filled up and formed some ponds. I am not sure which party formed the ponds. But the ponds where a great place for young boys like me to go fishing. The ponds were located right next to the Chattahoochee River. Since the ponds were located so close to where we lived, it was only natural for young anglers like me to be there every day trying to catch a lunker bass. We could see big bass swimming around the pond. But we couldn't get them to bite anything we tried. Brothers Bruce and Billy, and I would cast every bait we could at those big boys, but they wouldn't take our bait. Men gathered at Twin Tanks service station in the evenings to discuss the daily happenings. We were in the station and one of the men said, "You know they tell me that a big bass will hit an Alka-Seltzer. They say when those things fizz fish can't resist them". One of the other fellows said, "Well I heard that strawberry Ice Cream is good for bass too". The Adams boys made a direct travel to our Papa's store to get all the Alka-Seltzer we could find. We bored holes in those things and cast them into water. The bass didn't seem to like those things. We never caught a fish. We spent all of our money on Alka-Seltzers, so the strawberry ice cream would have to wait.   We did notice that when we gathered at twin tanks that evening several of the men were laughing, but we didn't know then, what we know now. We never tried Ice Cream. I always wondered if it would work.

RUN AWAY BOAT

The Westmoreland family lived at the bottom of the hill on the South side. The Magness family was at the bottom of the hill on the north side. Both families had kids about my age age so we played a lot together and enjoyed each other's company whenever we could. As we grew older and graduated from school most of us went our separate ways. One of the Westmoreland boys, Robert, went into the Army. He eventually owned a Dairy Queen in Toccoa, Ga. Between the Westmoreland's and Adams family were the Turners. Bill Turner was married to Robert's sister Jeannette. Bill and Jeannette lived next door to my Grandmother. They had two children, Laura and Mike. I saw Mike so much at our house; I thought that he was one of my brothers. It was a very tight community. I had graduated from college, and just started a teaching career in Lumpkin County High School in Dahlonega, Georgia. Robert Westmoreland was Mike's Uncle. Mike had purchased himself a speed boat. Robert had come home on leave from the Army. Mike had decided that he would take Robert down to Lake Lanier and they would do some water skiing behind Mike's new boat. Before they had left for the lake, Mike had seen my Brother Billy, and told him what they were going to do. Billy told Mike that he had just bought a boat and that he might come down to the lake to do some crappie fishing. They agreed to meet each other around the Little River Landing. Billy was a little later getting to the landing than he had anticipated. Mike and his Uncle Robert were nowhere to be seen. Billy waited a little while and decided that he would just go on fishing. But before he left the landing, one of our friends and fishing buddies, Mr. Wylie Brown came into the landing in his boat. Wylie had been crappie fishing. Billy asked Wylie if he had happened to see Mike and Robert. Billy described the boat for Wylie. Wylie said, "Yea, I have seen that boat. I sure hope the game warden doesn't see'em they are going around and around in that boat." He told Billy where he saw them so Billy decided he would ride up the lake and see if he could find them. It wasn't long before Billy had the boat in sight. He rode up to the boat but no one was in it. Billy heard someone yelling and he looked and there was Mike and Robert waving their arms. They were over on the bank. When Billy got over to our two friends, this is what he heard. Mike said that he was going to pull Robert up and since there was only him in the boat he was going to sit on the side of the boat so he could watch Robert ski. Mike said he sat down and opened his new boat up. He hadn't noticed but the steering wheel was turned to the left. It had a lot more power than he anticipated and it threw him over the side. The boat kept going around and around. Mike said that he and Robert had to swim like they were in the Olympics to get out of the way of that boat. Finally the boat ran out of gas. No one was hurt, but thank goodness there was not much gas in the run-away boat. I don't think that Robert ever got to ski behind Mike's boat, but he did get to play dodge boat with it.

WHITE BASS ARE A RUNNING

When I started coaching at Lumpkin County High School, it was hard to field a team of football players. I was always asking boys if they would like to come out for football. I had asked this one old boy that lived in the section of Lumpkin County known as Frogtown if he would come out for football, and he had decided he would. Now he was not the best player in the world but at least he was a body. He was a good kid and I had asked him to come out for football, so I had to take him home after practice each day. Spring training ran for three weeks and we had been going strong for about two of those three weeks. It was hot that spring and we had been giving the guys lots of breaks so they wouldn't over heat their bodies. We had just taken a break and the kid from Frogtown came up to me and said, "Coach I need to talk to you after practice". Since I had been carrying this boy home every day I said ok we will have time to talk. We finished our practice that day and the players were ready to hit the showers. The young man came after practice and got into my car. He looked at me and said, "Coach I am going to have to quite football." I said, "Well if you are going to have to quite, would you mind telling me why you are quitting." I will never forget his answer. He said, "Coach, the white bass are running up the Chestatee and I am going fishing." I told that young man that if that was what was important to him I didn't blame him for quitting. Good folks have their priorities in life, and he had his.

THE SPEED OF A NURSING MOTHER

Serving as the Superintendent of the Lumpkin County School System was a very challenging experience. You never knew what was going to happen. I woke up each day knowing there was going to be a new challenge right around the corner. I wouldn't have had it any other way. One of the things that made me really enjoy being the Superintendent of Schools was the fact that I had a great administrative staff. I found out very quickly that the people you have working for you can make or break you. Not only was the administrative staff wonderful but the secretarial staff was just as amazing. I was very fortunate to have as my secretary a lady that had served under several of the Lumpkin County School Superintendents, Mrs. Sammy Lane Sullens. Mrs. Sullens was someone that could have ran the entire office if need be. Sometimes I know she felt like she did.

I will never forget the time Ms. Sullens came into my office and said, "Mr. Adams there is a couple of ladies that would like to see you." Mrs. Sullens was stationed right outside of my office. Although she could not see me sitting in my chair, we were close enough to talk without raising our voices. Whenever someone asked to see me Mrs. Sullens would always come to my door, and ask if they could come into my office. On this particular day, I informed Mrs. Sullens to have the ladies to come on into my office. The ladies came in and I greeted them, and asked them to please have a seat. The first lady in said, "Mr. Adams I hope you remember me? I am not the one who wants to speak to you, but this lady here wants to talk to you", and she pointed to a lady that was holding a baby and had a toddler child by her side. I turned to the young lady and said, "How may I help you?" That was the last time I got to speak. The lady said, "Well, I tell you this, you blankeety, blanketty, blanketty, if that damn bus driver ever blanketty , I will whip that son-of- of blanketty. I can't believe that blanketty, blanketty, blank." I was trying to get a word in, but I couldn't. The lady that had brought her to see me was sitting there with a look of shock on her face. Her eyes were wide open in disbelief. The toddler started cry, then baby started crying, and the lady never stopped shaking a finger at me. Suddenly, she drops the top of her blouse and whips out her left breast and the baby instantly started nursing. Breast feeding is something I have seen many times, but never with the speed that this lady did it. She never missed a beat with her finger shaking it in my face as she placed her breast into the mouth of the baby. After finishing her rant, she immediately got up, and out the door she went. I never got to say a word. Her companion looked at me and said, "I am sorry Mr. Adams. I didn't know she was going to be like this." I told her not to worry about it. Mrs. Sullens had heard all of this, but she couldn't see what was going on in my office. Sammy Lane looked at me and said, "Now, Mr. Adams don't you think anything about that, at least that woman got it off her chest." I just thought to myself; yes Mrs. Sullens, she did get it off her chest.

SHOWING YOUR BUTT

I was going over some materials for a Board of Education meeting one day and my secretary said there was a lady that needed to talk to me for a minute. I told her to send the lady in to the office. The lady came in and I asked her to please be seated and I asked her if I could help her with anything. She told me that she hated to come and complain about anything but she felt as though she needed to tell me this. I told her to go right ahead and talk to me. I felt if she thought I should know something, it was pretty important. She said, "Well, I passed a bus today going out of Dahlonega on 115 East up near Wilson's Superette." She then kind of hesitated. I told her that was ok; there was a passing lane going up by there and it was a good place to pass the bus. She said, "Well, that is not what I really wanted to tell you." I said, "OH, I am sorry please continue." She said, "Well, something happened." "Yes, please tell me what happened," I replied. The lady looked around the room as if she was kind of embarrassed. She slowly began and said in a muffled voice, "Mr. Adams I got MOONED." I said, "Gosh, I don't know where you lived, but sometimes we all have to move." The lady looked and said, "Mooned, MOONED as in someone showing their ASS to me." "I am sorry. I thought you said you got moved," was my feeble reply. Then she said, "I know who it was." I really wanted to say "So you recognized the ass did you." But that is not what I said. However, by this time, she and I had gotten pretty tickled about the whole Mooning event. She told me who it was. I contacted the young man and told him rather than suspending him for a few days for showing his butt. He would have to apologize to the woman for what he did. He did. The lady was satisfied, and the young man has grown up to be a good young man. I guess we all have shown our posteriors on occasion, but it is nothing that an apology can't usually fix. Just don't show it so much that it becomes recognizable.

HOG KILLING TIME

My son, Brynnan was talking to me the other day and he said, "I sure will be glad when fall gets here, so I can start hunting with my bow, and looking for buck sign." Each year I am sure that his statement is probably repeated by several thousand young men and women who like the sport of hunting. For many years I am sure that I made similar statements. But unlike Brynnan, the fall of the year meant a whole lot more to me than hunting. One thing it meant was hog killing time was near. Daddy would always have a couple of pigs that we would start fatting up, so we could have fresh pork. We would feed the pigs a feed that was called shorts, and a lot of table scraps; referred by most country folks as slop. We would pour the feed in a five gallon bucket and then add water. After we stirred it up real good, we would then take it to the hog lot and pour it in the trough feeder where the fatting hogs were housed. We had to always wait for the first frost before we could kill the hogs. Dad would tell us not to plan anything on a Saturday morning, and if it had frost; a pig was going to die. Daddy would shoot the pigs and as soon as the pig hit the ground, he would stick the pig in the jugular vein with a sharp butcher knife, and bleed the hog out. Our job was to build a fire and keep plenty of wood around the old cast iron pots. We had to make sure that the cast iron pot was full of water. The fire would soon have the water boiling. Daddy always wanted us to bring the water to a boil, and then he would let it cool just a little before he would get an old coffee can, dip it into the water and carefully pour it over the hog. He would take his butcher knife and scrape the pig clean. There were usually several family members that helped with cleaning those pigs. After they were scraped clean and gutted, the pig would get a final wash and then it would be ready to cut up. Sometimes we would salt cure a ham or if we were lucky daddy would sugar cure one. Everything about a pig was used in some way or another. We did this every year for a long time. There may be someone in our county who raises a hog to slaughter, but I would bet that most folks that live in North Georgia get there pork from a local supermarket. Fattening and slaughtering a hog was not something I looked forward too, but the smell of fresh biscuits and ham frying in a pan made fall something a little bit more than just a time to start hunting. Dad thought that he had shot one of the fattened hogs once only to find out; he had missed. Daddy stuck that hog, and he bled out good. It wasn't until we had scraped and cleaned the pig that daddy noticed there was no bullet hole where he had been aiming. The pig had just slipped, and fell to his knees. Daddy said it didn't matter how the pig died. He was going to be bacon one way or another.

DOG VENISON

My friends, Gene Seabolt, and Donald Winkler, (better known as just Don) and I coon hunted about 5 nights a week. Once we got our dogs treeing raccoon, I guess we thought if they didn't tree about every night, they would quite treeing. Back in the 70's there were lots of places you could turn your hounds loose and tree a coon. Subdivisions now occupy the places where my coon hunting buddies once ran our old barking hounds. One cold January night the three of us decided that we would go hunting up the creek that ran down through the Moose family land and then through Garner and Emily Dyers farm. We had turned our dogs loose in The Dyer family's field where they sometimes planted a garden. After an hour or so of silence we decided that we would hike back out toward our vehicle that was parked in the Dyers garden spot. Don had a cold mine workers head light. They were called Wheat lights. They were an excellent light to find the shining eyes of an old sly raccoon. Gene had his six volt hand light and I had a two cell flash light. We had just entered the upper end of the field and someone brought up the topic of deer. Gene was talking about how he would love to have him some fresh venison. We walked about another hundred yards and Don shined his strong Wheat light down in the lower part of the Dyers bottom. Suddenly Don says, "Look there Gene, you see those deer's eyes?" Gene said, "I shore do. Man I would love to have that thing to eat." Winkler told Gene just be right still and hold the light and he would arrange for him to have some fresh venison. Don raised the little single shot 22 to his shoulder and BAM. Gene says, "I think you got that thing Don." Curiosity will make you walk faster than knowledge will. It didn't take us any time, and we were at the bottom of the field. There lying right where the

148

bright shining eyes had been, laid Genes dog. Gene looked down and said, "Well, I can't say anything Don. I was the one that told you to shoot and I was the one holding the light on my dog." We didn't tree a coon. We didn't see a deer, but we did manage to kill one of Gene's dogs. I always regretted the dog getting killed. I told Gene I hated it about his dog. Gene said not to worry about that dog, it wasn't any good anyway. I told him; I bet it was a lot better dog before it was shot. He agreed.

A BELATED THANK YOU

We were always hanging around Unicoi State Park when I was a teenager. That was the place to meet new girls. Lots of the campers were parents that would bring their daughters with them to the North Georgia Mountains. That suited the boys that lived around Helen and Roberts town just fine. Jimmy Tallent, Emory Brock, Royce Allison and yours truly had been up at the pavilion playing the juke box and dancing with some of the girls that were camping at the park. One of our friends, John Glen, also known as Boo, was like an assistant superintendent of Unicoi and John usually would be working behind the counter selling snacks and making change for the crowd. John Glen retired as a Georgia State Patrol. He recently passed away. Jimmy's mom, Inez and his Dad, Willard Tallent had just purchased a brand new Ford. It was about time to leave the park, so Emory, Royce, Jimmy and I got in the Tallent's new ford and was going to ride home. All of us boys either lived in Helen or Robertstown. There were two girls driving a little Chevy II. They were leaving in front of us. The driver stuck her head out of the car and said, "Hey y'all want to race." Well not having anything else to do; I guess Jimmy decided that would be something that we could do. So out the road the girls went with us close on their bumper. Now this road is crooked and narrow, and had no areas to pass another vehicle. Well I said, "Jimmy if you are going to pass her; this is the only place you can do it." That ford jumped out of passing gear at 70. I felt it jump out of passing gear. I also heard the gravel start hitting the side of the new ford. We went sideways. I was holding on to the arm rest. Suddenly, I could see stars. How could I see stars, if I was looking out the side window in the front seat? Then I realized we were up on our side. Trees were being knocked down. The car went off the road, rolled down toward the lake and stopped upside down. It was leaning on a little popular tree. Royce yelled, "Let me out of this SOB. It is going to turn over again." I asked if everyone was ok. The next response was Jimmy when he yelled, "Daddy is going to beat my ass." The car was totaled, but none of us were hurt. I got home that night thinking that maybe, just maybe, Dad and Mom would not find out about the wreck. Just as I slipped into the house, the phone rang. I quickly answered it and whispered, "Hello." It was Jimmy's Mom making sure I was ok. I whispered, "Yes, I am fine Inez, I wasn't hurt." I finally convinced her; I wasn't hurt. I hung the phone up turned around and there was Mom. She said, "You have been in another wreck haven't you?" The next day the Superintendent of the Park was telling John Glen that we may have to pay for those trees we knocked down. He told John that if it was a house where people lived we would have to pay for it. I will never forget what John told the man. John said, "Yes sir, but nobody was living in them trees." We didn't have to pay for the trees. I never got to thank John for what he did, so I am doing it now.

DRUNKS IN A VOLKESWAGAN

I was already in bed. It was 10 pm, and the spring of 1982 was in full force. The dog woods were in bloom, and pollen was still settling on peoples cars. My phone rang and I answered it. It was my buddy Lanier Chambers. Lanier said, "You know what tomorrow is?" Before I could answer he said, "The last day of turkey season. Do you realize you could get over here in about 30 minutes and we could go to Wilkes County, call us up a turkey, and we could be back by 9:30 or 10 in the morning." "I will be there shortly" was the reply he heard. I grabbed my gun, got my camo, and out the door I went. I was just coming down the hill below Cavender Creek Baptist Church, when my old car went Ka-Boom. Smoke filled the car, and I pulled to the side of the road. I realized that a water hose had busted. I started walking to a house that was about 200 yards away. Suddenly, I heard a vehicle coming off the hill from where I had just come. I looked and it had one head light. I thought; it must be a motorcycle. The sound that it made seemed to be like that of a road bike. The vehicle pulled in behind my smoking car. I rushed back to the car. There sat two guys in a Volkswagen. The driver said, "Hey thar buddy, (hic) looks like you (hic) need a ride." My two new friends had been in the beer pretty heavy. The guy on the passenger's side was completely passed out. I asked them if they could give me a ride back to my house, so I could get another vehicle. The driver got out and said, "(hic) Be glad to but you will have to keep your feet up in the (hic) back seat because my (hic) back floor board is rusted out." I got in, put my feet in the seat, and we were off. We had not made it to the bottom of the hill, when I suddenly smelled smoke. "Hey, buddy pull this thing over, it's on fire." I yelled. The driver said, "You are shortened me out." I said, "What?" He said again, "You are shortened me out." By this time it was getting hard to breath. The driver pulled to the side of the road, smoke was coming from under the seat I was seating on. I got out of the car, and quickly pulled the back seat out. There was fire coming out. The old boy said, "See thar I told ye. Ye was a shortened me out." My weight in the back seat had caused the battery to hit the metal in the seat. I said, "Get me something to pour on this seat so we can put this fire out." He said, "Alls (hic) I got is this here beer." He started handing me beer. I was popping the top on his beer; pouring it over the seat. The passenger has yet to wake up. Cars were coming by. All I could think was the headlines in the Dahlonega Nugget would read---SCHOOL SUPERINTENDENT ARRESTED WHILE TRYING TO POUR BEER ON BURNING CAR. I got the fire put out, loaded back up and we were off again. This time right in front of Cavender Creek Baptist Church; the car started to sputter. The driver turned and said, "(hic) this is plum embarsing. My darn old (hic) car is out of gas." I knew then that sometimes it is just better to stay in bed, than to be rescued by drunks in a Volkswagen.

MAGIC GIFT

My Mom and Dad always, and I mean always, showered us with presents every Christmas. After my cousins and friends had opened their presents they would all flock to the see what the Adams family was getting for Christmas. I had been sick and running a high fever. A five year old gets crazy things in his head. For some strange reason all I wanted was a magnet to play with. It was two days before Christmas and no one could find a magnet for my Christmas present. I remember crying and telling Mom and Dad how bad I wanted the magnet. They kept giving me medicine, but it didn't seem to be working. My fever was getting higher. I remember going to see what Santa had brought me on that Christmas morning. My Dad stuck his hand out and said, "Merry Christmas son, look what I got for you." I later found out that Dad had taken an old radio apart to get me that magnet. To this day I don't know if it was the medicine or the magnet my dad gave me that made me well. Merry Christmas Dad.

CHRISTMAS FIREWORKS

Bringing in a new year has always been a lot of fun for the Adams family. Sometimes we have had some awesome parties, at other times we have just stayed home and slept right through it. A new year has often been brought in with lots of fireworks. We would stay up late and at the stroke of 12 fireworks would be lit and Ka_Boom. You could hear those fire works for several hundred yard. But if one of my friends let one of those things go off in there hand: why you could hear them scream for miles. Perhaps the biggest Ka-Boom we ever had was when my grandpa Linton Adams decided that he was going to set some dynamite of in the big oak tree behind his house. Now papa may have been a little yankee godlin from that fire water he had been drinking, I kind of think he was. He climbed up on a latter, grabbed a limb and up that tree he went. He said he wanted to hear a big boom. There were two 8 inch sticks of dynamite in that tree. Well, papa heard a boom, a real big boom. In fact that boom knocked every window out of grannies house, and some of the neighbors. It was the last time by papa Linton got to do fireworks for the Adams family. But you know, it was also the last time granny got new windows for her house. Happy New Year to all.

STINKY FINGERS

Growing up in rural north Georgia was FUN. We had the entire area to ourselves. Most people thought we were a bunch of uneducated, backward thinking, country rednecks, and they were pretty much right. I heard a lot of the adults say things like, "we need more things for the young people to do", or "we will never have good roads, hospitals or schools until we get some industry in here." Pretty much the same thing that they say now. But what those folks didn't know was we were pretty content living the life that we had. Why, I remember once my cousin Clifford and Brother Bruce and I were going fishing. We had to dig our own worms, not go to some sporting goods store and buy them. We knew that the best place to find some worms was close to the cow manure. We could just about fill a prince albert tobacco can full of red wigglers in about 30 minutes, if we had a good shovel and madic. We learned a lot along the way. I learned that if Clifford hit my finger with the shovel just as I was picking up a worm, that the smell of cow manure on my finger would not keep me from thrusting it into my mouth. Things like that are hard to forget. But I think it was a lesson worth learning, don't you?

LIZARD IN MY BRITCHES

I remember helping a man cut timber for my Dad. He suddenly grabbed his overalls down about his thigh and yelled "a damn lizard is in my pants, reach in my pocket get my knife and cut my pants so I can get that ------ out of my britches." I did what he ask, and when I cut his britches his twist chewing tobacco dropped out of the hole I had just cut. I laughed and told him now he had two holes in his pants. The one the tobacco fell through, and the one I cut. Sometimes trying to help someone just makes things worse. Don't you think?

CANADA HERE I COME

There were several of my friends and me sitting around in the back of the service station. My Dad had leased Twin Tanks service station in Helen, Georgia, and he told me I was going to run it. There was usually a crowd that gathered in the late evening, and we would just listen to each other tell tales. There was an old fellow that came in occasionally and he always had an interesting story to share. You could tell from his speech that he was diffidently from the south. I sound like a Yankee compared to this guy. Someone in the crowd had found out that this old boy had been locked up over in Union County. The fellow that knew about the ordeal asked the man how he liked being in jail in Blairsville. That question led to the following. The fellow says, "Well hit twerte to awfully bad. Theys fed me good and were pretty dag gone good to me. Theys just had me fer being drunk in public. I told that thar sheff that I wooden't a been in public if my buddy haden't rund off and left me when I got out of the car to pee." There were several laughs and then he continued. He says but the damdist time I ever got locked up was when some of my friends and me wus up in Michegin. We's had decided to go across the border over in to Cannedie. I had bought an old 47 Plymerth and hit did't have a sign of brakes on that dag gone thang. You had to pump the day lights out of that thing to get er stopped. They wus one of them mounted men a lookin after the border into Cannedie, and they wus a long hill down to where the bridge wus that he were a guarding. My buddies and me were drunk, but we thought we could git that ole Plymerth stopped down at the bridge were that Mountie man wus. We came off of that thar hill and I could tell they weren't no way we were gonna git that blame car stopped. That Mountie man commence to a waving his arms and a hollerin HALT, HALT, IN THE NAME OF THE LAW HALT. Well I knewed we were in fer it. He drawned his gun and says stop er I'll shoot. All I could do wus stick my head out the winder and holler don't far a shot. We's pumping as damn hard as we can pump and she ain't er a gonna stop. Don't shoot we'll be backin er up as soon as we git er stopped. That Mountie man didn't far a shot, but when we backed up he locked er asses up for public drunkness. If we could of got er stopped, I don't think they would have locked us up in Cannedie. I had never been to Cannedie before and don't think I'll ever go back; unless, I've got a car that's got some good brakes on er. One of the boys listening to this story says, "How did ya'll get out of jail in Canada." The man, said, "Theys jus got tared of us, I reckon."

GUILTY AS CHARGED

Big Bud Duff was a very interesting character to say the least. There were many humorous tales told on Bud Duff. But the funniest thing I can ever remember about Bud Duff was in the fall of 1971. I had been teaching at Lumpkin County High School for a short period of time, when I learned that court week would take place in a few weeks. I made the necessary arrangements to take my US history class to see our court system in action. Judge A. R. Kenyon was the sitting Judge, and was a very well respected Judge. I really should have made an effort to find out what type case or cases would be tried. But being a beginning teacher, I simply didn't think of it. Plus, it probably wouldn't have mattered anyway. When we arrived at the courthouse court was already in session. My students entered the courtroom in a quiet and orderly fashion. It didn't take long for me to realize that the case involved Big Bud Duff being tried for bootlegging illegal beer and whiskey. It went something like this........ Mr. Duff are you guilty of selling illegal beer and whiskey? Bud asked, "No Sir." Well then Mr. Duff do you have a lawyer? Judge Kenyon asked. "No Sir" stated Bud Duff. Judge Kenyon then asked, "Well then can you afford a lawyer? Bud Replied, "No Sir, but if they had of left me a long a while, I would have a had er." The courtroom erupted in laughter. Judge Kenyon quickly restored order in the courtroom. He resumed his briefing to Bud Duff, "In that case," Judge Kenyon said. "Mr. Duff; the court will have to appoint you and attorney. Do you have one in mind Sir?" Bud said "Naw I ain't got nary a one in mind." Judge Kenyon then said in a very manner of fact way, "Well Mr. Duff since you don't have an attorney and can't afford one, the court will appoint you Lawyer Jim Wood of Dahlonega as your defense attorney. Evidently, Bud Duff didn't have much confidence in Mr. Wood as his defense attorney. Bud Duff looked at the Judge and said, "Ah Hell Judge, just change that to guilty, maybe the rope will break." This time Judge A. R. Kenyon put his head on the bench and laughed until he could say, "Ok, Ladies and gentlemen let's just get it out of our system." My students thought going to court was a lot more interesting than being in a classroom. I think they were right.

POURING CONCRETE

Jimmy Vandiver owned a concrete company. Jimmy poured a lot of concrete in the surrounding area and many people still tale stories of Jimmy's doing are saying things that were entertaining to say the least. I once heard Jimmy tell a fellow that a certain concrete company couldn't sell concrete for $19 a yard, which the concrete company was doing at the time. The man asked Jimmy, "Well how do they do it, because I just bought several yards of concrete from them." Jimmy just looked at the man and said, "Well, hell, I guess they just sell so much of it." Jimmy had been hired to pour some concrete at Camp Barny in White County. This camp is owned by the Atlanta Jewish community and they have a beautiful facility. It has been in White County for many years. Jimmy was finishing up his pour and had some concrete left over. One of the supervisors of the camp had told Jimmy if he had any concrete left he could put it on the dam of one of the lakes they have. Jimmy pulled his truck up to the dam and looked it over. He noticed a wet spot and decided that is where the concrete should go. He got his truck positioned and had that snout going back and forth slushing the concrete on the dam. One of the proprietors of the camp saw what Jimmy was doing. He rushed down to where Jimmy was pouring the concrete. Jimmy was standing there with one hand guiding the snout and the other holding his pipe. The gentleman says in a distraught manner, "Mr. Vandiver, Mr. Vandiver, I know that you know what you are doing, but sir, doing but don't you think that looks bad." Jimmy Vandiver took his pipe out of his mouth and looked at the gentleman and replied, "Well fellow I will tell you this, it's about like sewing a cows ass up with a log chain. It looks rougher ern hell, but I believe it will hold." That was the end of the conversation.

PECKED ON THE BUTT

In the early 50's there was a dance hall right up on a hill in Helen. When I was in high school, we lived on White Street and the old dance hall building was still partially standing. We would go down and play around the dance hall but we had to be careful when we were there because lots of the old boards had rusty nails in them, and Mom was afraid we would step on one of those nails and get lockjaw. I never did know exactly what lockjaw was, but I knew that I didn't want to get it. Mom also would tell us to be careful and watch for snakes. When I got a little older, I was talking to Benny Caudell about the old dance hall and how we would play and had to watch for nails and snakes. Benny started to chuckle as I was talking and said, "Let me tell you a story about the old dance hall, Bobby." He said, "We used to have some great times up at the dance hall. Just about all of the folks in the upper end of the county would come up on Saturday night and come to the square dance." Benny Continued, "A lot of us younger men would get about half lit, and I would call the square dances. We always had a great time. We had taken a break, probably to go out and get us a drink. Old Smith Crumbly came up to me and says, Benny I have got to go take a crap and I don't know exactly where I should go. I told Smith just to go up this trail and get way on up the hill out of site and do his business there. I told him he needed to take him some striking paper. Well, Smith hadn't been gone but about 6 or 8 minutes when I heard this loud scream, and I heard Smith holler, 'Come here Benny I been snake bit. Hurry Benny, Hurry'. I ran up to where Smith was standing holding his britches in one hand and turning around and around trying to look at his ass. He told me a snake had bit him on the butt. I said where did it bite you? Smith said right here Benny, look and see. I looked at old Smith butt, and there were two little red places but no broken skin. I said show me where you were Smith so I can find the snake to see what kind it was. Smith pointed to a log and said he had just sat down right over there and he pointed to the log. I walked up to the log very slow like and lit a match, there under that log was an old hen. She was sitting on her eggs. That old hen had pecked Smith on the ass. It just about scared him to death, and everybody there got to see Smith's old white butt." Benny said, "I got to thinking what if it had been a poisonous snake." I told Benny I guess he would have had to just cut Smith butt and suck the blood out of it. Benny laughed and said, "Hell, Smith Crumbly would have died right there. A friend might look to see if you had been bit, but there are some things a friend won't do." Benny was right.

GOLF LESSONS

My son plays golf on the White County High School team. He is a pretty good golfer. I remember the first time I saw someone hit a golf ball with a golf club. I thought to myself, that doesn't look so hard. It looked like all you had to do was swing the club, and anyone could hit a golf ball. Well, I later found out that it is harder to do than it looks. I finally got me an old golf club and decided I was going to give one of them golf balls a wack. I placed that ball on a mound of grass, gripped that club with my best baseball grip, and tried to frail that ball. I swung with enough force if I had connected with that darn ball; it would have gone through the gap of the mountain between Yonah and Pink. It would have landed near the Stovall's place down on Blue Creek. But thankfully, I missed the ball and everyone was safe. The next time I was trying to hit a golf ball, my neighbor came out with his hoe and said, "Where is the snake I will help you kill it." I finally got to where I could hit the ball occasionally, so I decided I would try to play a little golf. I was taking a P. E. class at Truett-McConnell College, and my golf instructor was one of my old buddies, Mr. Bill White. I would later find out that Bill knew about as much about golf, as I did about brain surgery. However, at the time it didn't make any difference because no one else knew anything about golf either. My friends, Gary Black and Jerry Dorsey and I decided that we would play a round of golf at the old Skitts Mountain Golf course. After receiving a great amount of instruction from our golf coach Bill White, we were ready to show the world what skills we had achieved in the game of golf. We were doing pretty well in this new game. When I say doing pretty well, I mean we had not hurt anyone on the golf course. We were hitting across the first pond back toward the club house. I think the hole was a par 5. I had hit my first shot into the lake. My second may have gone into the lake, but I had stopped counting after the first 58 strokes on the second hole, so I am not sure if it did or not. Jerry hit a beautiful shot 250 yards into the center of the fare way. My buddy Gary Black got up to hit. There were several fellows standing on the green just below us. They had seen Jerry hit his ball, and I guess they thought; these boys must be pretty good so they were watching Gary. Gary did a few exercises and teed his ball up. Knowing all eyes were upon him, he looked across the pond; he carefully brought his driver back, and came forward with the force of Samson. All you could hear was a swoosh, swoosh, swoosh. The club had come out of Gary's grip. All you could hear was the club turning over and over flying gracefully through the air, and then a cuu-chuk. It stuck up in the middle of the pond. I mean sticking straight up. The club head was sticking out of the water. It took about 30 minutes for play to resume. The men that had been watching from the nearby green were very slow getting up off the green and slower getting tears of laughter out of their eyes. I wanted to leave the club in the middle of the pond as a monument to show the whole world what good golfers we had become, but no, Jerry swam out and got Gary's club. Coach White was going to have to do a little better coaching to get us ready for Augusta.

PRINCIPAL'S OFFICE

I treasure my friends, each and every one of them. Friends are there for us when we need them. Friends call to ask us, what have you been doing? How are you doing? Did the cat get all right? How is your family? Is Paula riding her horses? Do you need any help with that? Friends ask about us. They truly want to be a part of our lives and for that reason; we should all value our friends. Some friends we feel so comfortable with they are like a family member, or a buddy that you can be relaxed with any time you're around them. One of my friends has been like that for me a long time. Barbara Armstrong was a student at Lumpkin County High School when I first started teaching. Barbara was a tall blonde with long legs and on occasion, would wear a short skirt and when she walked down the halls of that school, it was---well let's just say you noticed her. Over the years, Barbara and I have continued being friends and we have shared many wonderful laughs together. Barbara is like me in many ways; she can see humor a lot of times, where others don't. Being able to share stories about one another or with one another is always a testament to friendship. I would come in to school, and sometimes I couldn't wait to tell Barbara a joke I had heard. Many times those jokes where not exactly the kind you would want to tell the Sunday school class. As my granny used to say; them jokes might be a little on the nasty side. Barbara could tell me some that would make a sailor blush. Our high school Principal was Mr. Ralph McCrary. Ralph and I go a long way back. He was my coach and teacher at White County High School. Barbara was Ralph's secretary. Ralph had been the principal at the elementary school, and when he became the principal of the high school, he brought Barbara with him. This gave Barbara and me a lot of opportunities to share our jokes together. Barbara and I were always very careful to make sure that Ralph didn't hear our jokes. We feared he might not have as high opinion of us if he knew we were sharing a few naughty jokes. On one occasion, Barbara was standing just inside of Mr. McCrary's office and I said, "Barbara I got a good joke for you." We both looked to see if Mr. McCrary was around anywhere. Not seeing him, we pulled the door to his office shut. I don't remember the joke but I know it was a hoot. We both were laughing, when all of a sudden we heard the commode flush. Mr. McCrary was in the bathroom in his office. We quickly opened the door, but neither one of us could stop laughing. We thought we had shut the principal out of his office, but in reality, we had shut us up in the office with him. He only smiled when he came out of his bathroom. I think he liked the joke as good as we did. At least we didn't get fired.

COUSIN DALE

When I first learned that my cousin Dale Allen had a disease called Hodgkin's disease, I didn't know anything about it. I certainly didn't think that it could take my cousin from me. Dale was one of the strongest guys I knew. I had seen him lift motors, transmissions, the front end of a tractors, so to me; Dale was invincible. The first time I knew the disease was taking its toll on Dale, we were coming out of Mount Yonah Baptist Church and Dale whispered to me, "Bob, help me down the steps, and don't let anyone know I am leaning on you." He smiled and placed his hand on my right shoulder and together we eased down the steps. He got to his car and said he was going to need my help occasionally. I told him to call anytime he needed me. From that time until Dale passed away, I witnessed the horrible effects of how cancer could destroy a person. But I also witnessed how the human spirit can be inspired to do things that sometimes seem almost impossible. Once, my brother Billy, who was just a small boy, was cutting Dales grass. Two guys came down the road and threw a beer bottle at Billy. Billy didn't even see it, but Dale did. At this time in his life, he was confined to a wheel chair. Dale saw the bottle go by, narrowly missing Billy's head. Dale wheeled himself to his car, got in the car, and using his cane to mash the gas and breaks, he caught the guys in Cleveland and held them there until the law could come and get them. Having someone dying of cancer is not without an episode of humor. Dale was lying in his hospital bed with an oxygen mask on his face. The disease had just about taken everything it could from Dale. The once strong and powerful young man was now barely holding on to what life he had left. Dale's fever had been out of site. It would be so high; he would be delirious at times. So the nurses would have to constantly take his temp. The nurses' shift had end at midnight; new nurses would be working with Dale. I was staying with Dale that night. Dale was laboring to breathe. The new nurse came in and got a thermometer and was walking toward Dale, suddenly Dale's eyes were big and he had a frightened look on his face. He started to shake his head back and force. The nurse stopped and removed his oxygen mask to place the thermometer in his mouth. Dale became more frantic. He was only able to mumble, "No, no, no." With all of his energy he smiled and looked at me and said in an almost whisper, "I may be dying, but they are not going to put that rectal thermometer in my mouth." He was right. It was the wrong thermometer. That was the last time Dale and I laughed together. He passed away three days later. I can think back on that day and cry, or I can smile. Dale would want us to smile. So I smile with a tear in my eye.

BOYS AND BULLFROGS

It was early spring but the weather had been very warm so the bull frogs were already croaking and the spring flowers were in full bloom. The first full moon had arrived and the bream were on bed. We had dug up some red worms and we knew that with just a little luck we would be catching some of those bream. Uncle Ollie Turner had built a lake over on some of the property he owned and many of the local folks spent many enjoyable hours casting their baits out into the water. If we hadn't caught any of the pan fish by dark, we would then start fishing for catfish. As the summer air got warmer we would get out lights and start to shine the banks of Uncle Ollie's lake trying to find the eyes of the big bull frogs. Frog gigging was a lot of fun. Plus, mom could fry those frog legs and make biscuits and gravy and our mouths would water just thinking about it. I don't remember the first time I went frog gigging but I do know that it was something that I always looked forward to doing. I called my cousin Larry one evening and ask if he would like to go with us up to the frog ponds just beyond his house to see if we could get some frogs. We had already gigged Uncle Ollies' Lake. Larry told me just to stop by his house and pick him up. Jimmy Vandiver had a rock crusher on the Hardman property and he had created some fine small ponds. Larry and I had scouted the ponds. That meant we had asked Jimmy if he had heard any frogs. Jimmy had told us they were plenty of frogs, not just frogs but from the sound they were some giant bull frogs. We had a small flat bottom aluminum boat, a six volt light, and a good frog gig attached to the end of a stiff bamboo pole; everything you need to gig frogs. After picking up Larry, it didn't take long for us to have the boat in the water. We were beyond disbelief. All we could here was frogs croaking; saying to us, "Come and get us boys." Within 10 minutes we had three good size frogs. But the loudest croaks were coming from a small cavity looking place back in the farthest point of the cove. There were lots of overhanging branches; suddenly there he was the granddaddy of all bull frogs. His eyes looked 6 inches apart. The white of his throat looked like a roll of toilet paper floating in the water. The three young boys were spell bound by his size. Larry said, "Look at that monster. Be quiet boys we have to get that giant frog." Bruce never led the light leave his eyes. He said in a whisper, "Lift your paddles slowly so the dripping water will not spook him." We were getting closer and closer to our frog of a life time, when all at once the three frog men had to go under some low hanging bushes. A snake about the size of one of our oars fell into the boat. At that time it was every man for himself. Bruce went out to the right, Larry exited to the left and I chose to walk on the water behind the boat. My biblical endeavor only lasted for about two steps and then gravity took hold. Bruce was already at the bank when my head came out of the water. I was splashing around like a whale in a bath tub. Larry yelled, "You can put your feet down Bobby. It's not but about 2 feet deep." After we all got to the bank, we decided that maybe that frog wasn't as big as we thought it was. Plus it would have been hard to gig a frog without a gig, a light or a boat, especially if the boat had a snake the size of a log in it.

TALKING TO MYSELF

Growing up in the Adams house hold was not very difficult. I guess it wasn't, but sense it is the only place I ever had to grow up in; I guess--- well you know what I mean. Mom was at home and usually cleaning or fixing food. In the spring and summer Mom would be canning vegetables. When the strawberries were ripe she would make the best preserves and jam you ever tasted. Daddy was usually working. He would leave the house, and pick his sawmill crew up and try to get his mill running every morning by 8. They would work until 12 take 30 minutes for lunch and crank the mill back up at 12:30. They then would work until 4:30. Many days the only break the worker got was the lunch break. If the saw got dull the sawyer would stop the mill to file the saw, then right back to work. The log turner would roll the log on to the carriage and then he would dog the log. The sawyer would also dog the log. A good log turner would always make sure if the log had a bow in it, to turn the bow either in or out. The sawyer would then cut a slab off of the log. He wanted the bare side of the log to be at least 8 feet long. There was no market for lumber shorter than 8 feet. The sawyer would pull the log forward until he would cut either a two inch piece or a one inch piece. The rough side board would then fall on a roller carriage and taken by a man running the edger. The edger operator would determine the width of the board. The lumber would exit the edger usually with to strips cut off of the sides of the board. The lumber was stacked and the strips and slaps were sent to a fire pit. The men carrying the strips and slaps and stacking the lumber were called the off-bearers. On one occasion Smith Crumbly was carrying the strips and slaps to the fire pit. It was extremely hot. The sparks from the fire would spew as they hit the sweat on Smith's bare chest. The lumber was coming out of the mill and Dad was watching as the mill was running. He noticed that Smith was mumbling as he worked. Smith would walk to the edge of the fire pit drop his heavy load of strips and slaps and mumble all the way back to get yet another load. This had gone on for a long time. Finally, the mill had to be shut down so the saw could be sharpened. Before Smith could set down, Dad walked up and said, "Smith, why are mumbling when you work?" Old Smith sat down on the stack of lumber and looked at daddy and said, "Well, Herbert, I got to talk with somebody that's got some damn sense." I'll bet that is why I talk to myself some times.

KIDS AND DRUGS

I don't remember the exact time or place that someone told me about some kind of pungent smelling tobacco from Mexico. I think I was a student at the University of Georgia. I started hearing things on TV about marijuana. I had never seen or heard of it up until then, so I never gave it much thought. When I was hired as a history teacher and coach at Lumpkin County High School, I was asked to take a drug awareness class that was being offered by WSB-TV in Atlanta. Mr. Garner, the high school principal, ask me to take the class, and then I might be able to help educate other teachers about the increase of drug usage in schools, and how Lumpkin County might take some preventive steps to keep young students off of drugs. I made plans to take the class and start getting myself educated on this new tobacco called marijuana. I traveled to Atlanta and took the drug awareness class. It was very informative and I got a lot of good information from the speakers. When I returned to school, I couldn't wait to start teaching my students about the evils of drugs. It didn't take me long to discover that the students already knew a lot more about drugs than I did. I had come along when alcohol was the worst thing you had to worry about. So to say I was not up to par on drugs in our culture was an understatement. Not only did the students help educate me about drugs and the harmful effects on drugs, but they really made me realize that most of the students, not all, but most, didn't feel drawn to drug usage the way I had thought they might. I hear and read that some people think that our schools are just packed with drug users. Don't get me wrong, I know that we have students that use drugs, but I don't think it is a great number. If any are using drugs, that is too many, but the vast majority of students in the schools that I am familiar with are not using drugs. I actually think that today the number of students doing drugs is less than it was say 10 years ago. Since taking that class back in the early 70's, not only is there marijuana, but countless other drugs in our society that are very harmful. Some are so addictive that just to do them one time can mean a person can be hooked on them. That leads us to this question. Why do kids use drugs? I mean if you could point to one person and say; they use drugs and look how it has helped them. You can't. I can't. There is no easy answer. I decided to write this just to make people aware that we have students that might use drugs, but the majority of our kids are good decent kids. I hear of people that get on drugs that are in their 30's 40's and 50's. Last week we saw kids turning to religion, to help them cope with life. That issue was debated for several days. Perhaps some kids turn to drugs to cope with life. I think it is the role of parents and responsible citizens to show people that drugs are not a way to cope with daily difficulties. Drugs can very easily be the problem and not the solution. Drugs and drug usage in the schools are old issues. Just because they are old doesn't mean we should forget them.

INSURANCE SHORT COMINGS

Relay for Life comes to White County once a year. It is a great event and probably more people show up for this single event than anything held in White County. It is a time to turn in money raised to fight cancer and to recognize those that have been affected by this terrible disease. When we have the survivors walk, you can see many tears in the crowd as those that have so bravely fought this disease walk around the track at White county High School. We also get a chance to look back and realize that many that walked last year are not with us this year. Many of those that walk this year will unfortunately not be with us next year. We continue to do this in hopes that someday a cure will be found and this disease will not take the lives of so many good people. I try to always look on the bright side of things. I can find humor in anything. While having dinner one day, my Brother Billy, Brother Bradley, and my Nephew Austin were discussing how great the Relay for life program was. My Brother Billy and his Wife Sadie are both cancer survivors. We were talking about the cost associated with the treatment of cancer. The costs are usually astronomical, running into the hundreds of thousand dollars. Billy said, "You know I did have a cancer policy that paid several thousand dollars without question. The money came straight to us not to the doctor or hospital." I informed Billy that was usually not the case. Billy said, "Oh yea, there's one other thing it had in the policy. It said if you lost certain body parts it would pay a set price." Billy had prostate cancer, so I ask if it paid for the prostate gland. Billy said, "No but if a man had to have his penis removed it would pay $400.00. Austin said, "Four hundred dollars is that all? You would think that THAT body part would be worth more than that." Billy looked at Austin and said, "Austin, a woman obviously wrote that part of the policy." I am going home and review my policy. All you men had better do the same. And you women, stop laughing.

SHORT SKIRT AND PRAYERS

My friends Phil Price, Bill Christian and I were doing some work for one of my long time buddies, Roy Jr. Ash. Roy and his wife Jonnie Sue had hired us to paint their house. We had gotten the house painted and Roy wanted us to clean the stain off of his shingles. The oak trees had turned the white shingles almost black. Roy's wife, Jonnie Sue, is a deeply religious woman that I love dearly. She and I have shared lots of laughs over the years. Jonnie would tell me each day that she prayed for me on a regular basis. I would tell her that I appreciated her prayers, and I thought that I should get her a pair of knee pads. Just so her knees wouldn't get sore. Roy and Jonnie Sue came out of their house and informed us that they were going to go to the grocery store and would return shortly. We informed them that since they were going to be gone for a little while we would take a break and run up to a local gas station and get us a cold drink since it was 95+ degrees on that white roof. We returned from our trip and climbed back up on the roof of the Ash's house. About the time we got up there, Roy and Jonnie Sue drove up. As they were getting out of the car, I yelled and told Jonnie Sue that I thought those prayers were really working. She said, "Thank the good Lord. Why do you think that Bobby?" I told Jonnie Sue that while Phil, Bill and I were getting us a drink at the station, a beautiful young lady got out of a car and she was wearing an extremely short mini-skirt, and I didn't think that I lusted after her near as much as I should have. Jonnie laughed and looked up at me and said, "Bobby Adams, I am going right in hear and pray for you right now." I laughed and told her to go right ahead and get those painters knee pads out of the truck, just in case she felt she needed to spend a little bit more time on her knees. I told her I thought maybe she ought to do that because we were thinking we may have to go back to the store and if that pretty girl was still there; I was sure I was going to need those extra prayers, and while she was at it; she probably should say some prayers for Bill and Phil because their eyes looked like they were glued on to that mini-skirt. Good friends always pray for each other, as well as laugh with one another. I am glad I have good friends.

Grandmother Sims (Maude); L-R: Clifford Cox, Doris Cox, Bruce Adams, Bobby Adams

BONNIE SHEWBERT

When winter time came and the leaves had all been blown from the big oak trees in our yard, my brother Bruce and I would start to get our Rabbit boxes ready to place around the neighborhood. We had wonderful neighbors. Pearl Westmoreland and her brother Comer Westmoreland lived across the road from us. Bill Turner and his wife, Jeannette lived just below us and the rest of the folks were Aunts and Uncles. All of these folks would let the Adams boys place our rabbit boxes on their property. It was lots of fun to get up early at the crack of dawn and get ready for school, and then go check to see if any of the lids were down on our boxes. It wasn't unusual to catch one or two rabbits in the traps each night. Sometime we would get a surprise and find one box with two rabbits in it. We would rush home and tell mom and dad about our nightly catches. One of our neighbors was Mr. Vinson Shewbert. Mr. Shewbert and his wife Bonnie lived just below us on Asbestos Road. Mr. Shewbert gave me my first haircut with a pair of hand clippers that pulled more hair out than they cut. Mr. Shewbert passed away several years ago. Bonnie was a wonderful home maker. I went to the funeral home the other evening to say good bye to Mrs. Shewbert. She had a long and wonderful life. She had lost her site in her later years, but she could always recognize my voice. Bonnie, as all of her friends and family called her, was laid to rest recently after 103 years on this earth. Mr. and Mrs. Shewbert knew that the Adams boys set rabbit boxes during the winter. Besides catching rabbits, it also wasn't too uncommon to catch a big old possum. Mr. Shewbert would pay us 50 cents for each possum that we caught. Fifty cents was a quarter a piece. A quarter would get you in to the Princess Theater. When we found a possum in our box, we were tickled to death. Bruce or I would run home get a feed sack and run back to where the box was. We would then shake the possum into the sack and put it in a shed behind our house. As soon as we were home from school, we would carry that possum to the Shewberts. This would go on all winter. I remember going to the Shewbert's home one evening to deliver a possum and collect my loot. I knocked on the door and instead of Mr. Shewbert coming to the door; Mrs. Shewbert came to the door. I told her I had a possum for Mr. Shewbert. She told me to stay right there and she would get me some money. Mrs. Shewbert returned shortly and place fifty cents in my hand. Bonnie said, "He really likes to eat these things" I said, "Really?" She just smiled and said, "Yes, he likes to eat them a whole lot better than I like to cook them." I can only say that Bonnie Shewbert must have been one heck of a cook, because we caught several possums that winter. There's not many Bonnie Shewberts left in the world. She will be missed.

BRAVERY IN MY EYES

In 1963 we lived in a little white house on the Chattahoochee River near Roberts Town. My dad was in the process of building a chicken farm on some property that he had bought. Until the house was built we would have to live in the house on the river. It was a great place to live. Trout fishing was wonderful. Every day my brothers and I would be fishing or planning on going fishing. Helen, Georgia had not made the transition to a tourist town at that time. My dad had sold some property to Mr. George Ed Avery of Dahlonega. Mr. Avery had built a cabin on the river and his family would come over and stay in the cabin. Spring had brought lots of rain that year. The rains started coming down pretty hard one day and being right on the river you could tell that the water was beginning to rise. I walked back behind the house we were living in and I looked over at the Avery's cabin. There was a black 1956 ford parked at the cabin. I really didn't think much about the folks in the cabin at that time. But within a few hours it would be one of the most frightening things I ever had the privilege to watch. The rain never let up. I finally went inside and told my mom that we needed to let the people know that the water was up to the tires on the ford car. Momma assured me that they would get out if the water got to high.   More rain fell, and the Chattahoochee rose higher. After another hour of hard rain, I looked again at the car. By this time water was over the door handles of the car. I told Mom and she said we needed to find out who was in the cabin because there was no way the car would be able to get them out. It didn't take long to assemble a group of folks to see if they could help. The family that was in the cabin had been sleeping. The Chattahoochee was knocking on the bottom of the cabin. Mr. Camy Cantrell, his wife Pat, and their three children were trapped in the Cabin. The river was rolling. It would probably reach the highest level it had ever reached. The only thing to do was to try and get a boat over to rescue the Cantrell family. The first boat brought and put in the river wouldn't crank. Someone said Dwayne Taylor had a boat. Some of the men were gone for just a short time and returned with Dwayne and his boat. Dwayne and- I think it was Royce Allison- drove the boat over to the house and got the Cantrell family out of the house and brought them through the rolling water to the bank were several of us were standing. Just as the boat got to the bank where we were waiting, the current swept the rear of the boat under water. Dwayne literally threw the new born baby to the bank, and I caught her in my arms. I would find out 17 years later that the young girl I caught in my arms was one of my students at Lumpkin County High School, Camille Cantrell. I tell this story for one reason. Dwayne Taylor passed away recently. I have thought about that day many times. The bravery and heroism that was displayed that day by Dwayne Taylor and the other men that aided in that rescue should not be forgotten. In my eyes Dwayne Taylor was a real hero. I think he still is.

Papa Sims Store, Helen Georgia; John Walter Sims

SMITH THE COWBOY

I was thinking back on the work that I have done during my life and it seems I have done a lot of different things. Although I retired from an education career, I have had lots of different work experiences. One of the most enjoyable things I did as I was growing up, was to work for a man named Floyd Caudell. Floyd had lost the use of his legs in an automobile accident. He was confined to a wheel chair, but he was never still. He was one of those men that leave a lasting impression on you. Floyd

177

had a store that was located near Unicoi State Park. In fact the state bought Floyds' old store building and they use it as an office complex. Floyd not only ran a little store there, but he also had horses and he would rent the horses out for people to ride. My job was to take people around the trails and kind of serve as a trail boss. I had to saddle the horses in the morning and unsaddle them in the evening. Floyd paid me six dollars a day to work for him. I loved riding the horses and looking after them. I had been riding horses since I was about 6 years old so I was like an old pro around the horses. One of the men that like to hang out there with Floyd and me was Smith Crumley. I have told many stories on Smith and I will share this one as well. Floyd had purchased a 5 gaited spotted saddle bred gilding from the fellow that drove the Meritta bread truck. The horses name was Chief. I am surprised that I remember his name. Chief was a very spirited horse and Floyd had instructed me to not let anyone ride Chief but me. Chief had been trained to rare up when you raise your left arm. He also was trained to bow when you pulled down on the reins. Often I would make Chief do his tricks; after we had made our round on the trail. The people that paid to ride the horses always seem to enjoy seeing Chief do his tricks. Smith had watched me ride Chief several times. Floyd and I both could tell that Smith wanted to ride Chief so that he could impress some of the guest with his riding skills; skills that he really was lacking in. Floyd repeatedly told me to watch out for Smith and not let him get on Chief. He was afraid that Smith might get hurt. Smith constantly wanted me to let him ride Chief. I would always tell him no; Floyd only wanted me to ride the lead trail horse. One of my duties was to take the saddles off the horses if it started to rain, and then take the horses to their corral which was about a hundred yards above where the horses were tied. One day it had started to shower and I was getting the saddles off and leading horses to the corral. As I was returning to get the last two horses, I saw Smith place his foot in the stirrup of the saddle on Chief. Smith slung his right leg over the saddle and then raised his left arm. Chief immediately rose on his back feet. Smith dug his heels into the horses' flanks trying to hang on. This put old Chief in to high gear. When Smith and Chief came by me, I don't know whose eyes were the biggest- Smiths, the horse or mine. All I could hear was "Whao, whao, damn you whao." The run-away horse jumped the fence in to the corral and immediately stopped, sending Smith over the horses head and into the horse manure face first. Just as I got there Smith was spitting and cursing. When he handed me the reins, he pulled down on them as he was trying to get up. Chief bowed. Smith said, "Somebody gonna git kilt on that damn horse." Smith never wanted to ride Chief again.

TOM'S TURKEY

Turkey hunting is something that just about all my family has been involved in in some way or another. My Grandfather Sims would hold our attention when we were just young boys telling stories how he used to hear turkey gobbling on the Hamby Mountain which was located on the other side of the Chattahoochee River from his home in Helen, Georgia. My nephew operated a sporting goods store and manufactured his turkey calls for years. The Adams boys grew up turkey hunting. I lived for several years in the Northern part of Lumpkin County. My first home was located on top of a small mountain above Whitner's Lake. It was a beautiful place to live. I loved living in my little Chalet. I could get home in the evening and go fishing and during the winter; I could be hunting in five minutes.

Turkey season had been going for about three or four weeks and it had been a tough season. I had got one good gobbler, but my tag was not yet filled. I came in one Friday evening after a short baseball practice. I was thinking while driving home about going to see if I could hear a turkey. I got out of my truck and was going into my house, when all of a sudden, I heard a turkey gobble. The gobble was coming from my neighbor Tom McDonald's direction. I listened to make sure I was hearing a turkey gobbling. It gobbled again. I rushed into my house and quickly put on my camo, grabbed my shotgun and out the door I ran. I ran down the hill and crossed the little paved road at the bottom of the hill. I ran out into the field that was just below Tom McDonald's house. I stopped and the turkey gobbled again. This time it sound like it was behind Tom's house. I got to the edge of the field that ran behind Tom's house and looked but I couldn't see anything. There was another fence right behind Tom's place but I couldn't see into the field because of the honey suckle that had grown over the fence. I decided to crawl on my hands and knees to get closer so I could look over that last fence. I had gone about 50 or 60 yard and it suddenly dawned on me. What if that turkey was a tame turkey? But I came by the McDonald's house every day. Tom had not said anything about getting a turkey. I had talked to Tom on Monday and this was Friday. Surely I would have found out if Tom had gotten a yard turkey. As I inched closer to the fence the gobbler was giving it his all. He was gobbling just about every breath. I thought to myself, ok this is what I am going to do. I will get to the fence raise up real quick with my shotgun ready. If the turkey flies, it is wild and it will be fair game. If not it will just stand there and no one will know that I have ran 500 yards and crawled another 100 to try and kill a darned tame turkey. It was a good plan. I got to the fence. I placed my gun in the ready position and stood up immediately looked for my prey, and there he was. He looked at me. I looked at him. He gobbled and started walking toward me. I lowered my gun and there on the other side of the fence was Tom McDonald smoking a cigarette. He had been watching me the whole time. I rose up and said, "Tom, when did you get the turkey?" "Yesterday," he replied, trying to hide the laugh. I said, "Tom, what if I had shot that turkey?" Tom laughed and said, "We would have ate it and then I guess you would have bought me another one, wouldn't ya?" Yes, Tom I would have. I bet Tom McDonald laid in bed at night and laughed thinking about his neighbor trying to slip up on his tame turkey. I know I sure have. If you can't laugh at yourself, who can you laugh at?

CATCHING CHICKENS

When I purchased my first home, I was making $5600.00 a year teaching. My house payment was $131.00 a month. My take home pay was $356.00. At the end of the month after I paid my light bill, phone bill and all my other bills, I had absolutely nothing left. I quickly learned that I needed to earn some extra money. I was coaching football, basketball and baseball. There was no time for me to work on another job site, so I decided that I would let some guys at North Georgia College board with me. I got three guys to live there with me and they paid me $50.00 a month rent. It was a little crowded and trying to share a small bathroom proved to be a challenge, but we survived. One of the guys that rented a room was a fellow whose father was the owner of a poultry company and a feed mill in Summerville, Georgia. He came in on a Thursday afternoon and informed all of us that his dad wanted him to come home for the weekend and move some chickens. He told us that if we would help him not only would we get paid but we would go to Cleveland, Tennessee to some great night clubs. The pay didn't sound to inviting, but the thought of pretty girls and a juke joint got our attention. Now for those of you, who have never caught chickens, let me explain to you that it takes place after dark. You go into a chicken house, drive the birds into a netted off area, and bend down, and start grabbing legs. You put two to three chickens in each hand and stuff them in a chicken coop. The smell of the ammonia from the chicken manure will just about knock your head off. It is not fun. Chicken manure has a strong odor and will make your eyes water. We arrived in Summerville, Georgia about 5 PM in the evening and got all the instructions from the fellow's father that owned the chicken company. We left out all enthused and eager to go. We arrived at the chicken house which was located on top of a mountain. These chickens were laying hens, not broilers. Laying hens lay eggs. You eat broilers at Zaxby's Kentucky Fried Chicken or McDonald's, big difference. Broilers are going to the slaughter house when you catch them. Laying hens are going to be placed in another house in someone else's care. These were going to some place in Alabama to another chicken farmer. What started out as a fun trip was now going to be an all weekend of grabbing chicken legs. Not only did we work all weekend, but slept very little as well. I did find out one interesting fact. You can walk into a chicken house and look up in the dark. You will see chickens roosting on boards. A human being can see a chicken poop on the roost and you are just fast enough to close your eyes, look straight ahead, and the chicken poop will hit you right on the back of the neck. It will go down into your shirt without slowing down until it reaches your underwear, where it will stop. Your friends will laugh until a chicken does them the same way. All laughter will stop. Also chickens are not bashful;

they will poop in your hand when you are trying to grab their legs. They cluck with laughter. From that night on I have hated chickens, but I have a great appreciation for the guys that catch chickens. I don't think colonel Sanders started out that way.

MELTS IN YOUR PANTS NOT IN YOUR HAND

I have many great memories of my involvement with high school kids in Lumpkin County. Many of the young men and women are now parents and some are even grandparents. I don't know how they got so old so quick. I guess they just reached that great threshold in life called adulthood and then jumped right in to that period that we call old. I am glad that I have not entered that period as of yet. I keep putting getting old off. However during my maturing years I do have a few fun things that I remember happening in my classroom. There was a kid that kept coming into my classroom eating stuff just before the class would start. He did this every day. I always would ask him to please not bring stuff to eat in my class room. It wasn't that I wanted to let him go hungry, from the looks of him he was getting all he needed to eat at home. In fact he looked as though he could skip meals for about a week and still live while hibernating during the winter. Much like the way I look now. I remember him coming into my class and he was eating some M&M's. I told him that he would have to put his eats in his locker which was located just about twenty yards from my door. He said, "Sure Mr. Adams, I will be glad to put them in my locker." It was hot in the old Lumpkin County High School. There was no air conditioning. We had fuel oil heat in the winter, and when the kids would put a crayon down on the heater, it would smoke the entire room up. Needless to say in the summer, the rooms sometimes got extremely hot. The young man came back from his locker and sat down in class. He had on a pair of light brown pants. He was wearing a yellow tee shirt. I started my lecture and was getting my class in a motivated state. Most all of the students were participating. I noticed that the old boy that had been eating his M&Ms kept kind of squirming in his desk. It got pretty near the end of the class period and the young man raised his hand. I said, "Yes, ------------ what do you need?" He said, "Mr. Adams I need to leave the room quick." I looked at him and said, "May I ask why?" He stood up and said because this darn Chocolate is melting in my pants." When he stood up you could see that his front right pants pocket was a very dark chocolate. The kids start to giggle, and one girl said, "Gosh,--------- it looks like you have messed in your pocket." Everyone kind of laughed and the old boy just looked at the young lady and said, "M&Ms might not melt in your hands but that sure as heck will melt in your britches." He had a point. I let him leave class with a wad of M&M's melted in his britches. He never brought food to my class again.

RISING ABOVE

When my son comes in the house in the evening he and I always talk to each other and discuss what each one of us did during the day. It is something that I really look forward too. Having that conversation means a lot to me. I have always heard that your sins shall come back to haunt you. I am beginning to think that statement is true. Brynnan will come in at the end of a day and say something to the effect, "Daddy, I met one of your old friends today, and man did he tell some stories about you." My reply to Brynnan is usually, "Brynnan some of my friends mind are bad. They think the things that they did are things that I did." Or I will say, "Oh yea I remember them. We did have a lot of good times but they lied real bad back then, and I can tell they haven't quit lying yet." He told me the other day that he finds out a lot of stuff that I did when I was young. I told Brynnan this story. I was running for the Superintendent of Schools in Lumpkin County and I was campaigning pretty hard. One of my good friends who worked at the Lumpkin County Co-op was Fred Burns. Fred and several other locals that kind of hung out at the co-op were all talking when I walked in to the store. Fred looked at me and said, "Boy, you better get up in Yahoola they are telling a bunch of lies on you." I looked at Fred and said, "I can't Fred. I have got to go out to Wahoo. They're telling the truth on me. I got to stop that stuff first." I told Brynnan that some people think I make all of my stories up. Most people know I am just telling the truth. So if any of you are talking to my son and telling him something about me, he may start looking at you in a strange way. He will be trying to determine if your mind is bad, or if you are a compulsive liar. I wish I hadn't done all that stuff, denying it is harder than I thought. However, it was a lot of fun. But don't any of you worry, you will still be my friend, but my son may think you are a little nuts. That's what I am telling him.

KEEPING US SAFE

It seems there has been a great deal of concern about how private our phones, our emails or carrier pigeon's and smoke signals are now a days. Gee, I guess that means I have got to go back and apologize for all the things I have done with my telephone, my emails and by secret communication when I was just having fun. I had no idea that I was endangering our national security. Why I can remember when me and my cousins used to get Campbell soup cans, knock a hole in the bottom and tie a string in two cans and talk to each other. We should have probably been more careful about what we said. I told my cousin that I was going to be a fireman, but I got a degree in Social Studies and started teaching. I wonder if that will be held against me at some point and time. I can just hear some Sheriff saying to me, "Hey, buddy you are not what you started out to be. Pull it over I have your early Campbell soup can records." When I get to thinking about it I will have lots of things that I will need to ask forgiveness for. I remember the time I called a girl and pretended to be someone else just to see if the girl I was calling liked me as her boyfriend. She didn't. I hope she made some calls on her telephone that will get her arrested for impersonating a girlfriend. But she is happily married now, so I doubt it. Since this has all of the networks trying to decide which way they should lean on this topic, I kind of think that we may have to just decide for ourselves. As for me other than the time I called a Vice Principal at Dawson County and told him I was some news man from Channel 2 news and wanted some comments about some teacher that had exposed himself to someone in the school, or maybe the time I called the school and tried to convince them that it was snowing in Suches, and headed for Dahlonega, or just maybe the time I called the school and told them I was sick and the secretary said, "I can't hear you for the traffic in the back ground." Richard Sosebee and Phil Price had me held hostage, taking me fishing at Lake Fontana. Other than these and a few other misstatements of the phone, I have nothing to hide. I don't know about the rest America but as for me, if it has kept one SOB from being able to inflict harm on one person in my family, they can listen to anything I say. Just don't let Momma know I have said a bad word. She still believes in giving kids a whooping.

My beautiful wife, Dr. Paula-Early Adams. I'm a lucky man indeed!

LAMAZE

When I first heard that I was going to be a father, it was almost unbelievable. I found it very hard for me to think that I was going to have a child someone to call me Daddy. A man's life during the incubation stage, as I call it, is kind of like a rooster walking around the yard while the hen sets on the eggs. That sounds like a crude way to describe it, but to me that was kind of the way it was. I remember the first time I felt my daughter move. My wife, Paula was lying in bed and her bulging tummy was against my back. All at once it was like; hey, I am going to be out of here soon, and when I do I am going to pee all over you. I don't know if that is what my daughter was thinking but knowing her the way I do; it probably was. As this thing called a child grew, it was decided by the incubator that the rooster should take something call Lamaze. I had never heard of it. But I soon learned that it was what is called natural child birth. Being a rooster walking around the barn yard, you do not hear of things like that. I thought all child birth was natural. Before long I was enrolled in the Lamaze class, and learning to do the pant- blow technique. When I walked in to the Lamaze classroom there were several pregnant ladies in the classroom with a friend or relative. I noticed that I was the only rooster, Man, in the room. The instructor immediately told all the hens, ladies, to get on their backs. The she said, "You coaches will be giving the expecting mother encouragement and instructions while the baby is being born." She could have handed me a bull horn and I would have been glad to just stay outside and yell, "Yea Paula, Go Girl, push that little sucker right on out." But that was not what she meant. I have to admit after a while I got in to being the Coach. They told us we would have a monitor and we would be able to tell when a contraction would be starting and we could give our wives the necessary breathing instructions. We were told that the Coaches, please note I was no longer a rooster I had been promoted to being a coach, would stand at the head of the expecting mother until the child was born giving the breathing instructions as the birth was being carried out. When that long anticipated day came, nothing went as it was planned. They had no monitor, the air conditioning at the hospital was broken and I was so damn scared I was shaking. Since there was no monitor, I could only tell a contraction was taking place when my wife would grab me by the throat and say, "breath, tell me to breath or I am going to kill you." After saying, "you are doing fine, do your pant blow exercise" about a hundred times. A nurse that I am sure had been kicked out of the Marine Corp came in to that room and started barking out orders for Paula. She said something about the baby is crowning we need to get you to the delivery room. By this time I did not know if she was talking to Paula or me. We rushed down the hall in to the delivery room, the doctor said, "stand right here and you can see your baby's birth." All I could think was, "God, if I faint let me fall backwards not forwards; I would never be able to live falling on my wife down." Well I didn't faint and I did get to see my daughter brought into the world. Being a new father was everything it should have been. After Brooke was born, I went out into the hall of the hospital and crowed, and strutted around. That is what a proud Rooster will do.

UNCLE ROY GOT CAUGHT

Most people in North Georgia around my age- (which means all the old people) - knew someone that was always fooling with moonshine. They either drank it; they sold it, or made it. In my case all three of those circumstances occurred. Growing up around the old Adams store on Highway 75 north was quiet an experience. Many families in the 50's and 60's still led a very rural way of life. Houses were heated mostly by wood heaters in the winter and fans supplied all of the cooling the house got during the summer. Spring time brought a time to plant the gardens and enjoy leisurely hours on a pond or stream fishing. When the fall air started stirring, it was a time to start stacking up on the things that would carry the families through an unpredictable winter. Each one of the seasons meant different things for those involved in the moonshine business. You had to get all of your supplies ready, like your jars or jugs, your sugar, yeast and grains and other ingredients that were in the liquid corn. You had to make sure your mash was ready to run. Making moonshine was hard work. Since it was illegal, it was usually done in a very remote spot. The men that were involved in the whiskey business always faced the possibility of being caught and sent to prison. I remember my dad telling the story of his oldest brother, Roy taking a load of moonshine to some place in Jackson County. Uncle Roy had only gotten to about the Mossy Creek campground when the law got in a hot pursuit. Uncle Roy abandoned the car and took out on foot. The law officers gave chase. Uncle Roy hid in a brush pile, but was caught. Dad said that if Roy had not got to laughing so hard at the law man trying to catch him, he might have gotten away. It seems the officer got hung up in the brush pile and his pants ripped. The law officer said, "These are my damn new britches my wife bought me. And she is going to whip my ass." Uncle

Roy started laughing when he heard the man who thought he was talking to himself say what he did. Humor sometimes has its advantages, but this time it would have been better if it hadn't of been so funny. It is amazing the way we look back on things. I also remember thinking that drinking 7up was against the law. It seems that each time I saw men around the old store building drinking a 7up they were bending down trying to hide behind a car or sneaking around back of the building. I later figured out they were using the 7up as a chaser for the burning whiskey as it went down their throat. It always amazed me how those men would turn those jars up and guzzle that clear liquid down then make the worst face possible and say, "Man that is good whiskey." But then, I have never really understood how a television works.

JOKES

I remember some of the jokes that were told to me when I was growing up, but I don't remember who always told them. Some of the funny stuff I heard has been with me for a very long time. I know that some of the funny things will go with me to my grave. I am not as good at remembering jokes as some people. My oldest brother, Bruce, was someone who remembered jokes and love to tell them. I remember some. If you have heard them good that means you have not slipped in to dementia as far as some. There was this lady and she wanted to have a baby really bad. She and her husband had done all the things the doctor had said and still she could not get pregnant. She went to the doctor after going 10 or 15 times and each time she was told she couldn't have a baby. Well her and her husband finally decided that there was only one other doctor that might help them have a baby. So she goes to the doctor and the doctor examines her and she hears the same sad story. "I am sorry mam, but you have a deficiency in your birth canal and if you have a baby; it would be miracle." This time the women is so distraught that she goes by a local bar and sits there and tries to drown her sorrow in the booze. After several she staggers toward the door and takes a taxi home. She walks through the door and there is her husband waiting to hear the news. His wife looks at him and starts to cry. He says, "What is it honey? Please tell me what the doctor said." She looks at her husband and says in a slurring voice, "Well he said I had a fish in my canal. And if I had a baby it would be a mackerel." My Uncle Kary Cox told me one about a city fellow who had come up to north Georgia to lead a revival in one of the little county churches. The churches of the area were not exactly as modern as some of the churches from where the young city pastor was from. It was the first night of the revival and the young city preacher wanted to do a good job. The preacher got behind the pulpit and started preaching hell fire and brim stone. He really had the congregation going. There were some amens and halleluiahs' coming from the gathering. All at once the preacher said, "And God said to Abraham, and then Abraham said to God, and about that time the city preacher looked up and there is the rafters of the little country church was sitting a half grown possum;" the preacher's eyes got big and just as he said, And Abraham said to God he said, "Damn, What a Rat." These were some of the first jokes I remember being told. I guess I thought they were funny or I wouldn't have remembered them so long. A good joke makes us laugh, but the funniest things in life are the real things that have taken place, but we don't want anyone to know about them. We are afraid we might be treated like Paula Dean.

KRACKED UP COMMODE

Having a family that has always supported me in anything I wanted to do, has always been wonderful. I sometimes wonder why my brothers and sister always loved me the way they did. After I lost my oldest brother Bruce and my sister Brenda I would look back and know that their love for me was genuine. I remember one time I came home from School and didn't have a car to drive. My Brother, Bruce and his Wife Tia had just gotten their house built and I decided I would go see them. Seeing the house wasn't nearly as important as asking Bruce if I could borrow one of his cars. Chris Black was home for a few days and he and I had a lot of things to catch up on. Mostly drinking beer and partying. This was in my forming years, I guess you would say. I don't know what I was forming, but it is the only excuse I have. Bruce loaned me his ford for the night and Chris and I were soon on our way to catching up on our endeavors. I think we may have gotten a little ahead of where we should have been if I remember correctly. Chris had given me directions to take through some of the back streets in Cleveland. The number of drinks we had consumed might have influenced those directions to some degree. I was doing just fine when Chris says, "Bobby that looks like a commode in the road." Now you and I all know that there is no such thing as a commode in the road. Well, except this time there was. I ran over that commode and to this day I still believe that the car came off the ground. Chris was super excited because he and I for that matter had never run over a commode before. The commode was crushed. It is amazing how much noise a commode makes when you run over it, especially when you are in your brother's car. Well we came out into Hwy 129 where the present day huddle house sits. We turned left then we went around the square. I didn't know until the next day what our exact route was. However, Bruce and Tia's car soon started making a weird noise. I figured we had just enough power in the old car to get to Bruce and Tia's house. When we got there, I asked Bruce if we could borrow his other car. Looking back on that night was enough to convince me that I had one of the best Brothers in the world. Not many Brothers would really believe that you ran over a commode and demolished there car. Commodes are not the usual obstacle in the road. Bruce said, "Ok boys, but that is the last Car I have." One of the ways that Chris and I were able to trace ourselves the next day was by the transmission fluid that was on the Highway. We had busted the transmission pan and the fluid had drained through a hole in the bottom of the pan. Not only were we surprised to see that we had gone around the square in Cleveland, but we found out there was actually a new red light in Cleveland. I don't think we even saw the red light the previous night. I would say that if it was Red we ran it, and if it was green we didn't see it. I felt bad about tearing Bruce and Tia's car up that night, but sometimes a memory like that was probably worth it. After all Bruce paid to have his car fixed the next day; I was broke. Along with a commode I had met the night before.

TOO MANY FISH

There is nothing like a good fishing trip. You know one where you tell a buddy how you went over to a lake and caught a bunch of fish. Then your buddy says lets go back over and see if we can catch some. You get up the next morning real early and you take off. You get to the lake put your buddy's boat in the water and go out and start catching fish just like you told him you did a few days earlier. That is what all fishermen want. However, it usually doesn't work like that. Most of the time you tell your buddy how you caught the fish, he gets really excited and you and he go fishing and don't catch a darn thing. He looks at you and says things like; did you'll use them rooster tails? Or was you'll fishing this swallow. They just don't believe your fishing trip was as good as you told him it was. But the time that I told Lanier Chambers about catching all the trout in Lake Hartwell, well we went back and repeated the same type of catching experience, except better. In fact, we caught trout on everything we put in the water. It was one of those days when you could have put out an empty hook and caught a fish. That was kind of our problem. We had caught to many fish. We probably had caught double our limit. Finally fearing for the well-being of my friend I said, "Lanier, don't you think we did to take some of these fish back to our truck and put them in a safe place? Like where the game warden won't find them." Lanier says, "OK, just let me get this one in the boat and we will do that." As soon as I had netted the fish that Lanier had on his hook, we started heading to the boat ramp where we had launched our boat. We were slowly going into the ramp when all of a sudden I looked, and there was a game warden coming out of the cove we were going into. Neither Lanier nor I said a word. The game warden was slowing coming toward our boat. Lanier let his boat slide up on the sand to the right of the ramp. I place my foot on the side of the boat and jumped to shore. As soon as I touched land, I looked at Lanier and yelled, "I appreciate the ride mister. I will get somebody to take me back to my boat." I then started walking up the ramp. Old Lanier's face was red as all get out. His eyes looked like −I will kill you Bobby Adams as soon as I get the chance. Well evidently the game warden decided that he had given me a ride back to the ramp and we probably didn't have any catch to check. Just as suddenly as he was coming toward us; he turned and opened his outboard up and was gone in a flash. As soon as he was gone Lanier said, "Damn you Bobby Adams, was you going to leave me to get caught with all of this fish?" I told Lanier that I had thought about it, and felt that there was no sense in both of us going to jail. I thought it was good thinking. What do you think?

ICE SKATING

Some of the folks in Lumpkin County will remember this. Several years ago, Mr. George Elliot, the father of Nascar Legend Bill Elliot decided that he was going built an ice skating arena in Dahlonega. I ask Mr. Elliot why he was doing that and he informed me that he thought young people needed something to do. He was a big family values man and I thought that George was exactly right. The young people in our community needed something to do besides set in their cars and watch the traffic go around the square. Although I must admit, the way I saw some cars go around the square in Dahlonega was very entertaining for me. But I can't speak for everyone. Mr. Elliot proceeded to build his ice skating arena and it was something that most mountain people had never seen. Some maybe had seen an ice ring on TV, but that was about all. Several of my students would come in to the school and ask me to come down to the arena and give ice skating a try. It didn't look to difficult. I had been a roller skater for a number of years. I wasn't exactly a pro but I could maneuver most of the time without busting my tail too many times. After the students had encouraged me by telling me what a wuss I was, and calling me chicken, and few other choice names, I said. "By golly I will do it." That was the dumbest I will do it thing I ever said. I went down to the ice ring and got me a pair of ice skates. As soon as I stood up I felt my ankles begin to swell. My knees were straining to hold me upright. I could only go a few feet at a time. Finally after what seemed like an hour, I got on the ice. Have any of you ever seen a giraffe ice skate. Well that was about what I looked like as soon as my skates hit the ice. My butt would return to its natural color in three weeks. Let's just say to make a long painful story short. I quickly took the ice skates off my feet. Went home and soaked my ankles until the swelling went away. I answered to the name of "wuss" and "scaredie cat" for about two weeks." I never did learn to ice skate but I got to see lots of cars go around the square in Dahlonega. I thought it was fun and it didn't hurt.

STOVE PIPE

Working at a builders supply was a very good experience for me. I was used to working with lumber because my daddy had been in the sawmill business all of his life. My summers were usually spent working at dad's sawmill. I was really pleased, when instead of working at the sawmill; some of my friends had started a builders supply business in Cleveland and hired me to be the gofer. Working at that builders supply gave me the opportunity to go pretty much all over North Georgia. The new business was started in what was once an old garage. The building was very quickly filled with all kinds of supplies. Since we had no forklift all of the loading was done by hard work and lots of muscle. In the summer of 1966 I was a new graduate of White County High School and had been accepted at the University of Georgia as a future student. I knew that come fall work would end, and I would be off to Athens, Georgia. With that in mind I tried to have as much fun as I could before I departed to Athens. The builders supply job gave me the chance to be with three very entertaining men, Billy Wayne Chambers, his brother Lanier, and Jere Kimbrel. Each of them was a unique man. Put them three together, and you were going to have some laughs. I don't know if this really happened, maybe Billy Wayne just made it up. A customer came to the builders supply and Billy says, "Yes sir can I help you?" The gentleman told Billy that he would like to see if he could get some things for his wood stove in his house. Billy says, "OK, just tell me what you need." The man said he would like to see if he could buy a half a piece of stove pipe. Most of the building material was located in the rear of the building and that is where I usually worked, however I was making a delivery that day. Billy looks at the gentleman and says, "Just a minute and I will go see." Billy turned and started walking toward the back of the building. The gentleman was walking behind Billy Wayne, but Billy Wayne didn't know it. Lanier was in the back of the building and as soon as Billy Wayne saw Lanier he says, "Lanier some stupid asshole wants to buy a half a stick of stove pipe." Lanier's eyes were getting big and Billy quickly turned around to see the man standing right behind him. Without any hesitation Billy Wayne says, "And this nice gentleman wants to buy the other half of it." It was one of the few times a half of stick of stove pipe was sold at a builders supply business.

Grandpa Linton Adams. He was 6' 7" tall.

CATS AND SCIENCE

At the beginning of my junior year in high school I found out I was enrolled in a biology class that would be taught by a new teacher at White County High. His name was Harold Trull. Mr. Trull had lost one of his legs but walked with the aid of artificial leg from the knee down, and except for the slight limb you would never know Mr. Trull had lost his leg. I don't know much about Mr. Trull. I heard that he passed away. If he did, I am sorry, and if he didn't well there is still a good man in this world. Mr. Trull was a great biology teacher. He taught us by using frogs, earth worms and even cats. And that is the beginning of my story. Mr. Trull told us at the beginning of the school year we would have to do a lot of dissecting. Now I wasn't the smartest student in class so I kind of envisioned the school buying petrified frogs and rabbits or whatever else you use to dissect. This was supposed to help us learn about anatomy and body functions and whatever else you were supposed to learn. We had gone through the frogs, earth worms, and fish pretty quick. Mr. Trull told us we would be dissecting a cat before long and since there was no school fund to purchase embalmed cats, he wanted us to see if we could find a cat that wanted to donate its life to the world of science. I asked several cats but each one always gave me the same answer. Now all of you animal rights folks keep in mind that White County was very rural back in the 60's. There wasn't just a load of students that wanted to go into the field of science or medicine or for that matter go into anything that required a great deal of academic knowledge. But surprisingly, it soon became apparent that everyone was finding a cat that was going to donate its body for study. There were probably 20 025 students in that class and eventually everyone found a cat. My friend Jerry Dorsey told me that he had located us some cats that were in an old barn near his house. So taking a feed sack and a piece of string we went to catch the sacrificial cats. Those cats had other ideas about us catching them. It seems that wildcats are called wildcats because they are wild. As soon as we slammed the door shut in that corn crib we discovered that cats can be as mean as any wild animal. We thought for a while that the cats were going to put us in those sacks. They not only hiss at you; they will bite, claw and anything else they can do to get away.

But being determined and clawed all over, we finally got us a couple of wild cats in the bag and tied those suckers up. Now a lot of you will say how cruel it was to do that to those cats. This was the 60's. We did what we had to do to learn. Mr. Trull helped us embalm the cats with embalming fluid. Our entire school smelled like femaldihide embalming fluid. Teachers complained. The students complained. It was a very smelly time. Many people in today's society would have condemned and even prosecuted Mr. Trull, but I learned a lot about the human body and its functions from those cats. I think everyone else did as well. I don't think they would test that on the CRTC or SAT or any other test that seems to be so important, but by golly Mr. Trull taught us biology. I never realized what a great teacher he was until I was sitting in a class at the University of Georgia watching an instructor dissect a cat and knowing everything he was talking about. Mr. Trull was a teacher that used every resource he had to teach. I don't know where he got those worms or frogs and fish. But I bet they weren't as hard to get as those cats. Times have changed and my cat, Kingfish says; he is glad they have.

QUICK ON YOUR FEET

My son and I were talking the other day and he says to me, "Daddy how has things changed since you were a boy my age?" Brynnan is 17 and will be a senior this year and it seems like just the other day my daughter and her friends were all at the hospital waiting on Brynnan to arrive into the world. I told Brynnan that there had been a lot of changes in the world since I was his age. I pointed out that we didn't have cell phones. North Georgia was still pretty rural and taxes were fairly cheap. Then he says, "Yea, I know all of that, but did you have a lot more places to hunt?" This makes it obvious that he has taken some of his priorities after me. Hunting and Fishing are his favorite things to do in his spare time, and he seems to have lots of spare time once school starts. Of course we had more places to hunt. I explained to my son that many of the places we had to hunt are now subdivisions and there are a lot more people in our North Georgia Mountains. He said, "Did you ever get run off from a place that you used to hunt?" That brought to mine one of the times that we were going on a dove hunt. My friends all ways try to make the opening of dove season a big event. Usually we would go down to the Crumley Dairy and shoot doves. But on this particular opening day the folks at the Dairy had not harvested there silage. Since dove season didn't officially open until 12 noon we had a while to try to find a field that was going to have some doves. We were riding around and every place that we could think of that might have some doves just didn't pan out. It seemed that no one was going to be shooting doves. Between the Chambers Brothers Lanier and Billy and the Adams Brothers, me and my family we knew just about everyone in the county that was a farmer and might have a place to shoot doves. Well we had exhausted our list of potential places to shoot doves. Lanier and I were riding around and all of a sudden I saw what looked like a bunch of doves fly into the lower end of a partially gathered corn field. The rest of our cohorts were supposed to be following us. Lanier says, "Bobby you stay here on the road and wait for the other guys and I will ride through this field to see if those were doves." I got out of the Volkswagen and stood on the side of the road. Lanier had just gone of the bank and the other guys arrived. We were standing there and Lanier was going about 40 miles per hour through that field. All at once I looked and here came a man walking up from across the road from where Lanier was knocking corn stalks in the air. The man walked up and had a somewhat angry look on his face, and said, "You boys don't have permission to be in that field." Billy Wayne was standing the closet to the man and Billy said, "This is Mr. Cecil Crumley's field isn't it?" The gentleman said, "Hell no, Mr. Crumbly don't own this field. I do." All of us started yelling at Lanier who had by that time scared the blackbird out of the bottom of the field to get out of the man's cornfield. Lanier pulled up to where we were all standing with corn stalks still hanging from the Volkswagen, and says, "What's wrong?" Billy pointed to the gentleman and said, "Lanier, Cecil Crumbly don't own this field it belongs to this nice gentleman here." Without missing a beat Lanier said, "We sure are sorry. We will leave right now." I got into the Volkswagen and the other guys loaded into their vehicles and we drove off. I said to Lanier, "Where is Cecil Crumbly's field?" Lanier said, "I don't know but we don't have permission to hunt it either." I later asked Billy Wayne about his asking if the field was Cecil Crumblys. Billy said, "Well, I knew the man was mad, and I didn't say we had permission to hunt on Cecil Crumbly's property. I just ask if it belonged to Cecil Crumbly." Brynnan laughed, and so did I. We never found out who the man was that owned that property. It didn't matter; we had gotten away.

WATERMELONS AND CAMP MEETING

It was this time of year back in the early 1960's. People were starting to gather their crops out of the fields and the summer days were hot. People looked forwarded to the evenings and the sun would set and cooler air would be a welcome feeling. My folks would always have a garden, and Mom and Dad would have us gathering the green beans and getting the ripe tomatoes in the house where Mom could can and put the vegetables away for the winter. It was also a time of Camp Meeting. Camp Meeting would be held by the Baptist, Methodist, and Holiness churches in our communities. In the early years it was a time that people of common faith would come together and stay in simple buildings build primarily as sleeping quarters so they wouldn't have to make the long trip back to their homes by way of horse and wagon. But with the automobile now people just liked to camp and be with those folks to hear good singing, preaching and enjoy each other's fellowship. It is said that it was at Loudsville Camp Meeting where the legendary Babe Ruth met his wife. Lots of folks went to camp meeting to renew their spiritual strength. Unfortunately I was not one of them. I went to camp meeting because it was fun and we could get into all kind of stuff. One of our best tricks was to go down in the Mossy Creek and White Creek area and steal watermelons. The melons were usually coming in about the time the Holiness Camp ground was having Camp Meeting. Several farmers would have fields that would have been very productive had it not been for me and my friends. So while there was a large portion of the county's population renewing their spiritual self, there was a smaller portion of young boys that was sharpening our survival skills. That being, not getting caught, and shot to death by an angry farmer. I am sure that some of those farmers actually planted those watermelons knowing it was going to be too much temptation for the hooligans that I ran with. Now we didn't get all of the farmer watermelons; we just got some of them. After eating as much of the watermelons as we could, that is when the fun would really start. We would take the watermelon rimes find a car that was parked on an incline and place a rime under each of the back wheels. At the close of the nightly service many of the family would casually walk back to their cars saying good night as well as talking about what a good service it had been. We would be hid so none of the people getting in their cars could see us. The motors would crank, and suddenly it would sound like the Daytona 500. Engines would be revving up and exhaust smoke would fill the air. I always thought that some of those folks that had been renewing their spiritual wellbeing may have back slid a little when they got out of those cars to see those watermelons rimes under the wheels. I could have sworn that I heard a few unworthy words coming out of their mouths. It's Camp Meeting time again, but nobody grows watermelons. Oh well, I hope the singing and preaching is good.

FIRST LOVE

Sometimes we look back and realized we should have handled things differently. The things we do often hurt people we care about. We don't mean to hurt them but it just happens. My parents were very good parents although they never sat me down and told me about the birds and the bees. I think since we were country folks; I would learn about that stuff myself. I had started dating this young lady and she was absolutely gorgeous. She had the looks that drove young men like me wild. She had beautiful long black hair and the prettiest blue eyes I had ever seen. We met at a dance one night and started talking and it seemed like we had only talked for a few minutes and then I realized that we had been talking for over two hours. She gave me her number and we started dating. She came from a very nice family. Her mother and father were well thought of in their community. We started dating in the fall and before long it was Christmas. After Christmas things started getting well a little different if you know what I mean. She seemed to grow impatient. She wasn't her pleasant self. She seemed to want to argue a great deal. I just tried to be brave and go with the flow. Well it wasn't too much longer when we were on our way to a drive in movie. I think it was Thunder Road. I had seen it 10 times so I figured she would love it. We watched the movie and we were heading back in when she said that she wanted to break up with me. I asked her why and she started to cry. She said, "I can't believe the way you have been treating me. You are gone almost every week end and I never get to see you in the evenings. And just to think that I held out for a long time before, well before, I gave you what you wanted". Suddenly guilt hit me. She had held out longer than I had wanted and I had enjoyed it. I thought that it was a learning experience for both of us. I wasn't very experienced in that sort of thing. Oh, the feelings I had when she gave it to me. Well needless to say we broke up and it took me a few days to get over it. So ladies there is only one thing I can say and that is, ---- Never give a man a reel and rod for Christmas cause if he likes it; you will not see him near as much as you did. My next girlfriend gave me a tie.

WINNING ON A WHISTLE

When the fall of the year comes around Football season is in the air. I will be seeing and hearing the spirits of the game everywhere I go. Football has been a part of most everyone's life especially if you live in the South. I have friends that probably never attended a high school football game, but since they have become adults and have children they have become experts on the game and do not mind telling you what the University of Georgia will have to do to win the National

Championship. I love to hear people talk football. The amount of expertise one has makes no difference in how much they love the game. I really get a kick out of seeing the little fellows in the pee wee leagues or whatever they call the leagues that the small children play in. They look so determined to be a professional football player. I don't remember the first football game I ever attended, but I am sure it was a White County High School game. I have many memories of being a young boy sitting in the stands and watching the high school boys play football. I was attending a game at the White County stadium watching North Habersham and White County play. My math teacher, a Mr. Kimsey, died of a massive heart attack. I was sitting behind him when he fell over. He was a good man and well liked. The gentleman that would later take his place at the high school was Ralph McCrary. Ralph would be very instrumental in getting me to come to Lumpkin County as a teacher and Coach. Of all the memories about football, there is one that really sticks out. We were playing East Hall and they were supposed to be really good that year. I was probably in the 7th or 8th grade. We were sitting on the visitors' side in the bleachers. It was a tough game. The ball game was proving everything that it was expected to be. Both sides, the home side and the visitor's side were really in to cheering our players on to a victory. The score was 0 to 0. White County had a running back, his name was Jimmy Lockabee. Jimmy got the ball and ran in to line. It was a simple dive play. It looked like Jimmy was going to be held for no gain, suddenly and out of nowhere there was a whistle. Everyone stopped but Jimmy; he broke through the line when everyone stopped because they had heard the whistle. Jimmy scampered into the end zone. White County had scored. Who had blown the whistle? The officials said they had not blown a whistle. White County would win the ball game by scoring that one touchdown. The Coach for East Hall raised all matters of hell. He had heard a whistle. He was right there was a whistle. I along with many others heard a whistle. White County had won the ball game because of an undisclosed whistle. No one ever found out where the whistle came from. I know where that whistle came from, but I am not telling. No it wasn't me.

ART AT ITS BEST

One of the things I really enjoy is reading the newspapers and skimming the internet each day. I find some very interesting things. Recently I read an article that was about Lady Gaga. She is supporting some art institute. The way she is doing this is by stripping naked. It seems that she is stripping down to her birth day suite in order to support this art institute. It is some kind of a video. My less educated friends probably would call it a porno video. I will call it a performing naked arts video. I find that very informative, as well as inspiring. This art institute was founded by an actress whose name is Marina Abramovic. I am not sure exactly what Ms. Abramovic does at her performing art institute. In one of her last projects, it seems she got a bunch of folks to see how long they could sit and think with her. I don't know what they were thinking about. I don't think a fellow like me, who is so well refined in the performing arts, can really get in to the long sitting and thinking stuff. I was always more into the sitting and drinking stuff. When I was a young boy my mother said she had a very difficult time keeping my clothes on me. She said it was not uncommon for me to be seen running around the neighborhood showing my little white fanny and having what must have been a wonderful time. Thank goodness I matured and by the time I was 40; I stopped doing that. I really had to because I had a brother living on each side of me and they kept complaining about the dogs barking and their wife's smudging up the windows. Plus, the occasional visitors to their homes would blow their car horn and scare the livestock. Now I am not against Lady Gaga stripping down to her birthday suite, and I am sure that when she does they will be some of us, I mean some of those less educated in the arts than I am, will look at Lady Gaga's birthday suite. I have given this careful consideration. Not looking at this lady that will be naked as a jaybird, but considering how sincere her actions are. I know that the Nacoochee Art Center and the Historical Society here in Cleveland need funds. I wonder, since I have had a little experience running naked when I was about 5, if I volunteered to do a video in the buff if we could make any money. Naw, I think my friends would pay more for me to keep my clothes on. My friends are just not that much into the performing arts.

PRIVATIZATION

Over the years I have seen great changes in the mountain counties that make up North Georgia. I remember as a small boy riding with my daddy, Grandfather Sims, and Brother Bruce up to the place that would become the dam for Unicoi Lake. I heard the men talking about this thing they called a State Park and how it would provide some jobs and a place that would draw tourist to our area. I didn't know what a tourist was but it sound like it was something that you could catch or hunt. So naturally, I was all for it. As I got older Unicoi State Park became a big part of my life. Unicoi State Park did become a place that some of the local folks could find employment, even if it was just for the summer. A lot of the people that I grew up with had jobs at Unicoi during the summer. Some would work in the concession lodge; others would be life guards or work on maintenance of the park. It was also a great place for the young men and women to go. There were several arcade games plus a juke box in the lodge and you could waste your nickel and dimes in the machines. Naturally we guys figured out a way to gamble on the sliding bowling machine. We never lost too much money, mainly because we didn't have much money. By the time I had gotten to be a young man the State Park had become an experimental station in recreation. That's what the educated name was. For the locals it had become a tourist trap. A big lodge was built on the property that once belonged to Mandoe Vandiver. And in it is a nice restaurant. A lot of people came to our State Park and many still do come to enjoy the very things that we locals had held secret for so many years; the great life of living in the Mountains of North Georgia. As more people came to visit the North Georgia Mountain, more and more stayed. We had become a retirement haven. The State of Georgia has tried privatization of the park. The first time it didn't work. Now it is being tried again. I hope for the sake of the many who work there that it is successful. If not I guess it will go back to the state and run as good as it was run before. I did notice the price of a meal in our local gossip spreader. The ad was encouraging folks to come up after church and eat a dinner meal. The price of the meal is $14.95 plus tax, and if you have a drink, and all of us know that if you are from the South; you are going to have a sweet tea. The tea will be another $1.50 plus tax. That is about a Seventeen dollar meal. And of course if your wife goes with you it's twice that, and then you got to tip. I would say if you got out of there for around $40.00 bucks; you would be doing ok. I hope our State Park has lots of people to flock there every Sunday to eat, but I am afraid that most of the local folks that I know will probably just go home after church and cook a meal invite all the sons and daughters and son-in-laws and daughter-in-laws, and grandchildren, and feed them all on about twenty dollars. I have got to start saving my money so I can spend it on my future grandchild. So if privatization of Unicoi State park doesn't work this time, they can just blame it on me.

PAINT SPRAY FOR INSECTS

I have decided that for some reasons parasites love me. If I am outside and there is one mosquito in the world it will find me. When I walk in grass or go for a stroll in the woods, I will return with at least 10 chigger bites, and if I have been real lucky, I will have no more than 6 ticks trying to attach themselves to my body. I have friends that could sleep naked in the woods for 3 days and come out with not so much as a chigger bite. Many times I have noticed that while fishing in a boat at night that the mosquitoes will all be hovering around my head. Sometimes it will sound like a big helicopter buzzing over my head. I look at my fishing partner and there is not a single insect flying around their head. A bee will come across Yonah Mountain just to sting me. I do not understand why all of these little pests or so attracted to me. I think I must have blood that taste like cool aide or some sweet drink that all varmints that suck blood like. One time I was fishing with my old fishing buddy, Don Winkler. We were fishing in a bass fishing tournament on Lake Lanier. The tournament would start at 8pm in the evening and end at 12 o'clock that night. We had not been fishing very long when a squadron of mosquitoes began flying over my head. I would slap at the blood suckers that were trying to rid my body of my blood. There were several of them so I was doing more slapping at the mosquitoes than I was fishing. Don took his fishing seriously. When he fished in a tournament he fished to win. I was not being very helpful in catching fish that could be weighed in at the end of the tournament. Don looked back at me and said, "If you will quit beating the hell out of yourself, you might catch a fish." I told him the mosquitoes were eating me alive. Don said that he thought he might have a can of insect repellant in one of the boat compartments. We didn't have a flash lite but I felt around in the compartments until I felt a spray can. It was a dark night. I couldn't see the writing that was on the can. Don had said he thought he had some insect repellant so I started spraying that stuff all over my head, down my shoulders and around my belly, over my legs and plumb down to my ankles. We continued to fish. The bugs did seem to let off a little. I was only slapping myself about half as much as before. Before too long I began to notice that I felt a little sticky. However I continued to pick up the can and spray it on my body when I thought the blood suckers were attacking again. We returned to the ramp at the end of the tournament to weigh in the 5 fish we had. I caught one. Don caught four. We actually came in second place and won a little prize money. I felt like my skin was drawing up on me. We were getting the boat ready to return when I picked up the can I had thought was bug repellant. There was a big light in the parking lot at the ramp. It said "Clear Polyurethane High Gloss." By time Don stopped laughing and we got home I was the highest glossed fisherman in North Georgia. I may have been the highest glossed fisherman in the world. It took a lot of rubbing and a bunch of mineral spirits to get that stuff off of me. I do not recommend Clear Polyurethane as an insect repellant unless you want to be the glossiest person in the neighborhood.

RASBERRY DIET

Many of my fb friends have been asking how I got back on that Raspberry Diet thing. I feel compelled to tell you. You see, I was sitting in my recliner eating Cheetos and drinking beer when who do you think called me? It was the President of Raspberries International. He said that since I had eaten at least a ton of them Raspberries, and since I had helped the organization sell a lot of that Raspberry Diet stuff. Mr. President said he wanted me to travel abroad to promote his Raspberries. He might have said travel with a broad. I can't really remember; Gunsmoke was on, and old Marshall Dillion was in a real Jam. Well he started telling me that he needed a man of character to sell his berries. Maybe he said he needed a man that was a real character. Anyway, he said he had heard nothing but good things about me. I acted like I was surprised. I knew I was going to call momma later and see if he had called her. He said that he believed I could sell tooth brushes to a toothless man, which made me believe he knew some of my fishing buddies. He kept on about how I was the man they wanted to sell them raspberry diets. He kind of scared me because I thought for a minute there that he said he knew I was a wanted man. I was hoping he hadn't found out about them bad checks I wrote to old Bryson Wilkins. He was a talking real nice, and then he got to asking me some personal questions. He wanted to know what my political persuasion was. I told him Baptist or course, with a little Methodist thrown in there every now and then. That seemed to please him. He was kind of lost for words. He told me that he wanted me to represent his company in a big way. He said he could guarantee me to have all of the upper part of Towns County. He said if I was ready to go to work, why I could start right away. That's when I knew that Raspberry bunch was up to no good. When he said the

213

word work, I knew he must have dialed the wrong number. I said to that man, "Wait just a minute here fellar, just who do you think you are a talking to?" He started apologizing real fast. He said he was sorry if he had offended me. I told him not to be too hard on his self; there were several people that used that word work around me and I had only hit two of them. I told him that I use those berries all the time. They are pretty good. I use them in my pies, and when I make my high calorie, high cholesterol ice cream float, I use them then to. I convinced him that I use a good many of them raspberries. The President of Raspberries International said he was going to send me a free week's supply of that Raspberry diet stuff if I would just get off the phone. I told him he was the one who call me, if anyone needed to hang up it was him. He did. But he did send me some of that Raspberry diet stuff. They sure make a good pie. And that Facebook friends is how I got back on the Raspberry Diet.

NEW DOG

I had almost forgotten how trying it is to raise a puppy into a dog. Hudson, our Boykin Spaniel, is a remarkable little dog. He has already tried to commit suicide by eating rat poison. He does not know that a car will run over him. He thinks he can meet you in the driveway and run right under the wheels. Hudson likes to go everywhere I go. He follows me everywhere. When I go to the vehicle he goes and jumps in the seat. Hudson does not know that a muddy foot dog is not welcomed in the truck seat. Hudson lies down and goes to sleep immediately. I have never had a dog that could go to sleep as fast as Hudson. He dreams in his sleep. He will start twitching and all at once jump up growling and barking. He will scare the tar out of you.

214

Then he just lays down and goes back to sleep. He seems to be very smart. Hudson comes into the house and lies down on his little sheep skin pad and is out like a light. Hudson is not house trained. That is why I let him go over to my brother's house and play with their dog. They let him in, he plays until he has to go to the bathroom. He goes in their house and comes home. They have called me several times to tell me Hudson peed or pooped in their house on their floor. I have told them he doesn't do that in our house. I have tried to convince them that he feels secure in their house and that should make them feel proud. Joanna and Brad are just not into making my dog feel secure. They said they wish I would make him feel secure over here where he belongs, and they would like for him to crap on our floor. Little Hudson is a smart dog. If he sees any dog food over at my brothers; he just helps himself. I have told Brad and his wife that it is a sign that my animals feel content in their house. The dog obviously feels comfortable in their house or he wouldn't mess in their floor. They keep telling me that they want Hudson to feel comfortable in his own damn house. I think that is the way they put it the last time we spoke. O well, I just hope Hudson keeps being the loving dog that he is. I wonder if Brad and Joanna would let Hudson ride in the front seat of their car with muddy feet. I told Hudson not to be too pushy, but he might want to try it one day and if they don't scream too loud, hey, it may be an environment conducive to the development of a smart little dog. Now I have got to go over here and wake Hudson up; it's time for him to go over to my brother's house and do his business.

BAD DAY

Sometimes I have to just laugh at myself. This has been one of those weekends where everything I have done has been a wash out. It started early Friday morning. Did you know that when you get a little age on you; you have to realize that you can't see as well as you could when you were young? Well, at least I can't. I also have found out that the cortisone cream in the red tube looks a lot like Colgate tooth paste. If you get up at 5:30 am and start getting ready to leave to do some work at your deer lease, you really need to be awake before you brush your teeth. Or you need to make sure you have put on your glasses before you put anything on your tooth brush. The cortisone cream looked just like the Colgate tooth paste. However, it did taste a little different, but I made several ups and downs before I realized it didn't taste exactly right. Shucks, I am just glad it wasn't the Preparation H like it was the last time. My mouth was a little puckered for about a week. After spitting for 10 minutes and washing my mouth out several times to get the taste of cortisone cream out of my mouth, I decided that I would put a little hair spray on my hair. Fortunately, I still have a good bit of hair on my head. I sprayed my hair right after I had used my trusty hair dryer. I noticed that the smell of the hair spray had changed a little bit. In fact it didn't smell right at all. I did not know that my son had gotten a big can of Right Guard deodorant. I am glad that it wasn't the can of Lysol spray setting right next to it. I then go down to get a cup of coffee. I had poured the water in the coffee maker the night before. I just wish I had remembered to put the coffee in the coffee filter. Hot water with no coffee in it is not very satisfying. I finally made it out the door and there was my little dog, Hudson. Hudson looked up at me and I said ok you can go. He jumped in to my truck, and got over in the passenger's seat.

Have you ever ridden one hundred miles in a truck with a dog that is having terrible gas? Plus it wasn't raining in good old White County when I left, but as soon as I was going down Apple Pie Ridge road the bottom fell out. Maybe the cortisone cream was trying to tell me something. I believe that everything happens for a reason. So, I just laugh. Sometimes you just have to count your blessings.

REFINING ME

Being the connoisseur of fine art that I am, it came as no surprise that several of my redneck friends down at the local bar was interested in what I thought about the MTV awards? Since one of my specialties is art that shows excessive amounts of the human body, (Henry and Red call it pornography, but what do they know), it seems that they were pretty torn up about Miley Cyrus coming on the stage and looking like she had an alligator about half chewed up before she got out there. Knowing that I could offer an expert opinion on this artistic endeavor, my Brother Billy ask if I would review the entire episode so that those that were less informed on the art of nakedness, I mean nudity could except what little Miley had done. I told the boys that were congregated around the room that I would divulge my thoughts on this creative episode. Then nephew Steven says, "What the heck does divulge mean?" I could tell that I was going to have to get down on their level. In fact I may have to get in the basement to answer their questions. I began to tell them that throughout history music and dance have been used as a form of creative expression. I proceeded to tell them about musicians such as Elvis Pressley and how he brought not just Rock and Roll into the homes of millions, but also a lot of body movement in the dance routines.

I explained that in the beginning there were those that thought it was the music of the devil. My grandmother for one thought that if kids got to shaking and jerking like he was doing; why there wouldn't be enough hickory switches left in White County to make a shade for a bull frog. Moms and Daddy's would beat their kids to death. Granny wasn't a very good predictor but momma did trim a good size peach tree out behind the house. Now getting back to Miley Cyrus, I had to go on YouTube to watch little Miley try and eat that alligator because at the time she came on Live Wrestling was showing on my channel and I just couldn't bring myself to miss it. Well----after watching Miley come out on the stage and do her dance and song, I decided I would have to watch it more than once to get the true artistic meaning of the moment. Each time I watched it I could see the great musicians like Mozart, Beethoven, Louie Armstrong, Frank Sinatra, Otis Redding, Bill Monroe, Lester Flat, Earl Scrubs, Melvin Hawkins, Bryson Wilkins, the Soggie Mountain Boys and Loretta Lynn looking into the sky saying, "Holy bat crap, we ain't never seen anything like this." With that answer the boys just shuck their head and agreed. Now back to some real art on the TV. SEARCHING FOR BIGFOOT.

MISS MY BROTHER

I started writing this several times, and each time I started; I would stop. It would just be too hard to continue. So I have waited until I wasn't so emotional and I could reflect on this with open eyes and an open heart. I am writing about my oldest Brother, Bruce. Bruce wasn't just my oldest Brother; he was my best friend. From the first time I could remember Bruce was there for me. Bruce was almost two years older than me, but as we aged I realized that he was lots of years wiser.

Bruce concentrated on learning things, if he didn't know about something, he read about it or he would go to someone and get the information that he needed. Bruce has been gone for several years now, and each time I come by his house it seems like he is still there. Bruce was laid to rest in the church cemetery that his son Mark attends. His grave marker has wildlife on it which I know makes Bruce smile each time he looks down. Like all brothers we had fun. We had fights. But for some reason, but we never stayed mad and each other. Bruce protected me when I was a little boy. That would make me so mad. I didn't want anyone protecting me. Thankfully Bruce was there to watch over his younger Brother. My Brother was not without fault and I know that. But to me he was. When Bruce got married that made me kind of mad at him. I thought how could he not want to be with me all of the time? When you are young you are also dumb. I am writing this because in a few weeks it will be deer season. Bruce was so passionate about hunting that he got everyone of his friends as excited as he was. When hunting season comes around I think about my big Brother. I wish he were still here. I can just see him now talking to Saint Peter, Paul and anyone else that liked to hunt, and they are all getting excited.

WORDS OF WISDOM

Each day I read some post on fb that great or famous people have passed on. So I decided that I would put some of my sayings on this wonderful new media. We will call them "WORDS OF WISDOM FROM THE MIND OF BOBBY ADAMS AND FRIENDS". I already like the title. So now a few of those never before heard or stated words of wisdom. Please add your words of wisdom under the comment. I hope we get a bunch of them. Make them original words of wisdom. Humorous or whatever:

1. Never try to breathe while you are under water.
2. A pretty girl in the car is a whole lot better than passing 4 pretty girls on the sidewalk.
3. The first time I heard that rumor, it was coming out of my mouth.
4. You may be the life of the party tonight but a commode hugger in the morning.
5. Most people will do the right thing if the sentence is long enough.
6. If a man thinks he understands a woman, he needs to go fishing and think a little longer.
7. If you feel the weight of the world is on your shoulders, you may be the one holding it up.
8. Happiness comes when you least expect it, but so does diarrhea.
9. Money can't buy happiness, but you can rent a boat with it.
10. Live your life so that when you are gone, those that didn't like you will miss you just as much as those that did.
11. You can love animals and still be a hunter.
12. Talking bad about someone and looking in a mirror are both reflections.

Your turn-- now make some of your own words of wisdom. Do this at a family gathering and write them down. You might be surprised and how wise you and your family are.

KNOWING BETTER

When I started uses tree stands to hunt out of, they were not the kind that you sit down on and lift your legs up and stand up and then repeat the process until you are at the height you wish to be. The early tree stands let you pull yourself up with your arms and you pulled the bottom part of the stand with your legs. By the time you got to the place up the tree you wanted to be, you were completely warn out. Your arms would feel like you had been working out for about 4 hours. A deer could hear you breathing for a mile away. But you were at a lot better advantage of getting a deer if you were above the surface off the scent line. I had one of the dinosaurs of tree climbing. We were hunting in Wilkes County on some property that belonged to the Phillips family of Dahlonega. Ms. Phillips had given us permission to hunt on her property. After a few hours of scouting the property I found me a big yellow pine tree with no limbs on it for 30 or 40 feet up. I placed my dinosaur tree stand around that big pine and started up. Now there is one thing that all hunters knew about the old stands; you should all ways have a rope connecting the pulling up part with the foot part. This hunter knew that, but unfortunately, had forgotten to bring something to connect the two parts together, but after a short thought decided on taking the risk. It was a beautiful evening I had been watching for a nice deer to come along, however the deer had other plans that day and they never showed up. It was beginning to be sunset and the daylight was going away rapidly. I decided it was time to go down from the perch. I started down, the second time I lifted my feet to place the stand underneath me in came off of my foot and what they say can happen, happened. All the way to the bottom of the tree the stand rattled to the ground. There in the tree was a 230 pound fat man hanging in the tree. I decided that if I just let loose I would probably only break both legs with a possibility of a few more bones being broken. I decided that I would wrap my arms around that tree and try to ease my way down. I clung to that tree like it was my dancing partner. My mind kept saying you can do this Bobby. Occasionally it would say things like; how

221

could you be so stupid? What kind of idiot forgets to connect the two parts of the tree stand together? That part of the conversation with my mind I didn't want to listen to. I began my slow decent. I would hug the tree with my knees and then let my arms down just enough to grasp that ping again. Slowly I came down except for about the last 8 feet. That bark on the pine had cut my forearms so bad that I didn't get as good of a grip as I had been getting so it looked like a fireman sliding down a pole at a fire station, but the fire pole was not smooth and the landing was not very pretty. Lucky for me I wasn't hurt too bad. The cuts on my arms would heal over next few weeks. I had no broken bones. It was the last time I ever used a tree stand and not follow the recommended safety precautions. I sure was glad that no one was around to watch me come down that tree. I guess I am what you call a real "tree hugger."

The Sims brothers at Nora Mill in Helen, Georgia.

DOGGED OUT

Our new dog Hudson continues to impress me with his smarts. Hudson loves to retrieve and ride in the Polaris Ranger. In fact if he hears it crank up he will come running and jump right up in the seat. Not only does he like to ride in the Ranger, but he also likes to ride in my pickup truck. He knows if it is just me in the truck, he can ride in the front seat. If someone is riding with me Hudson will quickly get in the back seat. It doesn't matter where he rides in the Pickup, because he will immediately wad up and goes right to sleep. He can go to sleep the fastest of any dog I have ever seen. And when he sleeps, he sometimes snores. Having Hudson as a traveling companion is absolutely great; he doesn't take up a lot of space and he is always well behaved. There is one drawback to having Hudson travel with me. I will explain. Last week I knew it was going to be time to cut lots of grass. The weather had not been very co-operative to say the least. Rain has a way of making grass grow at an alarming rate. I had been told by my Brother Billy, that I needed to use 100% gas in my small engine pieces of equipment. Most all gas stations will have a warning that tells you that you are getting up to about 10% ethanol when you pump your gas. So I inquired as to where one would find the 100% gas. He told me that the station South of Cleveland on 129 sold it. So I got my plastic gas tank and threw it in the back of my pickup truck. When I opened my door Hudson jumped right in and was lying in the passenger's seat and before I got to town he was sound asleep. I pulled up to the station and sure enough there was a tank that had 100% gas written on it. However like most pumps you have to pre-pay before you pump. I walked into the station and told the young lady I wanted to get 5 gallons of the 100% gas. She said, "Go right ahead Mr. Adams and pump your gas." So I then go outside and I put 5 gallons in my plastic container. I placed the gas tank in the rear of the truck and then I tried to open the door. It would not open. Hudson had locked the door from the inside. Whenever I get out of the truck, Hudson will stand up on the arm rest to see where I go. I normally take my keys with me but Hudson was so quiet, I simply didn't think to get them. I called my Brother and my nephew Austin carried me to get my key. Before I left to get my spare key, I looked in my truck and there was Hudson in the backseat sleeping. I called, "Come here Hudson, come on boy, come here, Please Hudson unlock the door boy. Nice Dog." Austin looked in and said, "You know that is one smart little dog. Now if you can just teach him to unlock the door." I am positive that dog had a smile on his face. I know that was a fake snore. He is going to learn to unlock that door.

RADIATOR LEAK?

Back in the 70's I was going to a lot of car races. My Brother Billy and his business partner, and our brother -in-law, Ricky Robinson had dirt track race cars. Lanier Raceway was a dirt track and sometimes would have races on Friday and Saturday night. I loved going to the dirt tracts and coming home looking like someone had put makeup on me that made me look like an Indian in a John Wayne movie. I learned very quickly not to wash off with a white wash cloth. It would stain the cloth. Sometimes the red dust would be so bad that when you smiled you would have red streaks between your teeth. You could blow dirt balls out of your nose. You get the picture. It was dirty and dusty and lots of fun. A wreck usually resulted in a fight which meant more people the next weekend to see if there would be retaliation from the week before. The Cleveland Wood Preserve race team was usually in the mist of all the excitement whatever it was. One of the number 12 cars was driven by a fellow from over around Rome. His name was Johnny Jenkins. Johnny and his brother Author were both good race car drivers. Both had driven for Cleveland Wood Preserve. I remember on one of the weekend racing adventures Johnny Jenkins was going to be driving a 150 lab race at Lanier Raceway. Johnny was trying to think of all the things that he needed to prepare him for that long of a race. Johnny said, "Boys, I have got a slight kidney infection and I have been taking medicine for the last several days. What if I have to Pee during the race?" Well, we decided that Johnny could rig up a hose pipe with a modified urinal on the end of it and drive one handed until he relieved himself. The hose would just run out through the floor board of the race car. That sounded like a great idea and before long all the race cars were lined up ready to start. The green flag fell and before too long Johnny was driving toward the front. He was holding on to fourth place with a Number 9 car hot on his butt. With about 25 labs to go old Johnny slide into second place and the number 9 car was right on his rear bumper. The number 9 car began to drop back and another car came into the third spot. Then that car dropped back. Johnny didn't win the race but he came in second place. Immediately after the race here came the guy driving the number 9 car. He came up to Johnny and said, "Johnny I was going to try to pass you when I was right on your rear and then your car started to run hot and the water got on my windshield and I had to drop back, if it hadn't of been for that radiator spuming water all over me I believe I could have passed you. Yea, well when you got to go you got to go." Lucky for me my radiator got hot. We all knew that Johnny's radiator wasn't hot but we never let that other driver know it. Johnny Jenkins was later killed driving to work one morning. His killer has never been found.

JAKES POOL ROOM

I am sure that a lot of people in Dahlonega remember the pool room located on the West side of the street. Mr. Jake Palmer ran the pool room. Jake was a good man. He called me on more than one occasion to tell me that some young boys were skipping school and shooting pool in the pool hall. He would tell me that the boys were shooting pool and if I would come down there I could catch the entire crowd and give them a good talking too. Well I would go do to the pool hall and as soon as I walked in the young boys would dash for the back door. I did this several times. I told Jake that I was going to have to be able to come in without them knowing I was around. Jake said for me to park up the street from the pool hall and that way I come down and come in the back door. About two week later Jake called. He said, "Mr. Adams there's about 4 or 5 old boys down here shooting pool and I believe if you can get down here, you can catch em." I told him I would be there shortly. I did what Jake and I had talked about. I parked up the street and came in the back door. I came in and looked at the boys shooting pool. All of the boys shooting pool were about 20 to 25 years old. I said, "Jake where did them boys go?" Jake said, "Why that's them right there." I said, "Jake, I don't think any of those boys are in school. I think they are too old to be students at the High School." Jake Palmer gave me one of the best answers I ever got. He said, "Mr. Adams, they may be too old to be in school, but I know every one of them, and if they got out of school being that damn dumb, they need to go back." Jake Palmer was a wise man, but he couldn't guess age very well. Jake Palmer kept calling me whenever he thought a student was skipping school. He remained a friend until his death.

FLYING THE FRIENDLY SKIES

Day after tomorrow will be Thanksgiving Day. It will be a day that families and friends gather to eat, enjoy each other's company and to give thanks for the many blessings of life. My family has gathered and celebrated Thanksgiving as long as I can remember. When I was young, we would all gather at my grandmother Adams house and a feast would be had. There would be food that would put the Golden Coral to shame. My grandmother had nine children and her children and their spouse would all be there. Each of them would have several children to bring and of course there were always neighbors that would come and partake in the festive celebration. The grandchildren would all play outside until someone would yell for us to come in and eat. It was at one of these Thanksgiving dinners that I found out that I couldn't fly. I had told some of my cousins that I could fly off of the old chicken house located behind my grandmothers. They should have believed me without exception, but then one of my cousins who lived out of our county said something about me being crazy and it was impossible to fly. So being the brave young man I was, I told him that I could fly but I had to use an umbrella to prove it. I didn't have an umbrella so I thought that would settle the argument. Then one of the other cousins said, "I know where Granny Adams umbrella is and I am going to get it." Why is there always someone that just can't wait to settle an argument? I would have been perfectly satisfied to let it go and just let them think I could fly. That was not to be. In just a few minutes, while I was trying to decide how I was going to get out of this predicament, here came my cousin with a big black umbrella. "Here is an umbrella now let's see you fly." She said with a little smirk on her face. There was nothing left to do but get on top of that chicken house and fly off. With the aid of an old latter that was already leaned up on the chicken house, I was up there with granny's umbrella. I surveyed the distance from the top to the ground pretty quickly. In fact, I had been jumping off of that chicken house for several weeks just to show my brother that I could. I opened up that umbrella and when I did; I realized that granny's umbrella was huge. Being full of energy I thought the best thing I could do was to get a running start and jump off and with the umbrella I should float around until I could at least say that I had flown. Even if it was for a short distance. I backed up and pointed the umbrella the way I was going to run. I came running hard and just as I got to the edge I lifted that umbrella up and jumped. Needless to say, I didn't fly. My only excuse was that Granny's umbrella had been defective and folded up on my quick decent to the ground. I remember that Thanksgiving because my mom didn't give me an immediate whipping. She let me eat, and play, and then when I got home; I got my tail tanned for tearing up my grandmothers' umbrella. That was when I realized I couldn't fly; if I could have I would have been a jet because my tail was smoking. Happy Thanksgiving everyone.

ME, MYSELF, AND I

I remember many years ago, when I was a young guy, we would plan a big deer hunt on the Chattahoochee Management Area. It was always an exciting time for my family and friends. For a number of years Dr. Corbit Thigpen would come up from Augusta, Georgia and hunt with us. Dr. Thigpen had married a White County girl and knew lots of folks in this area. Dr. Thigpen was one of the authors of a book, The Three Faces of Eve. The book was based on the research and treatment of a lady who had multiple personalities. It was also made into a movie and Joan Woodward played the lead role. Ms. Woodward was actor Paul Newman's wife. I have thought a lot about those days of hunting with Corbit. He was an excellent hunter and we always had great discussions about any and all things. Not much was known about multiple personalities. It was something new and since those days a great deal of research has been done in that area. Although I have never been diagnosed with multiple personalities I am sure I have them. I know. You are saying, "Bobby, how in the name of Moses do you know you have multiple personalities?" Allow me to explain. This phenomenon didn't just occur to me out of the blue. No, it came to me over years of thinking. It really came on me hard when I retired. I bet it has come on some of my friends as well. They just haven't diagnosed themselves yet. You see when you retire; you start talking to yourself more. You will want to do something today but if you wait just a little while, something else better will come along. I think now there is the Good Bobby, and the Bad Bobby. Why just this morning I woke up and thought I needed to get out of that bed and get going. Suddenly the Bad Bobby spoke to me and said, "Why do you want to do that? This bed is warm. You have a remote for the TV. Just keep your ass in bed Bobby." Bad Bobby really knows how to argue. Good Bobby tried to find a comeback, but he couldn't. Good Bobby just the other day said, "Bobby, you need to rake the leaves in the yard." I walked down to where the rake was and grasped it in both hands, and you guessed it. Bad Bobby said, "Why rake the leaves Bobby? Just wait and the wind will blow the leaves away. Isn't that what you wanted; the leaves gone?" Hey, that Bad Bobby is good. He can really argue. This morning my wife Paula said, "Bobby, you have got to take the trash to the dumpster." Good Bobby replied, "Ok, I will be glad to do that." I waited for Bad Bobby take over. But all he said was, you are crazy, if you think I am going to argue with your wife." Bad Bobby still knows when to keep his mouth shut. I may have to research this a little more

BIBLE THUMPERS

I have never considered myself as someone that can judge someone else. I try to live my life the best I can and sometimes I know that it is not good enough. I have never been given the talent of judging other people. I do get amazed at the number of people that want to quote the bible and tell people that they are not going to go to heaven because of this or that. I have not read the bible in its entirety. I have read a good portion of it. It is a good book. It tells us a great deal about how we should try to live our lives. I leave the judging to the Judge. Recently this ordeal with the Duck Dynasty Patriarch is making the way those that are sticking up for their principles look as though they have no principles. Nowhere in the Bible that I have read, does Jesus condemn homosexuals. I am talking about Jesus. In fact, most of what I have read shows Jesus was more concerned with feeding and looking after the less fortunate and looking after the sick and afflicted. If it is in there; someone please show me and I will be glad to retract what I am saying. I know there are scriptures that say man should lay with only a woman, but Jesus didn't say it. Some want to pick and choose parts of the Bible to make their point. There are many who are saying that this is about freedom of speech. We all have freedom of speech but we don't have freedom of consequences from speech. As I understand, Mr. Phil had signed a contract saying he would not say inflammatory remarks against others. It paid the family a rather large sum of money. I would have signed it. I think most of the people I know would have signed it. Those that were paying the money thought he had violated his contract. I don't know if he did or didn't. I did read his remarks, all of them not just about his feelings toward gays but other things that he said and I could see how some would take offence to it. I don't judge Phil. I do think what he said is causing more hate to be spread than love. About the only thing left for someone to do to get more hate going is for the congress to investigate to see if President Obama had anything to do with it. As you do unto the least of these, you do unto me. But what do I know. For all have sinned and come short of the glory of God, this includes me.

DUCK TAPE AND HUNKIE STICKS

I have just read a post by one of my good friends. It was very informative and I can say that since reading her post. I have given great thought not only into the post, but also about how I am going to choke my dog Hudson the next time he has that terrible gas. The post I am referring to stated that the federal government spending over a $172 million dollars on penis pumps last year. I am sure that there are many out there that would say this is a waste of money. Of course if you are the one doing the pumping, it might not be. Before you rush to judgment let me speak to this expenditure. Being the creative man I am; I think I could save our government money and create new jobs while saving the money. I believe that we can save lots of money if they will follow my suggested advice. Instead of paying for penis pumps, I suggest that our government start handing out duct tape and and hunkie sticks. I know most of my friends know what I am talking about. I will let my friends on facebook figure it out. We would then create lots of jobs. People would have to have the duct tape and hunkie sticks delivered. Delivery drivers would be in great demand, more jobs. Companies would have to be built to make the sticks, more jobs. Trees would need to be cut to make the wood, more jobs. There would probably be a shortage of duct tape. So they would have to expand the duct tape factories, more jobs. And of course since there would be some dumb folks out there that wouldn't know how to properly use the duct tape and hunkie sticks, we would have to offer classes on proper splint procedures for the male penis, more jobs. I can see it now, television commercials running adds saying, "ORDER YOUR DUCT TAPE AND HUNKIE STICKS FROM US AND HAVE THEM DELIVERED TO YOUR HOME WITH OUT ANYONE KNOWING." I believe this could be done for only $171 million. A million here a million there, we would be saving money. Why hasn't this been thought of before? HUDSON, where are you? I know you are in here.

CALLING IN THE BUSES

It was a very cold winter; we had to cancel school several times that year. Calling school off before the students boarded buses or before mom's and dad's drop them off was not all the complicated if the weather would move in- -say at least 24 hours in advance. If the storms came in early we could determine if the condition of the roads would be so bad that school would have to be postponed. The problems of calling off school came when the snow would begin to fall early in the morning around 6 o'clock and then the bus drivers would start their routes. If they snow continued we would then have to call the drivers back with their buses to get the students back home before the roads would become hard to navigate. On one cold morning the buses had started arriving at the school and so had a heavy snow fall. Some of the early buses had already let the students out and headed for the bus shop. As Superintendent I made the decision that we needed to get the kids back home as soon as possible. I called each principal and told them that I would have the buses returning and that should get the kids back on the buses so we could get them home before the roads became too slick to travel. Everything seemed to have been carried out without any problems. I had already received word that one bus had slide out of the road near Ridley's Store on Hyw 19 North but the kids were safe and the driver had been able to navigate the bus onto the rest of his stops. It had been a very tense morning to say the least. I had just called each school to make sure that they had not experienced any problems. Each Principal confirmed that everything was good that the kids were gone from their campuses. I had hung up the phone thinking –Wow that was a close call. Suddenly my phone rang, I answered, "Superintendents office, Mr. Adams speaking." The voice on the other end said, "Hey Mr. Adams this is the PE instructor at the Middle School. I got all my kids in the gym here and how much longer do you think it will be before the buses get here?" I realized at that time that sometimes when you think you have done your best it is just not going to be good enough. We were able to get all of the kids in the gym home. And we made sure that the intercom system was working in all buildings from that time forward.

HEAVENLY DOCTOR

Sometimes when you hear of one of your friends passing from this life into glory, you can't help but look back on that friend and reminisce. Dr. Tommy Lumsden of Habersham County was the first Doctor that ever gave me a shot. I was only 5 years old and my Grandmother Sims told me if I didn't cry, she would give me a quarter. I walked up the street to where Doctor Lumsden's office was went in there and turned my head away from him, and I still remember him saying, "Ok, a little sting." I didn't cry and got my quarter from my Grandmother. Mom and Granny Sims were so proud of me for not crying. I must have pitched some holy fits before that bribe from Granny. As the years went by, Dr. Lumsden delivered my sister Brenda, Brother Billy and Brother Brad. I remember being in the hospital in Habersham County in 1956. I had my appendix taken out. I was in the third grade. Dr. Lumsden didn't operate on me but he came by to check on me every day. He always left me with a smile on his face. Dr. Lumsden was loved by just about everyone in the Helen and Nacoochee Valley area. He, like a lot of the first Doctors in the Mountains of North Georgia made many house calls to care for the sick and afflicted. I had the privilege of seeing Dr. Lumsden not too long ago. He would say, "Right here is one that I delivered at the Charm House in Clarkesville". He said, "Bobby, I remember your mother Frances and her sister Louise, but there was one other sister, and I can't remember her name?" I told him that Momma's baby sister was Thelma. He said that the reason he wanted to remember her was because in 1954 there was two cases of polio in White County and both of them were his patients. One of those patients was my cousin Flowetta Gaddis, who was Aunt Thelma's daughter and I think the other was Mike Turner who now lives in Lumpkin County. That brought me to remembering the little sugar cubes that was handed out to all the kids in my school. It was the way that Polio was brought under control in America. Dr. Lumsden severed the people of North Georgia well. He helped keep my family members well for many years. He was not only a good Doctor but he knew the history of our area as well as anyone I know. Mark Twain once said, "Every man is a grindstone, and someone will always be bringing an axe to us." Doctor Lumsden had lots of those axe brought to him, and he never turned any away. He was a good Man.

OLD SMOKY THE CAT

My Aunt Louise Cox can make the best cornbread this side of heaven. When I was a young boy growing up in the Asbestos Community of White County I spent many nights with my cousins at Aunt Louise and Uncle Kary's house. The first time I slept on flannel sheets was at Uncle Kary's. My cousin Clifford, Brother Bruce, Wayne Sims and usually Lamar Sosebee and myself could be found all sleeping in the same bed at the Cox house on any given Saturday or Sunday. I always looked forward to staying with my Aunt and Uncle because not only was the cornbread good; Aunt Louise made great sweet tea. In Their house was a wood saver heater. Lots of families had this kind of wood heater in their living rooms at that time in history. You could stuff that thing full of wood and turn the air down low and the next morning you didn't have to restart your fire. Their house would stay warm and cozy all night long. We were sitting around that heater one night and Uncle Kary rolled him a Prince Albert cigarette. Uncle Kary used big ole diamond matches to start his fires with, and to light a cigarette with every now and then. These matches were so darn big that it took a wind tunnel machine to blow them suckers out. Most people that warmed their homes with wood and at that time most all homes were heated by a fire of some sort, either a fireplace or a wood heater. They would buy a box of these and they usually placed them close to where the fire was. Uncle Kary got his cigarette rolled and struck that match to the side of that wood heater and the match lit up. After taking two or three quick puffs Uncle Kary shook it in his hand a time or two and then through it on the metal thing that the wood heater was sitting on. Laying on that same metal sheet was one of Aunt Louise's cats. The match landed right at the end of that cat's tail. Suddenly there was a blue flame that went from the end of the cat's tail to the top of its head. That cat squalled, and then took off like a rocket. Zooom out from under that heater at about 100 miles an hour came that cat. It didn't hurt the cat, but you could smell the smoking hair as it left out of there. Uncle Kary just looked in the direction the cat was going and said, "That match must not have gone out." The next morning the cat was right back under that heater. Uncle Kary started calling that cat old smoky. Years later my uncle and I were laughing about that incident and he said what was really funny was from that time on if he lit a match; the cat would leave the room.

DATING SITES

One thing I have discovered that when you are retired, you can watch a whole lot of television. I never thought about what comes on TV a great deal. I mean, you know; I would turn on the tube, and watch a good western or a comedy. It was just taken for granted that something good would be on the big eye. Since I have retired the TV has taken on a new role. I like to see what types of commercials are on the entertainment machine. I have noticed that dating sites are really big right now. I mean you can find a date in any category you want. You want a farmers date. Farmersonly.Com. You want a religious date, Christianmingle.Com. Then of course there is the take anything site, Eharmony.Com. That is the one that you usually meet your relatives on. You can even get a race date site, Whiteonly.Com. or Blackpeoplemeet.Com. What has happened to our society? Have we turned so technologically dependent that we use a machine to say, "Hey, this girl or this guy is for me?" I know some of my friends might think this is nothing out of the ordinary. However, some of my friends, that are not as sophisticated as me; may be taking these dating sites too far. I had one friend ask me if there was a dating site called Beerdrinkeronly.Com. Another wanted to establish one called Richchicksonly.Com. That sounded like it might have lots of promise. You want a rich guy or rich women. Hey, sign up. Unfortunately we don't know any rich folks available. We did discuss a Football loversonly.Com site but the two girls we knew that would sign up still hadn't found anyone to go on their bond to get them out of jail. Hunterslikeme.com sounds like a good one. You want someone that hunts go right to this site. I mean you could find out what caliber gun he or she owns and who knows love may be waiting right out there in the big outdoors with someone who has a gun bigger than yours. My friend Bill told me if I could find a site that met this poem he would sign up. I met the perfect women. I cannot ask for more. She is rich, deaf and dumb, and over sexed and owns a liquor store. It may be hard to find old Bill a match. Let me know if any of you hear of one.

PREDICTING DOG

My dog Hudson is trying to make a name for himself. Since he found out about the ground hog, General Beauregard Lee, coming out every year on February 2nd to try and see his shadow, and make his weather prediction, Hudson has been thinking that maybe he has some super powers that the world needs to take advantage of. He doesn't like the idea of trying to see his shadow. That would require him to get up off of his bed and go outside. Plus trying to upstage a ground hog would be pretty darn near impossible. He thought about making political predictions, but in the South if he didn't pick a Republican, some would start calling him a socialist, or even worse, maybe even a Collie. He quickly threw that idea right out of the dog house. I did see some potential last night as the Super Bowl was playing. I placed two bowls of food on the floor, one had the Bronco's emblem, and the other had the Seahawks. Each time I placed them down he would eat out of the one that had the Seahawks emblem on it. This proved to be quite amazing. So naturally I told my Son, Brynnan, that Hudson had picked the

Seahawks to win. We were admiring this new found talent of our canine companion, wondering if the bookies in Vegas would pay to have this dog do his incredible feat for them. We were admiring an animal with limitless potential. Hudson was standing proud watching the TV as though he knew what the outcome would be. My wife Paula walked into the room, as she sometimes does, and I told her of our dog Hudson newly acquired skill. She only said, "Well that is nice Bobby. But next time put food in both of the feed bowls. And don't do it when one team is losing by 35 in the 4th quarter." Hudson returned to his bed and said if she hadn't of noticed how our experiment was going; he could have been famous. It is time for Hudson to get up and go see his shadow but he says it is raining outside so he can't see it. Weather may still be his thing.

JUST A SWINGING

I have lots of fond memories growing up in White County. My Grandfather Sims ran a store in Helen and my Grandmother Adams and her family had the old Adams store right out of Cleveland on the Helen Highway. As a child I remember making many trips to Helen to visit my Granny Sims and Papa Sims. It was like going on a vacation each time we made that 8 mile journey. When we entered Helen, the bottoms along the river had massive stacks of lumber all up the River. My Grandfather was a foreman at the big sawmill that was located on the banks of the Chattahoochee River there in Helen. The mill and most of the lumber would be lost in a fire, and it never reopened. That is when my Papa started operating his country store. One of my most treasured memories is that of the trout fishing that me and my brothers did on the Chattahoochee River. From Nora mill to the headwaters of the Chattahoochee is where I spent many of my days trying to catch the Rainbow and Brown trout that were so tasty when mom fried them up. For some reason it always seemed like the best fishing was on the other side of the river. It was a time when all things were peaceful and everything was right in the world. There were no "POSTED" signs. There were only the smiles and the friendly waves to us boys that tramped along the banks of the river. One of the things I remember was the swinging bridges that crossed the Chattahoochee. There was one there in Helen just below the concrete bridge that goes over to where Orbit Manufacturing plant was located. The other swinging bridges where in Robertstown, and just North of Robertstown just passed the bend in the river where Trey Mountain road is. The swinging bridges served most families that lived on the side of the River where there was not much traffic. The children could walk across those bridges and catch a school bus. I remember after the flooring rotted from the bridge there in Robertstown; we would walk the cables across the river to test our skills of balance which sometimes wasn't too good and we would end up falling in the Chattahoochee. I also remember letting one of the Abernathy boys out of a vehicle that dad was driving and he walked across the swinging bridge to his house on the other side of the River. The old swinging bridges are gone. In fact most of those that remember them or used them are also gone. But there is still one red headed boy that smiles when he thinks back in time about the swinging bridges on the Chattahoochee when everything was right with the world, and all you wanted to do was catch that fish on the other side of the river.

WATCH YOUR STEP

Since Mom passed away recently, I find myself thinking about her a great deal. She was not only my mother but she was my friend, my hero, my inspiration, and the source of lots of memories. When we were young boys growing up around the old Adams store on the Helen Highway; it was a new experience every day. My uncles were characters in their own right, and something was usually going on around that store. Men were usually buying whiskey or helping each other drink what they had already bought. My father built a two story chicken house when we were just small kids and our job was to get up in the morning go feed the 2000 chickens down stairs and then feed the 2000 chickens upstairs. When we first started feeding those chickens I hated it. It was the summer of 1955. Since it was summer and school was out, Mom would not let my brother, Bruce and I wear our shoes to go feed the chickens. She told us we would have to go barefooted to the chicken house so we wouldn't ruin our shoes. I hated to go barefooted worse than I hated feeding those chickens. The first time I went into the chicken house barefooted the sawdust on the floor of that chicken house kind of felt good to my tender feet. But as those chickens got older the poop got bigger and much more of it. If you have never stepped barefooted in chicken crap in a chicken house and felt the warm, mushy, chicken shit come up between your toes---Well, you may not be as country as you think. I did not like that warm, mushy, stuff coming up between my toes. Once I was coming out of the chicken house and of course I had enough chicken manure on my feet to fertilize the garden and being a small boy I was just venting my frustration to my brother. I looked at my brother Bruce and said, "I hate stepping in that old chicken shit." I thought that it was an honest statement. How was I to know that Mom was standing at the corner of the chicken house, and she heard those words come right out of her little red headed boy's mouth? I only felt her grab me by my shirt and say, "I heard what you said little boy and I am going to tear your tail up. You know better than to talk like that." Needless to say I got the peach tree limb. Years later, when I was a young teacher; Mom and I were walking through her yard and she stepped in a pile of dog manure. She said, "Dang I stepped in a pile of dog crap." I looked at her and told her, "You know better than to step in that, you might get a whipping. She said, I didn't whip you for stepping in it. I whipped you for saying shit." It is strange the things we remember when we lose someone that gave us so many memories.

LIFE AFTER DEATH

A couple made a deal that whoever died first would come back and ... inform the other if there is sex after death. Their biggest fear was that there was no after life at all.

After a long life together, the husband was the
first to die. True to his word, he made the first contact,
"Joanne ... Joanne "
  "Is that you, Earl?"
  "Yes, I've come back like we agreed."
  "That's wonderful! What's it like?"
  "Well, I get up in the morning, I have sex. I have breakfast and then it's off to the golf course. I have sex again, bathe in the warm sun and then have sex a couple of more times.

Then I have lunch. In fact, you'd be proud of me – I eat lots of green vegetables. Then, another romp around the golf course, then pretty much have sex the rest of the afternoon. After supper, it's back to golf course again.

Then it's more sex until late at night. I catch some much needed sleep and then the next day it starts all over again."

"Oh, Earl! Are you in Heaven?"

"No -- I'm a rabbit somewhere in South Carolina."

MR. CANNON

Every time I hear of someone passing for some reason, it will always bring a memory of that person back to my mind like it was just yesterday. Recently I have been having too many memories being brought back to me. When I was a student in the White County Public schools here in White County, I was privileged to have as one of my teacher a man by the name of J.C. Cannon. Mr. Cannon taught in the science department of the High School. Mr. Cannon could always get your attention by taking his fingers placing them on your head and somehow he would knock a knot on your head. That finger on the head either got your attention or it would knock you slap out. Thankfully Mr. Cannon would usually try to just get your attention. I liked Mr. Cannon. He was a pretty good teacher. He would often tell me stories about when he was a prisoner of war during World War II. One story he told me was of a young troop who was going to try and escape by jumping off a bridge and staying under water so the German troops couldn't see him. He told me the young troop jumped off the bridge but the water was only about a foot deep, and he died of a broken neck. He said he always was thinking about escaping but every time he would think about it he would think about the guy breaking his neck. Mr. Cannon like to do a lot of experiments in class. On one occasion he decided that we would heat some chlorine and make some chlorine gas. The experiment was very simple.

After making the gas, we were to pass around a glass tumbler with the gas in it and take a quick sniff of the gas. We did. Of course when it got my turn I grabbed that tumbler and put it under my nose. The smell was so strong it actually startled me and I took a deep breath. Well that gas went into my lungs and I started coughing and I couldn't stop coughing. Mr. Cannon was so afraid that I had injured myself that he carried me home and explained to my mother what happened. He told me many years later that he never did that experiment again. Being a former POW he knew that the Germans had used chlorine gas in the war. The chlorine would cause vapor to come in to the lungs and it basically made the person drown in is on fluids. Mr. Cannon and I would laugh about that episode each time we had the opportunity to get together. JC would say, "Bobby didn't know the difference between a sniff and a snort." After that when he said a sniff I knew he meant a sniff. Mr. JC Cannon was a teacher, POW, hero, decorated soldier, but mostly a friend. RIP

BEAR DOG

Well I guess I can say that the month of March is a good month for me and my family. My son, Brynnan was born on March 6, my brother, Billy was born March 10, my new grandson, Wilder was born March 20, and I was born on March 22. Many of my friends and some kin folks were born in the month of March. Of course our new dog, Hudson celebrated his 1 year birthday on March 11. I think Hudson is by far one of the more trusted members of our family. Hudson has worked pretty hard to earn the respect of each family member. Hudson is one of those dogs that if he were a human; people would say he is just laid back. Hudson loves to be with people. If he sees you go to the barn he will be there by the time you get there. When he comes into the house he finds a place and flops down. If it is not where you want him all you have to do is point and he will move to where you are pointing.

The other night my son decided that he and his cousin Spencer, would go over to his cousin's house and get in the hot tub. After staying over there for a couple of hours his mother said, "Don't you think you should call Brynnan tell him to come home?" I don't know why I am the one that should call but in order to maintain peace and tranquility in the house I agreed to call and request that he come in. I called and Brynnan told me he was on his way. Not long after that Brynnan came running into my bed room and said, "Daddy you should have seen the bear that just came out of Uncle Bruce's driveway." "That thing was huge." I asked him how big is huge and from the description it did seem to be a rather large bear. However, after he told me what happened after they saw the bear; it may have had a bearing on just how big that bear was. It may have made it grow a little. It seems that Brynnan and Spencer took off after the bear in Spencer's truck. The bear very quickly jumped into the pine thicket located on the left side of my driveway. Brynnan decided that he would get out and see if he could see the bear. He gets out comes around the truck but unknowing to Brynnan, Hudson our four legged friend decided he would greet Brynnan before he got up the driveway. Brynnan had just said to Spencer, "Gosh man I hope that thing doesn't get me when I get out of the truck at the house." It was about that time that Hudson came up behind Brynnan and rubbed the back of Brynnan's leg. By the time my son realized it was Hudson touching his leg and not the bear I would bet that bear grew by several hundred pounds. It didn't take Brynnan very long to get from the truck to the house. March has been a good month.

EASTER PRAYER

Have you ever noticed how some people say they want government out of their lives but in the next breath they want government to pass a law to make some things illegal or to make something legal? I am not saying this is wrong but I do think it is kind of the way people are. Some even go so far as to want the government to legislate morality. Some things in our lives should be left between man and God. Now I know that many think that if laws are not passed or not declared illegal that the whole world is going to hell in a hand basket. I don't mean to be the bearer of bad news; laws are one of the things that make us a civilized world. I have said many times to my friends a statement like this; well if you don't think we need laws then the next time someone hurts you or your families don't call the law. They say something back like this. I don't need the law. I can take care of my family myself. This proves my point, because of that mentality we have to have laws. Sometimes I don't like it, but that is the way it is. Our nation is a nation that has been built on tolerance. This Easter is a time for Christians to give thanks to our Savior, Jesus Christ. In recognizing the resurrection, we should remember that Jesus was a very tolerate man. He commanded us to look after the hungry, the sick and the poor. I remember one of my Sunday school teachers, Ms. Blanch Thurmond telling me when I was just a small boy in the old Mount Yonah School house that Jesus wants us to pray for everyone. That was a mighty big statement, but I think Blanch Thurmond was right. Happy Easter

REDUCING YOUR DEBT

I was sitting on the sofa watching old Hoss Cartwright knock a bad guy's nose around, when the phone began to ring. I looked at the call indicator and he stated it was one of those toll free 800 numbers that was not supposed to be calling my house. I don't know if any of you ever get one of those calls that says, "this is a very important call and this is your finally notice (Which it never is the final notice) if you would like to completely eliminate your credit card debt please mash the number 1 now, if you do not wish to get this notification again, please mash the 2." I have just about worn old number 2 out mashing him so much but to no avail. They keep calling. I thought well I am going to answer this call just to see if it was the same robot I had talked to before? It was. So I decided I would mash that number one to see if there was a human on the other end or if it was another robot. It was a human. She sounded as though she had been in the US about two weeks, but she was very pleasant. She said, "Haw low Miter Abbums. So you want to redsus credkit cod debt". I thought; I just have to do this. So I said in all of my Southern charm, "Why yes Honey child I would love for you to help me get these old credit card bills caught up. What is your mailing address Honey? I will just send them to you". She then ask, Miter Abumms about how much credit card you owe?" I said, "Why darling I don't owe much but I think it is about $178 thousand dollars on about 4 different cards". She said, "You o one thousand seventy eight dalla?" I said, "No honey child, I said one hundred seventy eight thousand dollars." She said, "Wow Miter Abums you a lots of money." Don't know if can help. Wow that lots of money." That is when I said, "Just tell me your address and I will send this bills to you". She very quickly said, Miter Abums I have talk to supervisor. I call you brack." I said to her, "No wait, if you won't let me mail my bills to you, just take my name off of your call list. Can you do that without speaking to your supervisor?" The young lady informed me that she could. For some reason I don't think she did. Maybe I should have made up a higher number. I sure hope she took my number off her list. The number 2 on my phone is starting to stick.

LOVING PARENTS

This is not a funny story, but maybe a historical one. This is just being written because I wanted to pay tribute to my Mom, Frances Ella Sims. Mom was born to John Walter Sims and Maude Stamey Sims of Helen, Ga. On that day September 19, 1928 she was born on a fireplace hearth at the Sims house that was located on Dukes Creek. I do not know who delivered my Mom. That is a question I now wished I had ask. There were six children born to Walt and Maude. The boys were Ralph, James, and Charles. The three girls were Louise, Frances, and Thelma. My mom met Charles Herbert Adams when she was 15. She said their first date was in an old lumber truck that Dad had just bought. They were married after a quick romance and they would begin to raise their own family. Herbert and Frances would have six children. Those children would be Bruce, Bobby Brenda, Billy, Bradley and Becky. Becky only lived a short time after her birth.

This Sunday May 11, 2014 is the first Mother's day that the three living children of Herbert and Frances Adams will celebrate without one of our parents being here with us. Dad has been gone several years. Mom passed away on Valentine's Day, February 14th of this year, 2014. I think she was Dad, Bruce and Brenda's Valentine gift. Although Mom is gone; I wanted to just tell her how much she meant to us. She never failed to provide all the love that she could to her family. She protected us. She spoiled us. She laughed with us. She fished with us. She sang with us. She cooked for us. She worshipped with us, and God knows she always tried to be the best Mom she could be. I once overheard her telling someone in her house that she never whipped her kids very much and then she hesitated a little and said, "Well, except for Bobby." Mom we miss you and if I needed a spanking today, I know you would give it to me, and then tell me how much you love me. Sometimes a son just wants to tell his Mom how much he loves her. On this Sunday just know that your children love you just as much as we did when you were here. Happy Mother's Day Mom. PS- Mom when and if I get this book completed, this will be in it.

GRADUATION SON

I have put this off not because I didn't want to share this on this social network but because I am an emotional type guy. You know the kind that cries at sad movies and laughs out loud when everyone else is quiet. A little over 18 year ago I came home and my wife Paula was crying. I ask her what was wrong and she said, "Oh Bobby sit down I have something to tell you. We are going to have another baby." Then I began to cry, and asked her "Are you sure?" Now, I wanted to know for sure, not because I didn't want another child, but because I was getting old. After two weeks of crying, then came the happiness when we decided that this child was a gift from God. I am a person that believes that God doesn't really give us a child. I think God loans us one, because I know that someday we will go back to him. Having lots of Bs in our family we decided to name him,

Brynnan. My daughter, Brooke, insisted that we spell it with a y not Brennan. On March 6 of 1996, my son was born. Well shortly after he came into the world, I had some health issues. I prayed that the good Lord would let me live long enough so that he would remember me. Those prayers have been answered plus some more. I have watched Brynnan become a man. I know that if I am not here with him, that he can carry on with his life and become whatever he wants to be. He will graduate on Friday May 23, 2014 from the same High School that I graduated from in 1966. He has been a good son. I tell people that Bryn has made me a better person. Nothing makes a father any prouder of their children than to hear others brag on their child. I have stuck my chest out a lot. There is one thing that I want to do, and that is thank all of the people that have helped my son mold himself into the person he is and will be. Good friends, good teachers, great family members, and a loving community all contribute to the development of a person. Brynnan has been blessed with all of those. A special shout out goes to all of the seniors at White County High School; you have added so much to our family's life. You have slept on our floors, in uncomfortable chairs, and in our barn, and it has been a blast. Maybe there is a lot of truth to the statement, "they will keep you young." Thanks and congratulations guys we love you. If you have a child or know one that is graduating please share this.

DANCING BEAR

This morning my son, Brynnan came in the house and ask his mom how she got mud all over the side of his truck and the top of it. Paula told him she had no idea what he was talking about. And of course in order to not enter this argument yours truly just kept my mouth shut. Well fast forward to this afternoon. Paula comes in and asks if I would go down to the barn where I have two big dog lots. I mean these lots are 44 by 38. We have one dog, Ruger, in one of the lots. He has a self-feeder in his lot. And we keep dog food in a metal trash can by the door of the vacant lot. Well it seems that the bears have decided that since I am not going to put any more feed in my deer feeder that they would just help themselves to my dog food. Not only out of the trash can, but they climbed over the fence and got in the lot with our dog Ruger and proceeded to eat the dog food out of Ruger's self-feeder. Ruger has been seeing these bears for so long that they don't seem to bother him. I think he thinks they belong to us. We have horses that we put in the stalls at night and I sure hope that those bear do not decide that they like Oats. If they get in there with those horses I know one lady that might decide that the only good bear is a dead bear. We have lights on, and a radio playing. Paula asked if I thought that would keep them away. I told her I wasn't sure but at least they could see real well while dancing to the music. Paula just didn't see the humor in that. Oh, and the mud on Brynnan's truck, yep it was the bear. Big paw print right on top of the truck. Maybe they were trying to get a ride to the dance.

THE CLAN

If you know the Adams family, you also know that we are a very tight group. We're a clan, I guess you could say. We grew up around our grandparents and most of us have been within rock throwing distance of our parents, and believe it or not; we have gotten along pretty well. Usually, if someone in the family gets mad at someone else in the family; it is usually over in say about week. However, if someone does something bad to someone in our family, we will stay mad at them until their well runs dry or their cows go dry whichever comes first. That is just the way my family is, and it is about the same way other folks that grew up in rural north Georgia are. We have all worked hard and we play hard. If someone needs a helping hand we are always willing to give it. Our Dads and our Moms were always respected and honored. We try to show respect to those that deserve it. We try to pass down all of our values to our children and we cherish every day that God gives us here on earth. This week will draw my family even tighter. My Nephew Spencer has been given a lot of attention as a potential professional baseball player. Last night we watched the top fifty professional prospects on the MLB channel. Spencer was number 27. The major league draft will be held Thursday of this week. My family will be watching the draft with Spencer and giving him the support and love that has come so naturally for such a great young man. We don't know which team will get him, but we hope that whoever gets Spencer realizes that with him they get an entire family. I say this with all sincerity.   If they don't want a family that looks after each other and loves each other then I don't know if Spencer would be a good choice for that team. They will be getting a daddy that has watched his son play ball from the time he could pick one up. They will be getting a Mom that is like a wooping bird shouting woo woo woo woo each time she sees her son play. They will get a bunch of Uncles and Aunts that have watched him play since he got out of his diapers. They will get a bunch of cousins and friends that love Spencer whether he plays ball or not. It is going to be an exciting time Thursday around the Adams Clan. The entire White County community will be rooting for Spencer. Go get that dream Spencer, your family has got your back. The team that gets you also gets us.

GO IT ALONE

Well by this time all that know the Adams family have heard the good news about Spencer and his great opportunity. It is of course an opportunity that not many young men get. Playing a professional sport is very unlikely for most kids Spencer's age. But he now has a door open that can bring him a very happy, and yes, prosperous life. That happiness and success will depend on lots of different things. Some say they are praying for Spencer. Prayers are always welcome in our family, however, I don't think the good Lord cares whether he plays sports or not; plus God may not be a White Sox fan. I do think that Spencer has a great challenge in front of him. Of those few young men that get the chance to play professional baseball; a lot of them never make it into the big leagues. Only those individuals that work hard, make their own luck, and keep their dream in their lives make in to the top of that sport called Baseball. Morning rides on buses, playing in small unknown ball parks, and sometimes looking into the stands and not seeing one familiar face. Lots of those young men will get homesick. Many decide that this opportunity is just not what they expected. The folks here in White County know Spencer is a good young man. He is polite, courteous, and addresses people by saying, yes mam, and yes sir. Thank you very much, he is the kind of guy that all of us want him to be. We want him to be a professional baseball player, but only Spencer can step through that door of opportunity. We can only walk so far with him. The rest of the journey is up to Spencer. Show them what you got Spence. All of us know you can do it.

FATHER'S DAY

He was never famous. He never acquired lots of money, and he grew up in a time of hardship. America was still in a great depression when he was a boy. At that time in history lots of young boys had to become young men before their time. Working hard and helping his family was what was expected of him and so that is what he did. He helped his dad plant crops and worked at cousins lumber mills when he could. He was in the CCC camp near Lake Seed. He told me he got $16 dollars a month and they sent $16 home to his parents. He would tell me that the bunions' on his feet came from walking the hot roads from there back to the Asbestos Community where his Mom and Dad lived. At the age of 19 he became a saw miller. Because of his occupation he never had to go to the military. The government told him the need for the lumber was greater than the need for him to serve in the military. He married my Mom, Frances Ella Sims and they would have six children. The last child died shortly after birth. He worked hard his entire life providing for his family. He would always be the last to eat at the table just so he would make sure that his children had all they wanted from the food prepared by Mom. He never raised his voice in anger, and if he said no that was it. When never dared to try to get him to change his mind. He was a handsome man 6 feet and one inch tall. He had sandy blond hair and a smile that would melt anyone's heart. He worked for 42 years as a lumber man. When he finally realized his kids were all grown and he didn't have to work as hard, he started running a small restaurant called the Yonah Burger. He was always very proud of his little place of business. When his health started to decline he would rent his business to other folks. But Dad sat on his front porch and would gaze across highway 75 to see that everything was going ok. More than once he would pick up the phone and tell someone that a custom seems to have been standing at the serving counter longer than he should. We would laugh when we would find out usually the customer was a friend of one of the young ladies working in the restaurant. After science could do no more to keep my dad alive, he decided that he wanted to go home from the Emory Heart Center and that he would die in the home that he had shared with his wife and children. It has been 16 years since his passing and I miss him today as much as I did the day he left. But when you are a father that loves and is loved, that is the way it should be. Happy Father's Day Pop.

Mon & Dad (I placed this picture here as a way of honoring them, as I recount the stories that are reflective of them. I apologize for inserting this picture more than once.)

THE LYLE LOVETT LOOK

When I was born I was naked and I think I had a little hair on my head. Since I can't remember that far back I just have to think that is the way it was. I do know that I was born with red hair. All of my early pictures indicate that was the color of my hair. I also know that I was born a boy. That probably explains why they gave me a good Southern name, Bobby Lee Adams. If you are born in the South, chances are you are going to have a middle name. Of course some kids are given a mouthful of names like my son, Brynnan. His full name is Robert Brynnan Paul Adams. It is just not with the boys. We also give our daughters full names like Ashley Brooke Adams. If I had known how many forms I was going to fill out that ask for the names of my children I would have named them differently. I would have named them Her Adams, and Him Adams. That would have saved a lot of writing over my life span. Since we teach bathroom procedures by numbers, (do you have to number one or do you have to number two) naming them One and Two would have never worked out. Kids at school would have started calling them, Pee or Poop. My kids would have later grown to hate their parent for giving them such easy names to write on forms. Well any way, back to my hair. I have never giving a great deal of thought about my hair. I don't comb my hair anymore. However there was a time when I got haircuts anywhere I could. I would walk in and say, "Trim me up." The man or lady would cut my hair then turn me to the mirror and say, "Is that ok?" Usually without looking I would pay and out the door I would go. Once many years ago I had just walked into a newly opened Walmart. I looked and saw a sign that said, "Walk Ins Welcome." It was about time to get a haircut so I walked in. A very nice lady asks me if she could help me and as I sat down in a chair; I said sure "trim me up." She was very excited. It didn't take her very long to get behind me and start cutting my hair. She said I was her first customer. I mean I was her first ever to cut hair customer. She cut and cut and cut and then cut a little more. She turned me to the mirror and said, "Is that ok?" And typical me, I paid and out the door I went. I noticed I got a few stares as I shopped in the store. I got in my truck and decided I would look in the mirror. There were no two hairs on my head the same length. I was convinced it was not me. It was Lyle Lovett on a bad hair day. Being a very optimistic, person I told myself it wasn't too bad. After all, the hair would grow back eventually. I traveled over to my Brother Billy's house and walked into his living room. There were my two adorable nieces, Brelan and Darla. Brelan looked up and said, as she started to laugh, "You look like Lyle Lovette." Since then, when I get a haircut, I just ask, "Do I look like Lyle Lovette?" Then I pay.

WHAT WOULD YOU DO?

Since I was a little boy every year when the 4th of July came around I have always remembered some kind of celebration. I am sure it will be no different this year. I will celebrate the 4th in some form or another. Most Americans will do the same. In fact not only the Americans but there will be some that are here that have not yet become Americans celebrating the greatness of our Country. I know that many have lots of fears about the influx of people coming into America. I certainly don't have all the answers, but I do know that our greatness, our compassion and our way of life is envied by many people in many lands. I saw the buses that were stopped by the people in California. To tell you the truth if you were proud of what those people did I wonder if you have really given thought to why they were here. Those buses didn't contain illegals that had just drifted into Texas or crossed into a border town from Mexico. There were children with their mothers that had gotten them out of dangerous places in Latin America. Many children are killed. Mothers and daughters are raped and many savagely beaten by people that want to take over their country. Those people had made a long a dangerous journey to get to what they saw as a safe place for their children. The way they were greeted was very un-American like. I know that many of my friends don't feel the way that I do, but I believe that had Jesus Christ being standing there he would have welcomed those folks into a safe environment. We celebrate our Independence from what we saw as an oppressive British Government. On the Statue of Liberty are still the words "Give me your tired and your huddled masses yearning to breathe free, the wretched refused of your teeming shore. Send these the homeless, tempest tossed to me; I lift my lamp beside the golden door." I think when people risk not only their life but the life of their children to get away from an oppressive government the words on that statue still ring true. Happy 4th of July to everyone and it is still the greatest country on earth.

ATTEMPTED SUICIDE

I come from a very big family. I am not only talking about brothers and sisters. I am also talking about Aunts Uncles, Cousins and people that are blood relations. One of my distant cousins was a fellow by the name of Charlie Thurmond. Charlie was said to always have a great sense of humor. Charlie was a true salesman. He sold furniture and anything else that people would buy. Old Charlie had quite a reputation for being a ladies man. Someone once told me if a man and woman came into the furniture store where Charlie worked when he was a young man that Charlie would not only sell the couple a new bed but would also help most of the women see if they liked laying in the bed. I remember one time going up to a warehouse where we kept sheet rock, shingles and other items like sand. I was supposed to go behind the warehouse and load a ton of sand. When I turned in and drove behind the warehouse there was Charlie's car and all I could see was a ladies leg over one of the seats, and another leg on the dash with a pair of feet with black socks and britches hanging on the ankles sticking out of the car. Needless to say I very quickly put it in reverse and left whatever was going on--well to go on. Charlie would develop throat and tongue cancer in his later years. He had several surgeries and each one affected his speech a little more. While sitting at his house one evening he told his wife Fanny that if he had a gun he would just kill himself. Well Fanny decided to call his bluff, she went to the bedroom and returned with a 22 caliber pistol and told Charlie there was the gun and if you going to kill yourself just go ahead. Charlie wasn't bluffing. He put the pistol in his mouth and pulled the trigger. Fortunately or unfortunately --he didn't succeed in killing himself. Fanny called the ambulance and they rushed him to the hospital in Gainesville. Dad came in from his sawmill, and wanted to go see Charlie. So down to Gainesville he and I went. When we walked into Charlies room he looked up and said, "Why Hubut uo and Bobay tum on in." Daddy said, "Well Charlie someone said you tried to kill yourself. Did you?" Charlie looked at dad and said, "Yea I did hubut, but I ain't doonn ta do dat a din. Hit tears Fanny up to bad." He looked and dad and laughed and said, "I tank I passed dat bullet. I hurd it hit de tamode when I shits this moaning." He never lost his since of humor. Charlie never tried to kill himself again and died a peaceful death three weeks later.

Daddy always believed that kin folks should go to funerals to show there respect for the deceased. When Charlie Thurmond had passed away, dad came in from a long day's work at the sawmill and said, "Bob you need to take me down to Tom Hoods store to get me a pair of shoes to wear to Charlie Thurmonds funeral." So that is what I did. Dad and I walked into Tom Hoods store on the square there in Cleveland and Tom met us at the door. Tom was a well-liked man and had once served in the Georgia Legislature. Tom Hood was a wonderful fellow. Tom inquired as to what he could help us with. Daddy told Tom he needed a pair of shoes to wear to Charlie's funeral. "Well just come on back here Herbert and let's see if we can find you a pair." Tom said. My daddy had the worst smelling feet in the county. Daddy had been wearing his old work boots and probably had been wearing the same pair of socks for a couple of days. His feet were ripe. I mean a buzzard would have gaged had one smelled daddy's feet. As soon as daddy took his shoes off the smell of those feet would float through the air and make anyone that smelled them sick. I am sure if the smell had gotten outside of Tom's store it would have stopped traffic right there on the square of Cleveland, Georgia. About the time that daddy took his shoes off a lady came in the front door of Tom's store. Suddenly she turned her nose up and said, "My goodness Tom what in the world is that smell?" Without missing a beat Tom looked up and said, "Why that's smell is from that old Orkin man. He just sprayed for insects. It will be gone soon." The lady said well I will just wait outside. Tom looked at daddy and smiled and said, "Hell Herbert I bet she don't want to buy nothing but a pair of socks anyway." Daddy got his shoes. Tom made a sale. But I bet that lady never called Orkin to come spray her house for bugs.

WILLIE VS JOE

In the 1950's the old Adams store on the Helen highway was running full steam ahead. It was a gathering place for lots of the folks in our small community. You would usually find many of the men sitting outside on one of the benches that were located against the entrance wall of the store. People would stop and buy their gas for 26 cents a gallon. A coke was 5 cents. Then they went to 6 cents. I think Back in the 1950's the old Adams store on the Helen highway was running full steam. It was a gathering most people were like me and wondered why in the world you would raise the price a penny. That meant you had to have two coins to get that coke. Anyway back to my story, on any given day you probably would find one of the fellows sitting on that bench smelling a lot like moonshine and for a good reason; they were drunk. I used watch those men go behind the building with a pint bottle sticking out of their back overalls pocket and a 7-up in their hand. Many times those men would get that pint bottle out of their pants, squat down behind a car, turn that whisky up and chug a big drink down, then they would make an awful face and drink a big drink of that 7-up. I thought drinking 7-up was illegal for a long time. One of the patrons that sat on the bench was a fellow by the name of Joe Magness. Joe was a hardworking man that liked to indulge in the spirits. Joe was sitting there one day and one of our neighbors, Mrs. Willie Belle Thomas drove up in a brand new car. Mrs. Thomas was a fiery little lady. She was once band for Live Atlanta Wrestling because she hit one of the Wrestlers across the head with her pocket book. Mrs. Thomas got out of her car and Joe was about to fall off of the bench. He was mumbling something and Willie turned and said, "Ain't you a purty looking thang, sitting there drunk?" In a drunken slur Joe says, "Why I have kicked purtier women than you out of my bed." Mrs. Thomas turns and said, "You wait right here I am going to get my gun and I will shoot you." Everyone in our community that had been to a wrestling match knew Mrs. Thomas could get mad. She jumped in her car and toward her house she went. My Uncle came out of the store and told me to take Joe behind the store into the field and make him lay down. I did as I was told. In a few minutes Mrs. Thomas was back and had a hog leg pistol that looked as big as any gun I had ever saw. After several minutes of talking, my Uncle finally got Mrs. Thomas calmed down. When she left I asked my Uncle why he made me take Joe to the field and make him lay down. He said there were three reasons. 1. She said she was going to get her gun. 2. She was going to shoot Joe. 3. She was a woman that usually kept her word. Needless to say after sleeping the whiskey off old Joe avoided Willie for a long time. He said he liked breathing.

STIRRING THE MASH

Back in the 60's there was quite a few folks that would go to a dirt track car race for their weekend entertainment. I was one of them. There would be a race at Toccoa speedway on Friday night and one at the Banks County speedway on Saturday night. It was a beautiful summer day. Friday had gotten here and my friend Franklin Cathy and I had decided that we would go over to the Toccoa Speedway. It was a quarter mile dirt track and we usually knew some of the guys that would be racing. Dirt track racing was lots of fun. Usually you would see some great driving and occasional car turn over, and of course if you were really lucky; you would get to see some darned good fist fights. My friend Franklin came over to our house and picked me up. Franklin informed me that Lloyd Allen had told him that he would like to go with us to the track and watch the race. Lloyd was another one of my friends. Lloyd lived in a small frame house just across Sautee Creek in Nacoochee Valley. Franklin and I pulled up into Lloyd's yard and it wasn't long until Lloyd came out of the house. But instead of getting in on the passenger's side, he lend up against the car and said, "Boys I would like to go with you guys to the race, but I have got to go over to a still and stir some mash." That might shock some people, but several of my friends in those days were making corn to drink instead of to eat. Both Franklin and I decided we could help Lloyd stir the corn mash and get to the race in plenty of time. Lloyd said that would be great if we could help him. We walked a pretty good distance over to where the still was located, and there were several 55 gallon barrels full of fermenting products. As we were stirring the mash Franklin decided that he was going to drink some of the beer that had already worked off and was ready to run. One drink led to another, and then another. Finally Lloyd reached in a stump hole and pulled out a half gallon jar. Here try this and see what you think? We thought it tasted like it would need tasting again and again. So we did. We tasted it so much that we ended up spending the night and sleeping on the floor at Lloyd's place. I don't know who won the race in Toccoa that night but since Franklin had been the one drinking that beer mash; He won the race to the outhouse the next morning. I don't think it was even close.

A SAWMILL MEMORY

In the summer of 1967 my Daddy, Herbert Adams bought 10 Acres of pine trees from Mr. Tom Blackstock. Mr. Blackstock was a farmer that lived just South of Gainesville right off of Hyw 129. He at one time had a grape vineyard out on the highway.

When dad bought that timber I wondered why he would pay such a high price for just 10 acres of pines. After I saw the timber, I knew why. The pine trees were thick on the ground and long and beautiful. That was probably the best looking patch of timber I remember seeing. We had been sawing a patch of timber on a Mr. Parks farm which was also located on Hyw 129 South of Gainesville, Georgia. After the mill was set up in Mr. Blackstocks pasture near the edge of the timber, the timber cutters started falling those big slick bark pines. The way the lumber was stacked when it came out of the edger or off of the sawmill carriage; it was on pine logs that were called skid poles. There was usually room to stack two stacks of lumber on those skid poles. Once the lumber stack was considered to be about all our lumber truck could haul, we would put a cable around the lumber and pull the stack of lumber on to the lumber truck which was in a hole so the sliding lumber would go right on the truck. Then we would put a couple of chains around the lumber and buck it down. The men that worked at dad's mill would all bring their lunch to eat on the thirty minute lunch break. Most of those sandwiches and eats would usually be in a brown paper sack or a poke, as we called them. One day we were going to put the cable under a stack of lumber and as one of the off bears (the men that stacked the lumber) slid the cable under the lumber stack and about 8 or 9 little hound pups came running out from under the lumber stack. Their little bellies looked like they couldn't get any fuller. They were as round as they were long. They had got Shorty Gilstrap and Shorty's son, Cecil's sack lunches and ate all 8 of their sandwiches and several biscuits. Shorty was a thin man that drove the mule to bunch logs so the tractor driver could drive grabs into them and bring them to the mill. Shorty always had a chew and he was very level headed man because the tobacco juice ran down both sides of his mouth. Shorty said, "Well I guess little old dogs have got to eat too hain't I'am right?" I said, "Well Shorty I guess you are." Cecil just kept staring at one of the bags and reached over and pulled out a banana. He looked at his dad and said, "Well pap I guess you are glad them little dogs weren't a monkey." Shorty replied, "Why fer son?" Cecil said, "Why Pap if them thangs had been monkeys they would have ate this here banana." I guess you would have just had to of been there.

BABIES FIRST WORDS

When you become a parent it is not only exciting but in some ways a little scary. You realize that you must take responsibility for another human being that has been added to your life. Both of my children have been far better than I was when I was a child. My wife is an outstanding mother. She is by far a lot better mother than I am a father. When my grandson was born I thought back to the days when both of them were small and thought a great deal about how they have developed into two unique individuals. My daughter Brooke was never shy and she was never a picky eater. Brooke seemed to never meet a stranger and would eat anything you gave her. Brynnan, on the other hand, was a little bit shy and was a very picky eater. He has grown out of the shyness and has become a lot less contrary in his eating habits. We are finding that John Wilder, the grandson, is developing his own personality and I am sure he will have some quirks that we will have to live with as he grows into the person he will become. Brooke has been trying to get John Wilder to say Momma. Brooke's first word was Momma and then progressed to Dado. We were beginning to worry a little about Brynnan. He seemed very vocal but had not been saying Momma or Daddy or anything other than saying Joulwe. He would be lying on the bed and he would say, "Joulwe, Joulwe, Joulwe." This went on for several weeks. Finally I told Paula and Brooke that he was trying to say something, but I just couldn't figure out what it was. Occasionally he would be sitting at the table and look and his Mom or Me and say, "Joulwe, Joulwe, Joulwe." It was a very puzzling thing. Then one day I came in and Paula was not there; Brooke was supposed to be watching her baby brother. Keep in mind that Brynnan was born almost 18 years after his sister. I went upstairs and there sitting at the foot of the bed was Brooke and Brynnan. And on the television was the JERRY SPRINGER SHOW. I walked in to the tune of JERRY, JERRY, JERRY. The puzzle was solved. My son whom I dearly love, first words were JERRY, JERRY, JERRY. Who says kids don't learn from Television?

POULTRY ECONOMY

It took the rural South a good while to catch up with the rest of the country economically back in the 40's 50's and 60's. We were mostly an agricultural area and industries were few and far between in the mountainous counties of North Georgia. My father, like lots of people in North Georgia was a saw miller. Even though he owned a saw mill, it was still hard to carve a living out for his family. Dad, like a lot of men, heard about the chicken business coming into North Georgia. He built a two story chicken house for his wife and sons to look after chickens while he sawed timber all over the North Georgia area. Just about everywhere you looked a chicken house was being built. My Brother, Bruce and I had to feed the chickens before school and as soon as we got off the bus from school; it was back in the chicken house. The feed came in sacks. We had half gallon jars for their water and the feed had to go in medal feeders that were about six feet long. We would put the feed in a five gallon bucket and we would take feed scoop and put feed in the long feeders. There were 2000 chickens in the bottom and 2000 chickens in the top. In the winter we burned coal in our heaters so the chickens wouldn't freeze to death. If it was really cold we would have to get up during the night to put more coal in the heaters. They were just not big enough to burn all night and keep the chickens warm. There was a man from Dahlonega who would come every now and then to buy the feed sacks. His name was Mr. Robert Hughes. After I started teaching in Lumpkin County I found that Mr. Hughes was from Dahlonega and I had some of his children in my classes. Selling those feed sacks to Mr. Hughes was a big deal. Sometimes it would give my Mom the extra money that she would need to buy her children some needed school clothes or maybe a pair of shoes for herself. Sometimes the sacks would have pretty flowers on them and the women in our community would make beautiful quilts out of the feed sacks. Several years ago I had my Real Estate License and dappled in selling real estate. A lady from Florida wanted to find her and her family a home in North Georgia. I told her that there were several beautiful places that I could show her. The first thing she said to me was this, "I want a place that I can't see a chicken house going to are coming from my home. I hate chicken houses." I assured her that we would find her a home that met her criteria. Later that day I thought to myself if she had known how hard people in these old red hills had worked and how much the chicken industry had done to bring North Georgia out of a depressed economy, maybe- just maybe, she wouldn't of mind driving by and old abandoned chicken house that at one time meant so much to those families of long ago. As one of my friends said once, "It may smell like chicken manure to some, but it smelled like money to others. Times have changed don't you think?

CAR IN THE DITCH

My wife Paula was born and raised in Dahlonega. She was very active in High School. She was in lots of the High School clubs and she was a cheerleader. Of course and being very attractive girl, I am sure there were lots of guys hanging out around Paul and Lois Early's house hoping to catch Paula's eye. Paula doesn't share lots of the crazy stuff she has done with me. I guess she figures that having one crazy in the house is enough. Paula did share one story with me that I thought was great. Now I know that people don't like to hear stories about themselves, especially if I am the one telling the story. But I think this story bears repeating so that it can remain in the hearts and minds of the people who lots of us know and love. It seems that one of Paula's friends, JoAnn Avery's (the wife of Tom Rainey), mother had just gotten a brand new car. Gertrude Avery has been a great blessing to Lumpkin County. Not only has she got some great kids and grandkids but Mrs. Avery just has a big heart. Gertrude and George Avery welcomed lots of teens into their home when Joann and Paula were in High School. It seems that Paula and JoAnn were going to take Mrs. Avery's brand new car for a test drive. Driving a new car was a big experience if you have never driven one and Paula had never driven one. JoAnn is sitting beside Paula and as any excited teenager who is witnessing another teenager drive their mothers car, that by this time has become the teenagers car; she is giving Paula driving instructions. It started to rain so the girls decided it would be best if they just turned on to a little dirt road that just so happened to be getting worked on by the county road department. JoAnn was giving good instructions and telling Paula not to wreck her mother's new vehicle, and for a while it worked, but that mud was just too much and the car slide into a ditch. It was raining. The road was muddy and there were two young ladies sitting in the ditch. "Oh, no Paula, You have ditched my mamma's new car," said JoAnn. JoAnn by this time was in tears. Paula was close behind her. But the good Lord looks after people and as luck would have it; Mr. Fred Burns just so happened to come by in his old Pickup truck with a chain in it. Fred recognizes immediately that the girls needed a little assistance and quickly hooked the chain to the car and pulled them back onto the road. They thanked Fred for his kindly service and at that time JoAnn says with a few tears in her eyes, "Paula you are not driving my Mother's car anymore." Since they were still on the dirt road Paula did not contest JoAnn's advice. JoAnn got behind the wheel and starts out only to go about 100 yards and right back into the ditch. Now the girls are really upset. But once again a fine Lumpkin County Samaritan showed up. Mr. Pat Wimpy happens to come by and the mud, the rain and two crying girls indicate that they need help. Pat hooks his truck to the ditched new car and pulled them back on the road. The girls were thanking Mr. Wimpy for his kind gesture and they still had tears in their eyes. Mr. Wimpy looked at the girls and said, "Ah, you girls don't feel so bad about gitting in that ditch, why somebody told me Fred Burns was down here a little earlier getting two damn fools out of the ditch on the other side of the road." No, they didn't tell him.

GETTING BETTER RECEPTION

Even watching television has gotten expensive. I was looking through my monthly bill box and noticed that my satellite provider is charging me about a hundred dollars a month to watch the big Eye. I know that kids and most grownups can't remember a time when they didn't have Television to entertain the household. In 1951 my dad bought our first TV. It was a Philco. Man, we soon became the most popular family on the Helen Highway. Once word got out that dad had purchased the television all of our family members and a lot of the neighbors would come by on Friday and Saturday evening to watch that box that dad was so proud of. We watched programs like the Friday night boxing sponsored by Gillette, Amos and Andy, and on Saturday morning the cartoons was always a favorite. No one that had a TV at that time could get by without watching Roy Rogers, or Rin Tin Tin, with a little of Lassie thrown in for added entertainment. I am sure not many remember the Howdy Doodie show, or Captain Kangaroo but they were all ways great to watch. Television was different at that time. There were no remote controls. The parents use their kids to turn the channels. Since you couldn't get but 3 channels, you were pretty limited as to what you could watch. Dad would say, "Turn it to channel 2," or "I believe the news is on channel 11." Of course 2, 5 and 11 were it. If they didn't have it, you didn't get it. I remember a great deal about those early television days. The Ed Sullivan Show was one of Mom's favorite. She knew who Ed was going to have on just about every week. The family would all gather in one small room where the TV was located and watch that magic box like it was the most important thing in the world. There was no High Definition, no surround sound, and no auto tune. About the only thing you really could depend on was someone in the family yelling, "Turn it just a little bit more, no, that's too far. Back up a bit. That's about as good as it's going to get." If you remember a conversation that sound like that, let's just say; you may be starting to show your age.

HIDING THE FISH

I got my little female Boykin this weekend. Mr. Jeff Parker brought her up from Bowdon, Georgia. Little Ms. Jesse is a beautiful little puppy and already shows signs of being a smart little dog. Jeff and one of his fishing buddies were coming to Helen and do a little trout fishing. After Jeff dropped Jesse off I started to think back about many years ago when we lived in Helen and trout fishing was one of the most fun things that the Adams boys did. One of the Game Wardens of long ago, Mr. Arthur Abernathy, remarked to some of the guys at Warren Browns service station there in Helen, that there would be plenty of trout in the Chattahoochee River if them darned little Adams boys wouldn't catch them as fast as the DNR put them in. Looking back Ranger Abernathy was probably right. We knew when and where every stocking truck from the fish hatcheries would be bringing the fish. Arthur was not only a game warden, but he knew little boys pretty good. Once Bruce and I was fishing on the Chattahoochee and we had found the spot where the stocking truck had unloaded about half of its load of hungry trout. We were well on our way of catching enough to have a big fish fry. We looked up and there sat Arthur. He said, "Boys, I am going to go up here and check these boys up ahead of y'all but I will be back to check you two in a few minutes." As soon as that truck was out of site we began stuffing fish under logs, covering some up with grass and if there was a stump whole close; it was soon filled with fresh caught trout. True to his word Ranger Abernathy was back down in a few minutes to check our fish. Bruce and I were smiling knowing that we had gotten rid of the evidence. We counted out our trout. Each one of us was supposed to have 7 the limit was 8. That way we could continue to fish. Bruce was checked first. Seven fish exactly and they were all rainbows. I was next. Seven then eight. How did that happen? Arthur said, "Well boys, looks like you son can keep fishing. Now you young man will have to stop. Or you could put one of these trout up there where that one just happened to flop out of the leaves when I walked down through that trail, and then you can keep fishing or both of you can quite fishing and as soon as I am gone gather up the fish and not fish any more today. That way some of these other fisherman will have a better chance of catching a few trout." Needless to say we stopped fishing, gathered up our trout, and had a big fish fry. We didn't go back to fishing for two whole days. Ranger Abernathy was proud of us. I could tell.

MOM AND THE CIA

Recently we have been hearing a great deal about torture. It seems that we are guilty of torturing some guys that were thought to have information that might help us find the people who were responsible of harming our country or people who want to do harm to our country. Now before I get everyone that reads this angry or before you all start wondering why I decided to elaborate on a topic that I have no knowledge of or expect training in, let me assure you; I know a little about torture. After all I was in education and I had to go to lots of those meeting that were going to make me a lot smarter and a whole lot better at what I was doing. I am sure that some of those meetings would fall under the heading of torture. Also I have had to go to functions with my wife when she was a full time therapist and I sat through those meeting and held a smile on my face until it would sometimes start to twix. Also I might add that I think I may have been the first to ever know what water boarding was. Yes sir re, my grandfather Sims had a little country store in Helen, Georgia and just about every weekend you would find us visiting my Granny and Papa Sims. Papa sold Coal. Now lots of you don't know it but people in the fifties and sixties used a good bit of coal in there heaters. It was brought up from a Coal supplier in Gainesville and unloaded in Papa's coal hopper. Another thing you probably don't know is that little kids like to play in those coal bins. We could use coal to make little rock walls that were supposed to keep the Indians out of our Forts. Children do not look at their hands when they are playing with those shiny black rocks. Only mommas look at the children's hands, but that is right after the mother has looked at the face of the child that has been playing so hard and running so fast that the sweat from the kids body is running down their face and into their shirts until it is all absorbed. The children will wipe their face with their hands to keep the sweat out of their eyes. They can't see what the mother is looking at when she screams, "What in tar nations have y'all been doing?" She then grabs her little black face white boy by the arm and smacks him on he but about every two steps. She goes into my Grandmothers bathroom and starts water boarding the poor little boy. That wash cloth is pressed so tight to his face that his nose and ears look a little distorted. That is just the first round of water boarding. She then realizes that first child she washed was not hers, so she grabs another and proceeds to do the same all over again. So you see I know a little about torture. I think my Mom was working with the CIA (Children Immediate Attention). She may have help train people in water boarding. We can only say that sometimes we do wrong by trying to do right. I don't know for sure that Mom's water boarding me ever made me a better person, but it did help clean me up.

PAY IT FORWARD

The Pay It Forward thing is absolutely fantastic. The other day I was going through the drive thru at one on the fast food places here in good old Cleveland, Ga and to my surprise when I got to the pay window, I said, "How much." And to my surprise the cashier said, "Nothing, someone has already paid for yours." I don't know who it was but it made me say thanks to whomever, and hope that the person that did that wonderful deed had a great day. I had heard of this happening but it had never happened to me. I had shared my good deed with several of my friends and family members and had told them what a great feeling it gave me. I was so touched by the Pay It Forward moment that I did the same thing for a person at one of the drive troughs the other day. It was like 5 bucks or close to that amount. I once again shared what I had done with family and friends. Now I have some wonderful Nephews and Nieces. I love every one of them with all my heart. I think that sometimes when we tell people about how good it makes you feel to do something like the Ice Bucket Challenge or the Pay It Forward deed that they are inspired and they want to do something that make them feel good about themselves. This brings me to telling you about my Nephew Austin Adams feel good moment. Austin was recently married and has a wonderful young lady for his bride. Carly is just great. She fits right in with the Adams clan, which might mean that she is little tetched (as granny used to say) or just simply a great young lady. I choose to believe that she is a great young lady. Austin was in one of the fast food places to get him and Carly a breakfast biscuit. Austin saw a little old lady coming to the counter and told the cashier, "I will pay for what she gets." Well Austin comes out to the car in a few minutes and says to Carly, "I need about 4 more dollars." Carly says, "Austin, I thought you had twenty bucks?" He says, "I did Carly but I was going to do the Pay It Forward deed and I told the cashier I would pay for the little old ladies bill." Carly say, "Well did you?" Austin says, 'How the Hell did I know she was going to order 14 biscuits to go." Good deeds are always worth doing. Sometimes we just have to do a little better than what we thought.

NUDE CELEBRITIES

I don't know what is up with all these celebrities taking nude pictures of themselves, and then getting angry when someone somehow gets a hold of their nude shots and post them on the social media. Now I do have to point out that I haven't looked at any of those nude pictures but then no one has told me who they were of or how to find them. Not that I would look, but information is not as easy to find as some thinks that it is. I mean, if I want to go look at some thinly clad people or almost naked people all I got to do is to go down to Walmart and some of the folks that come in there barely have their bare covered up. Of course some of them would have to work overtime just to cover all that skin up. I had thought that since only celebrities were doing the nude photo thing that this might be a chance for me to bring myself up to celebrity status if I could just take a few nude selfies of me. Then I could post them on here and get feedback from friends and family and who knows what fortune that might bring me? Well I stripped down to my birthday suit then I sat my phone down and had the camera set to take pictures on a time lapsed sequence. The first few shots you could only see my head and shoulder. So I decided I would have to back way up so I could get all of my body in the shot. Well that didn't work either. When you get old and out of shape it is hard to take a nude selfie. I had to back up so far that by the time I got all of me in the picture; it looked like one of the whales from Disney World had washed up on the asphalt. You couldn't tell who that handsome red headed devil was; So much for me trying to make myself a celebrity by posing nude. I guess I will just have to stick to running naked around my vehicle on top of the Richard Russell Highway on the coldest night of the winter. That just might be my best chance of being a celebrity. See y'all there.

JUST SAY NOTHING

Sometimes saying nothing might be better than saying something. I know that is true especially when a man is talking to a woman. Like the other night when I was watching TV my wife Paula said, "Do you think this looks better with this dress, or do you think this looks better." Well-being hard of hearing and very interested in the western that was on TV, I just said something to the effect of move you are blocking the screen. How did I know that was going to erupt into an angry woman? I then got lectured about how I don't pay attention to her when she is asking me an important question. I followed up with a good apology and told her how sorry I was but I thought she had ask something about old Hoss Cartwright and since she was standing in front of me I couldn't see the TV. That answer didn't get a good response either. Things like that are good reasons that a man should just say nothing. Let the female repeat the question at least two or three times and then a man should smile and say, "Let me think about that."   One of my old drinking buddies was watching TV the other night and his wife came in and said, "Do you like this red dress?" Being a lot smarter than me, he just nodded his head. His wife then said, "You know I wish I had big boobs. I think I will ask the doctor what he can do to enhance my bust line." My friend just kept watching the TV and said to her, "Why don't you try rubbing toilet paper between them that will make em bigger." His wife had a smile on her face and said, "How will rubbing toilet paper between my breasts make them bigger?" My old buddy said, "I really don't know, but look what it has done for your butt." As soon as the swelling in his eye goes down he is going to buy her a new dress. He should have just said nothing.

COUNTRY DOCTOR

Having lived in North Georgia all of my life has given me the opportunity to meet many amazing people. One of the great men that I had the honor of knowing was our neighbor for many years. Dr. Myron Eberhart was a country Doctor. Myron came from a hard working family and went to medical school and became a physician. Myron was one of the few doctors that would make a house call if need be. Many times he would come by my parents' home to give my mom a shot. He also would come by if Mom or Dad told him one of their children was too sick to go see the doctor. I remember Myron coming by the house one afternoon on his way home to give me a shot. I was running a very high fever and had an extremely sore throat. Myron was not only our doctor but he was a friend to all that knew him. After I had grown up, Myron and I spent many hours on the back of our horses riding in the mountains of North Georgia. He and I both loved to ride. I introduced my friend David Wilkins to Myron and they soon became good friends and riding partners. David and Myron would ride four or five days a week some times. They traveled all of Georgia, North Carolina and South Carolina riding their horses. On one of the rides that David, Myron and I were on; we were sitting on a log taking a break. We always carried some snacks with us. David would have the Apples; Myron would have the nuts, almonds, peanuts, etc. I would have the drinks in my saddle bag. It was an enjoyable time. I ask Myron if he ever got frustrated with patients. He said that sometimes he did, but sometimes there was lots of humor in the sick. He told me that once when he first started practicing medicine an elderly lady who was a new patient came in to see him and she had several nice looking eggs with her. She told Myron that she didn't have a lot of money but would give him the eggs if he would be her doctor. Myron told the lady why of course he would be her Doctor. He then asks her if those eggs were those big double yolk eggs he had heard so much about. The old lady looked at Myron and said, "No those are not the good double yolk eggs, I didn't bring you any of them cause I don't know that you are that good of a doctor yet." He said that she lived many years after that first visit, and she never gave him any of those double yolks, but she did give him a laying hen. I think she must have decided that he was a good Doctor.

DREAMS

Well it is Valentine Day, and it started with an incredible event. There I was lying in bed, sleep still holding on to me. I had forgotten about it being February 14. That is the day that you sent flowers, chocolate, and for some, diamonds to the one person that you truly love. Back to my morning--- laying there with soft music playing in the back ground, and fragrant candles placed in a beautiful arrangement on the small tables around the room. I heard someone's feet slowly moving toward the room I was in. As the door knob began to turn, I could see a beautiful cheek and white teeth behind the smile on the face of a stunning looking women. Then she pushed one leg into the room. She had long silk like legs. As my eyes slowly began to focus, I see that this lady had on a beautiful pink negligée. It probably had been purchased at Victoria's Secret. Then out of nowhere I heard my darned old cat, Kingfish start MEOWING. Meow, meow, meow. He could have been screaming in a bull horn and it wouldn't have been any louder. I woke up from my dream and it is then that I realized; I hadn't bought a card, a flower or anything for Valentine's Day. I rushed down to the local place where I buy flowers and cards and got that done. Now I am going back to bed and see if I can have another dream. This time I locked the door and Kingfish will not spoil my dream again. I hope I start right when the door opens again.

DOG SHOW

I have had hound dogs for as long as I can remember. My grandfather Sims had coon hounds and then he had Rabbit dogs. Some folks used to tell about how their coonhounds would run coon at night and the next day; they would take the same dogs rabbit hunting and they would run rabbit. I never had quiet so versatile dogs. However I have had dogs that would tree just about anything that would go up a tree. Having a good hound is something that some folks just cannot comprehend why men want to have a smelly old dog to take out into the woods and listen to him bark. I must confess it is hard to explain why I have always loved to hear the sound of hounds running that old raccoon up the creeks and across the mountains. It is something that I think is just special to certain people and quite frankly those folks really don't give a damn if people understand it or not. I have rabbit dogs at present and I really enjoy listening and watching those dogs run a rabbit. I am sure that many of the dog lovers in the world know that at this year's Westminster Dog Show the winning dog was a Beagle. Just think, all those dogs, owners spending thousands of dollars on a fine bred dog and a little old beagle - as my granddaddy used to say "Whupped em Good." For a man like me, that brings lots of satisfaction. Knowing that Fe Fe the perfectly groomed dog didn't win kind of brings a smile to my face. However, that win by that little beagle has brought a little problem to me. Since his win my beagles are starting to think that maybe they may be related to that dog. I have tried, to no avail to convince my dogs that they are not related to the winner of the Westminster Dog Show. Now they are complaining about it being too cold to hunt or that they think they need to be brushed more. Good grief those beagles of mine have never been brushed a time in their lives. My little beagle named Jesse is positive that he is related to that Champion Beagle. I finally got tired of telling them they were in no way related. I ask Jesse why he thought that he was related to that Champion Beagle and he said, "Remember last weekend when we all dug out of the lot that you had us in and you didn't get to go hunting?" Well I did remember that. He said his great, great, great grandmother was in a kennel near the daddy of that Champion Beagle and he dug out and met his great, great, great grandmother on the trail of a rabbit, and there was more than just a rabbit race that took place. I still don't think my dogs are related to that Champion Beagle but Jesse does have a point. Naw, you can't believe a beagle.

FULL DIAPERS

There is something magic about a grandchild. They look up at you and you can feel the love that they have for a Poppa or a Nanny or Meme or Pops or whatever the Grandparent wishes to be called. The grandparent waits with excitement building each time they know that the grandchild will come for a visit. To see that smile on the face of the little one just as they see Pop or Nanna feels your heart with joy. The magic that is there goes farther than just the smile or the love that is felt, it carries on to include body functions. I am firmly convinced that if my grandson John Wilder Henry Nix is constipated; all my wonderful daughter has to do to get those bowels moving freely again is to call her father and say, "Deadie,(she is a southern girl) can you keep John Wilder for a little while so I can go to my Doctor appointment?" Who could resist seeing that wonderful little bundle of joy? Not this Granddad that is for sure. I am always eager to see little Wilder. He is never any trouble, well most of the time anyway. When people ask if he is spoiled I can only say if he isn't, he will be. I get the instructions on what to do and how to do it from Wilder's mom, and I agree to all of the terms for keeping little Wilder. If he doesn't see his Mom leave he will not cry a bit. However, if Brooke places him down on the floor and he sees his Mom get out of his sight, he might fuss for a short period of time but that is soon stopped and he goes back to being his cheerful self. Having kept JW several times it has been brought to my attention that when John Wilder hears his mother drive off he immediately starts leaning on is right side, the face starts to turn red, and then it happens. The one thing that granddads are not good at is cleaning up a little boy after he has freed his bowels up so that everything that he has eaten in the last 6 days is going into that diaper that is equipped to handle about 4 pounds of crap, shew shew dirty, pew pew or du du or whatever you choose to call it. The diaper cannot hold all of the 6 days' worth. No, the rest of the radioactive material goes up the back, and down each leg. Wilder starts to laugh and kick when his grandparent tries to hold his nose with one hand and undo the diaper with the other; one must then take a deep breath and hold it because this takes both hands and sometimes help from another person. This is what I call a four wash cloth bowel movement. It takes two to clean John Wilder and two to clean up his grandfather. When grandfather gets through there are sheets to be removed, towels, and wash clothes to be burned and air freshener used by the gallons. The magic that the grandparent has goes well beyond that smile of love; it can go right on to be a scientific cure for constipation. It happens every time, but we can't wait till we get to keep him the next time. Love runs deep even when you are up that creek.

GLAD ANDERSON

When I started my teaching and coaching career at Lumpkin County High School there was a lot of last names that were what I call fixed in the history of the county. One of those names was "Anderson." We had several Andersons' in our school so I knew that there must be a lot of folks that grew up in the county with the last name of Anderson. It didn't take me long to learn that I was right. One of those Andersons that I soon got acquainted with was Mr. Glad Anderson. Glad's whole family was farmers and most liked to enjoy the outdoors. Glad loved to hunt and fish. It was said that Glad always wanted to kill the biggest deer or catch the biggest fish of anyone in the county. I learned over the years that Glad Anderson was a very good outdoorsman. If you told Glad were there were some good buck sign, he would check it out and if it showed that a big buck was doing it; Glad would hunt that buck down. The same thing was true about big trout. Glad loved to fish the streams for big Rainbow or Brown trout. I remember one time I told Glad that I had been fishing below the Tate Bridge in the Chestatee River and a big fish came up to look at my Mepps spinner. Glad kept asking questions until he figured he had the where a bouts down pat. Even though I had not been fishing, I figured it would be a good one to pull on old Glad. The next day I drove through the Town Creek Rd where the Tate Bridge is located and sure enough there was Glad's Truck. The next day I saw Glad and ask him if he had caught any fish? Glad said," Well I caught a good Brown Trout. He was about 22 inches long." So much for trying to pull one on Glad, if I had known that fish was there; I wouldn't have told Glad. Glad offered to take me fishing on a lake called Lake Jocassee in South Carolina. The Lake had some huge Brown and Glad had caught several of them. I had never been to the Lake. We trolled that lake for several hours. I put on an old lure that I had never caught a fish on before. We hadn't gone a hundred yards when a big Brown took that lure and ran with it. Glad wanted to know if I had another one of those lures. I told him no and that was the truth. I don't know if Glad believed me. It was the biggest fish we caught all day. Glad never invited me back to go fishing with him. We laughed about that fishing trip many times. Thanks Glad for those memories may you rest in peace knowing you had many friends that loved you. Glad, I saw a big Rainbow the other day. I am sure God will tell you where it is. You were my friend.

GIVING THANKS

Thanksgiving always makes me thankful for the many wonderful thing and people that I have in my life. I am thankful for my Wife. She is a good person. She cares about others and has been a great mother to my children. I am thankful for my children. They take after their mother. That is something to be really thankful for. I am thankful for my Grandson. He brightens the day just by smiling. I am thankful that I had good parents that provided for me and helped me realize that helping others should be a high priority for all of us. I am thankful for all of my wonderful friends and family. They add so much to my life. I am thankful that I was able react quick enough to miss the young lady that pulled out in front of me on the way to Gainesville. I am sure she is thankful for that as well. I am thankful for my material possessions. I enjoy fishing and hunting. I am thankful for my dogs. They love me unconditionally. I am thankful for my health. Not as good as it used to be but still hanging in there. I am thankful that I have lived in site of Yonah Mountain all of my life. I am thankful that we have clean air to breathe and clean water to drink. I am thankful for the laughs that we share. I am thankful that everyone doesn't think like me. Everyone should be thankful for that; Happy Thanksgiving to all.

SPECIAL FRYING PAN

The Christmas Holiday will be upon us soon. And most families will be sitting at the table enjoying all of the bountiful food that will be sitting on a table. That food more than likely will have been prepared by someone that we love or respect or both. Otherwise you would not be sitting at the table. When my Grandmother Adams was living we would celebrate Christmas at her house. It was all so a celebration of her birthday, and all of her children and all of the grandchildren and many close friends would gather around that table and many would be sitting outside on the porch waiting their turn to get a plate and fill it with some food that was fit for a King. I was watching my grandmother cooking up some corn bread and she opened the oven door and slid that old black skillet into the oven. When she shut the door, I heard her say, "Now I will wait for that corn bread to get done and I will fry some chicken in it." I saw several other pans in the kitchen and so being a young know nothing about cooking boy I said, "Why don't you use one of the other pans Granny?" She looked down at me and said, "Honey I like to use the old black skillet in the oven for making my bread and frying stuff in, because it is my favorite thing to cook in." Well I couldn't understand that answer until I got to be a grown man. I love to cook and it shows I know, but my Grandmothers answer is right on target. This morning I was cooking some breakfast and that old black skillet that I all ways use was out of my site in the cabinet. While I was feeling around in the dark for my black skillet my son said, "What are you doing Dad? I told him I was looking for my black skillet. He replied, "Why don't you use one of the others?" Yes, he got the same answer as my Grandmother Adams had given me. I am proud of the things that my Grandparents and Parents passed on to me. I know there is lots of cookware that is 10 times better than my old black skillet, but I am glad that I reached a little farther in the cabinet and found that old black skillet of mine. It is still my favorite.

February 2nd was always a special day in the Adams house when we were growing up. Mom and Dad would be up with a smile on their face and usually both would be in the kitchen cooking their children some gravy and biscuits and of course it might be served with whatever meat was on hand. Could be ham, could be rabbit, squirrel, quail, and deer which ever meat was thawed and out of the freezer. It usually started with someone asking if the groundhog saw his shadow. There would be a little conversation about that and of course us kids didn't care one way or the other about what that ground hog saw. Most of the time we were hoping to see a ground hog so that he wouldn't be seeing anything else if he had been getting in our garden or under one of dad's sheds. Predicting the weather may have been the responsibility of one groundhog but his cousins and relatives were not welcome around the Adams house. We didn't care if it was going to be an early spring or not. We wanted to just get through the winter and start plowing fields for planting. The real reason it was always a special day was because it was mom and dad's wedding anniversary. Yes they were married on ground hog day and they never let us forget it. Each ground hog day dad would say "I don't know if that old ground hog saw his shadow or not but that's the day your mom and I got married. The only shadow I saw was the one of the man that married us." Both are gone, but never so far away that we can't say "Happy Anniversary Mom and Dad. The ground hog saw his shadow, and its blowing snow; we still don't care what that ground hog saw, but we miss you."

This is me (Bobby) trying to get my horse, Molly, to talk. I would ask her if she had eaten all her oats. She would raise her tail and say a fffeeewwwww. Farmers joke.

To all those who have purchased this book, I hope you enjoyed reading it as much as I enjoyed writing it.

Bobby Adams

www.ingramcontent.com/pod-product-compliance
Lightning Source LLC
LaVergne TN
LVHW051457080426
835509LV00017B/1789